MUSLIM PREACHING IN THE MIDDLE EAST AND BEYOND

MUSLIM PREACHING IN THE MIDDLE EAST AND BEYOND

Historical and Contemporary Case Studies

Edited by Simon Stjernholm and Elisabeth Özdalga

EDINBURGH
University Press

Edinburgh University Press is one of the leading university presses in the UK. We publish academic books and journals in our selected subject areas across the humanities and social sciences, combining cutting-edge scholarship with high editorial and production values to produce academic works of lasting importance. For more information visit our website: edinburghuniversitypress.com

Edinburgh University Press Ltd
The Tun – Holyrood Road, 12(2f) Jackson's Entry, Edinburgh EH8 8PJ

First published in hardback by Edinburgh University Press 2020

Typeset in 11/15 Adobe Garamond by
Servis Filmsetting Ltd, Stockport, Cheshire

A CIP record for this book is available from the British Library

ISBN 978 1 4744 6747 6 (hardback)
ISBN 978 1 4744 6748 3 (paperback)
ISBN 978 1 4744 6749 0 (webready PDF)
ISBN 978 1 4744 6750 6 (epub)

CONTENTS

Acknowledgements vii
About the Authors viii
Note on Transliteration x

Introduction 1
Simon Stjernholm and Elisabeth Özdalga

Part I Ritual and Performance

1 The Framework of Islamic Rhetoric: The Ritual of the *Khuṭba* and its Origin 19
Jan Retsö

2 The *Khuṭba* Scene in Arab Religious Films and TV Dramas 30
Jakob Skovgaard-Petersen

3 Instructive Speech among Bosnian Muslim Women: Sermons, Lessons or Guidance? 48
Catharina Raudvere

Part II Power and Authority

4 Preaching and the Problem of Religious Authority in Medieval Islam 67
Jonathan P. Berkey

5 Friday Sermons in a Secular State: Religious Institution-building in Modern Turkey 83
Elisabeth Özdalga

Part III Mediation

6 Going Online: Saudi Female Intellectual Preachers in the New Media 107
Laila Makboul

7 Brief Reminders: Muslim Preachers, Mediation and Time 132
Simon Stjernholm

Part IV Identities

8 Advising and Warning the People: Swedish Salafis on Violence, Renunciation and Life in the Suburbs 155
Susanne Olsson

9 Discourses on Marriage, Religious Identity and Gender in Medieval and Contemporary Islamic Preaching: Continuities and Adaptations 173
Linda G. Jones

Epilogue 201
Simon Stjernholm and Elisabeth Özdalga

Index 206

ACKNOWLEDGEMENTS

The editors would like to thank Riksbankens Jubileumsfond: The Swedish Foundation for Humanities and Social Sciences, for generously supporting this project. We are also grateful to the Department of Cross-Cultural and Regional Studies, University of Copenhagen, as well as the Swedish Research Institute in Istanbul. A special thanks is also due to Maria Lindebæk Lyngsøe for practical support.

ABOUT THE AUTHORS

Jonathan P. Berkey is James B. Duke Professor of History at Davidson College, North Carolina, USA.

Linda G. Jones is Associate Professor of History at Universitat Pompeu Fabra, Barcelona, Spain.

Laila Makboul is MSCA post-doctoral fellow at the American University in Cairo and the University of Oslo, Norway.

Susanne Olsson is Professor of History of Religions at Stockholm University, Sweden.

Elisabeth Özdalga is Professor of Sociology and Senior Researcher at the Swedish Research Institute in Istanbul.

Catharina Raudvere is Professor of History of Religions at University of Copenhagen, Denmark.

Jan Retsö is Professor Emeritus of Arabic at University of Gothenburg, Sweden.

Jakob Skovgaard-Petersen is Professor of Middle Eastern Studies at University of Copenhagen, Denmark.

Simon Stjernholm is Associate Professor of History of Religions at University of Copenhagen, Denmark.

NOTE ON TRANSLITERATION

Throughout this book, we have generally used the Arabic transliteration standard of the *International Journal of Middle East Studies* (IJMES). However, in case studies where languages other than Arabic are used, such as in Bosnia and Turkey, the respective language's spelling of terms has been applied. We have refrained from transliterating in detail terms that are commonly used in English, such as Muhammad, the Qurʾan, hadith and jihad.

INTRODUCTION

Simon Stjernholm and Elisabeth Özdalga

On 4 July 2014, about a month after Islamic State had conquered the northern Iraqi city of Mosul, the jihadist group's leader Abu Bakr al-Baghdadi (1971–2019), now declaring himself caliph, led the Friday sermon – the *khuṭbat al-jumʿa* – from the city's famous al-Nuri mosque. The fact that this *khuṭba* (pl. *khuṭab*) was widely used in a political propaganda war may have hidden from the public gaze its ritual and religious significance. Muslims around the world would have known about it, but for vast audiences of non-Muslims it may not have been so obvious that al-Baghdadi's performance was joining the chorus of Friday noon sermons, rolling like a wave over the global time zones from Indonesia in the east to California in the west. What knits these hundreds of thousands of *khuṭab* together is a common ritual, with long historical roots. Thus, al-Baghdadi's *khuṭba*, in spite of his and Islamic State's extremist agendas, did not only resonate with Friday sermons held elsewhere in the world that same day, it also resonated with a liturgical tradition going back to the days of the Prophet Muhammad. The choice al-Baghdadi made to use the ritual of the Friday sermon in order to claim his caliphate and announce himself as an aspiring leader for Muslims globally was not random. The form of the *khuṭba* itself, echoing the classical Islamic oratorical tradition in the way it was performed (Qutbuddin 2019: 477), is a communicative act with distinct connotations to its audience.

Preaching is among those Islamic practices that appears to have been continuous since the days of Muhammad until today (Qutbuddin 2008, 2019). Every Friday, millions of Muslims around the world listen to the liturgical Friday sermon being delivered from the pulpit (minbar) of a mosque. It is a pillar of stability in Muslim religious life. *Khuṭba* preaching also accompanies both calendrical religious festivals like *ʿīd al-fiṭr* and *ʿīd al-aḍḥā* and family festivities such as weddings and circumcisions (Millie 2017). In addition, there are many other forms of Muslim religiously instructive speech – or preaching – than the *khuṭba*. Examples include the freer form of preaching that can take place in many settings – such as mosques, Sufi lodges, university campuses, street corners or cafés – known as *waʿẓ*; the religious lesson (*dars*); leadership of a study group (*ḥalqa*); and more informal lectures given on special occasions, at conferences or, in particular, media like television and radio. Muslim preaching, as we approach it in this volume, is not limited to a particular time, place, structure or degree of formality. It is a type of oral religious discourse that, due to its particular features and forms of mediation, can reach far into people's everyday lives.

This volume aims to highlight the great variety of preaching in Muslim religious environments, historically as well as in contemporary times. The book also offers analytical perspectives on how Muslim preaching has been practised, as well as how its pervasiveness has been established and maintained. For that purpose, we have invited a broad range of cases of preaching – spanning several genres and forms of mediation – from a number of countries and historical periods. Thus, the book does not take as its starting point a particular country, region, language or historical period. With inspiration from previous scholarship concerning important aspects of the history of Muslim preaching (for example, Armstrong 2016; Berkey 2001; Halldén 2005; Jones 2012; Qutbuddin 2008, 2019), as well as in-depth studies of preaching practices in contemporary Muslim-majority contexts (for example, Antoun 1989; Gaffney 1994; Halldén 2001; Hirschkind 2006; Brinton 2016; Millie 2017), this book has been conceived in an exploratory spirit. We have been interested in seeing what the bringing together of highly diverse cases of Muslim preaching can offer: what does it allow us to see in a new light, which similarities and discrepancies come to the fore, and what promising trajectories for further inquiry can be gleaned from this collection of essays? Our aim is that the whole will be larger than the sum of its parts, offering readers who may be familiar with individual contexts and cases the chance to engage with comparable practices and problematics in other contexts. The book also strives to open up possible fields of inquiry to researchers who have not previously made preaching an integral part of their work.

Muslim preaching can be analysed using theoretical insights from multiple disciplines, including (but not limited to) the study of religion, anthropology, media and communication studies, rhetorical criticism, literary studies and history.[1] This means that a number of analytical approaches and methods, including ones that have been developing across the humanities and social sciences in recent years, can offer relevant perspectives. Among these are discursively oriented approaches to the power plays and competing authority claims that are central to the oratorical tradition of Islam, historically as well as contemporarily (for example, Asad 1986; Eickelman and Piscatori 1996; Gaffney 1994). It is also useful to consider ritual- and performance-oriented perspectives on religious orations, as preaching, on the one hand, can be highly ritualised, with detailed prescriptions while, on the other hand, it is always a specific person, in a particular setting, that performs the actual preaching, giving a certain character to it (for example, Grimes 2008; Kalmbach 2015; Millie 2017). A further analytical field of relevance to the study of Muslim preaching is its circulation in various forms of media, including print media, cassettes and television, as well as mediation more broadly understood, such as embodied oratory and its sensory perception by the audience (for example, Hirschkind 2006; Meyer 2011; Schulz 2012). As preaching often – explicitly or implicitly – treats issues of identity, individual as well as collective, it is also important to consider topics concerning, for example, how in-groups and out-groups are constructed, what rhetorical devices are used in this construction, and how various audiences are addressed (for example, Berkey 2001; Jones 2012; Millie 2017). These are only some possible useful approaches, which have been used in order to thematically structure this book. In the following, we offer an introduction to the particular form of discourse that we take Muslim preaching to be.

A Hortatory Discourse

Preaching, by definition, has a normative dimension. The concern of a preacher is to instruct, or exhort – do this, don't do that, be like this, avoid the company of those. But the preacher's task often also includes to explain what should be regarded as right and wrong, and why. In order to explain that, they need to give an account of the central narratives, figures and ideas of the tradition to which they belong. In Islamic tradition, normative aspects have always weighed heavily, as the practice of commanding right and forbidding wrong illustrates (Cook 2000). In order to communicate norms effectively, preachers cannot simply issue lists and instructions. In addition to informing, preachers need to engage and persuade the audience. Various rhetorical strategies are used to achieve this, including narratives, vocal and visual performances, and uses of cultural resources which go beyond the strictly religious. The most engaging preacher is not necessarily the most highly educated or theologically sophisticated. In fact, preachers who become popular might speak in ways that are seen as contrary to, or at least challenging of, established authorities or traditional norms. The role of popular preachers (see Berkey in this volume) points to the necessary interactive dimension of preaching. This is a relevant perspective regardless of historical period, cultural context or which language the preacher uses. Medieval as well as contemporary preachers must engage with the needs and concerns of their audiences, or they risk being regarded as uninteresting or irrelevant.

Using narratives gives preachers a chance to do more than simply state what is right and wrong, what listeners should and should not do. Narratives engage listeners in a relational process where certain characters serve as moral models, positive as well as negative, which listeners can use to make, apply and interpret meaning that resonates with their own experiences. Narratives also have the ability to engage and entertain an audience. In addition, preaching involves material and embodied aspects, especially preachers' voices, meaning that senses are engaged to a high degree. The importance of the human voice in Islamic tradition can be illustrated by two practices that are somehow emblematic: the call to prayer from a minaret and inside the mosque, and the elaborate rules for and training that is spent on learning how to recite the Qur'an (Turkish *tilavet*, Arabic *tajwīd*).

Voices are highly personal and can be moulded in various ways through intonation, shouts and whispers; the use of alliteration and other rhetorical figures also affects oral delivery. Even though these aspects of preaching are not always available to us in the sources we have access to – for example sermon transcripts – it is nevertheless a dimension that needs to be reckoned with in the analysis of preaching. Preaching is different from writing, although the documentation of or instructions on preaching often takes the form of writing. In addition to speech, preachers can employ gestures and paraphernalia – for example clothing and books – and sometimes additional visual and audio media.

All of this means that it is not just the preacher's senses that are engaged, but also those of the audience. Listening to preaching is not a passive reception of a message that is completely controlled by the sender; it is an active and sensory engagement, which means that preaching is often highly interactive. This is not limited to the modern period. No matter which period or local context, a preacher is dependent on the audience's response. In a position quite different from more textually oriented religious scholars, or groups of religious scholars whose mode of discourse is mainly kept within their own ranks, preachers are, if they are to be successful, required to communicate successfully. This means developing and performing characteristics dependent on personal and corporeal qualities rather than – or in addition to – rationally acquired forms of knowledge. This includes the 'ability to make complex ideas understandable or to be an engaging performer' (Brinton 2016: 64). In this respect, a preacher has similarities not just with the educated class of Muslim religious scholars (ʿulamaʾ), but also with teachers and entertainers.

As mentioned, this hortatory discourse of Muslim preaching can be approached and analysed in many ways. We have chosen four analytical themes as the organising principle for the chapters of this volume: ritual and performance; power and authority; mediation; and identities. These themes are not mutually excluding categories; rather, they partly overlap with each other. For example, performance is dependent on forms of mediation, ritual and power are closely related, and identities both shape and are shaped by authority structures and engagement with various media. Nonetheless, we have arranged the volume's chapters according to what we see as their dominant theme, while at the same time acknowledging that they also relate to and can be put into conversation with themes dealt with in other sections.

Ritual and Performance

Perhaps the first association that comes to mind when contemplating the term 'Muslim preaching' is the highly ritualised weekly oral address given from the minbar of mosques around the world in relation to the Friday noon prayer (*ṣalāt al-jumʿa*). Along with other practices, including what is known as the five pillars of Islam, the Friday sermon is distinctly recognisable: with long-established norms and rules for how it should be carried out, there are limits for how spontaneous and extemporaneous it can be. In order to be recognised as a *khuṭbat al-jumʿa*, the ritual script needs to be followed (see Retsö, in this volume, for a summary of classical requirements of a Friday sermon). This ritualised form is simultaneously its strength and its limitation. On the one hand, the rules and their legitimation in scripture has no doubt facilitated the survival of this type of address through the centuries. This gives individual speakers the possibility to perform their role as *khaṭīb* in a way that can be directly related to reports of the earliest generations of Muslims, indeed reports about the conduct of the Prophet Muhammad himself. On the other hand, this can prevent the speaker in the Friday sermon from using rhetorically more original, colourful or local expressions.[2] What may be lost in originality, then, can be gained in legitimate performance.

Thanks to the formality and official status of the Friday sermon, it has been put to a number of uses, not least politically. In the earliest stage of Islam's history, it was the religious and political leader who delivered the *khuṭba*, which was then not limited to the Friday religious liturgy but encompassed a number of different public speech situations and topics. The Prophet Muhammad and the early caliphs – in particular ʿAli – are remembered for their oratorical eloquence; their speeches are still studied as models and sometimes memorised. Early on, it also became customary to pronounce blessings not just on Muhammad and his family, but also on the political ruler, who was named; failure to do so could be seen as dangerously oppositional. There are also examples of ritual cursing of enemies as part of the sermon's ending, for example Umayyad cursing of ʿAli and Salafi-oriented preachers' maledictions on allegedly heretical groups (Qutbuddin 2019: 85f, 474). In modern times, states have attempted to boost their legitimacy and persuade citizens to behave in ways beneficial to the regime's interests through imposing control of and centralising content in Friday sermons (see, for example, Hashem 2010; Samuri and Hopkins 2017; Özdalga, this volume).

In his chapter, Jan Retsö discusses how the formal structuring of the Islamic *khuṭbat al-jumʿa* can be seen as evolving from pre-existing regional models of kingship, conflict-solving and public oratory. Drawing on scriptural and archaeological evidence, not least from ancient Ethiopia, Retsö's analysis challenges the way that later Islamic tradition has framed the practices of Muhammad and his followers as fundamentally different from what went on in pre-Islamic Arabia and its surroundings. This chapter raises issues concerning what kind of work the office and speech of the preacher was expected to perform. Rather than having an exclusively religious character, analysis of the ancient *khuṭba* ritual shows how important worldly matters were for the development of this practice.

This early phase of Islam's development has fascinated Muslims throughout the centuries. One of the ways that it has been represented is through films and TV serials. By analysing *khuṭba* scenes in Arab films and TV serials, Jakob Skovgaard-Petersen contributes an analysis of fictionalised accounts of preachers and their audiences, in both historical and contemporary settings. We encounter situations and characters like the Prophet's farewell sermon and his early followers, a fraudster *khaṭīb* and the militant missionary preacher (*dāʿī*). Through sampling material from the mid-twentieth century onwards, Skovgaard-Petersen is able to show a development regarding the type of preacher that is shown in films and on television, as well as the imagined consequences of preachers' speech acts.

Moreover, in many instances, preaching accompanies or is part of a larger ritual practice, rather than being a separate ritual in and of itself. Example of this include marriages, circumcisions and *mawlid* celebrations. Here, the act of preaching – its content, tone and form – is not primarily required to follow a ritual script, but rather to fit within its particular ritual setting. A skilful preacher will adapt to the audience's needs and level of knowledge, the occasion's emotional and thematic key (grieving, celebratory, educational, and so on), as well as the time and space available. In Catharina Raudvere's study of contemporary Bosnian women's preaching (Chapter 3), she analyses such an occasion. The setting is not overtly formal but has its own ritual and performative scripts that need to be followed. In this case, it is a women-only gathering in a Sarajevan mosque, where a sermon was held by a woman trained in the Islamic sciences. Her ability to combine material from the Qurʾan and hadith with topics and scenes from the daily life of the participating women, enabled this preacher to relate everyday concerns and local lives to eternal ideals and models.

Power and Authority

Questions concerning power and authority are central for analyses of Muslim preaching.[3] Who is allowed to preach, where, and how? Who is listened to, by whom, and why? What kind of effects do the speeches of a preacher have on its audience? Mirroring the relatively open category of Islamic religious scholars, there have generally not been fixed restrictions on who can speak publicly on religious matters. As Jonathan P. Berkey's chapter shows, there have been many opinions regarding the suitability of certain preachers, types of oratory and styles of address. But the actual power to curtail and shut down the platform of individual speakers has been less common, not least due to their popularity. When it comes to historical judgements of preaching, it is not simply the case that those who delivered *khuṭab* were considered legitimate, while others, such as 'storytellers' (*quṣṣāṣ*) were not. The category of storyteller was used more ambivalently in the early history of Islam than such a neat division would suggest (Armstrong 2016).

The office of *khaṭīb* came to be an official appointment, related to the political ruler of the day. Still, debates around the power and authority of preachers continue unabated. Several modern Muslim-majority states have tried to curtail and control Muslim preachers. It is also noteworthy that the role and influence of Muslim preachers is often discussed – and feared – in countries where Muslims are a religious minority. This can be seen in, for example, legal efforts to either ban certain travelling foreign preachers from entering the country, or to deport imam-preachers whose activity is seen to be a threat to national security. These tendencies show that Muslim preachers, in particular preachers who are deemed to be radical, are expected to wield substantial authority and have great power to influence supposedly compliant audiences. Their power of persuasion is often more or less taken for granted.

Yet the authority of a preacher is not as self-evident, stable or obvious as such control efforts might imply. In fact, there are many obstacles to – even forms of resistance against – preachers' ability to move audiences in a desired direction. In his study of authority, Bruce Lincoln (1994) chooses to focus on instances of when attempts to speak authoritatively fails – for example, when an expected exercise of authority is challenged. Authority is not something a person 'has', like a personal gift or quality. Rather, it is an intensely interactional potential outcome of particular, contextually situated interactions between a speaker and an audience. Various audiences will therefore ascribe different speakers with authority, based on criteria and expectations that reflect their collective identity. What works for a preacher in one social context, might not be successful in another. Ability to perform culturally esteemed ritual roles – such as performing the Friday sermon according to the traditional requirements or mastering authoritative texts like the Qur'an and hadith – will increase the likelihood of succeeding in speaking authoritatively to an audience accustomed to these particular norms.

The development of modern states, with their complex bureaucratic structures, has offered renewed possibilities as well as challenges in terms of regulating and centralising preaching, in particular the *khuṭbat al-jumʿa*, thus 'putting preaching to work' (cf. Starrett 1998) in order to accomplish social and cultural change. Increased centralisation and institutionalisation of religious life is a complicated and afflicting process. The Muslim-majority country that has gone furthest along that road is without doubt Turkey. In Elisabeth Özdalga's chapter, focus is on the Turkish Directorate of Religious Affairs (Diyanet) and the sometimes harsh negotiations between this institution, other state institutions like the military, various governmental offices and representatives of religious professions with ambitions to promote religious interests. The Turkish case offers valuable insights into the dilemmas encountered when Friday sermons are standardised to the degree that the same sermon is offered to all mosque congregations – on the one hand, making efforts to unify the whole nation around the same homily and, on the other, having to realise that the contents are so trite in order to please everyone that, in fact, they miss the active interest of any of the heterogeneous audiences.

Mediation

This theme, on the one hand, includes attention to particular forms of dissemination and interaction in contemporary media landscapes – for example radio, social media and television – and how these have been used in relation to Muslim preaching. On the other hand, the theme of mediation acknowledges and engages with the mediated quality of preaching (and other forms of discourse) in a broader sense, as it is dependent on material factors like the human voice and the senses, meaning that it also 'shapes the making of religious subjects' (Hirschkind and Larkin 2008: 4). Preaching is generally a form of oratory, which means that the human voice and an audience's sense of hearing are central to its production, circulation and reception. Voices are in themselves not neutral carriers of meaning or evaluated equally. They are listened to differently, whether due to culturally informed gender ideologies (Schulz 2012), evaluations of different languages, dialects and idioms (Millie 2017), or because of their sound effects and the soundscapes within which they are listened to (Hirschkind 2006). However, when studying preaching in past periods (before audio recordings became common), we have to use written accounts – and critiques – of preaching and preachers. Sermons preserved in writing can – and do – serve as ideals, models for living preachers to use, inhabit and allude to in order to enhance their own authority.

In contemporary times, there is a variety of media formats through which preaching can be disseminated. Sometimes, the preaching is adapted specifically to a particular media genre and type of audience (see, for example, contributions in Lynch 2017). Elaborate analyses of the processes, strategies and struggles of utilising the affordances of a particular media form are found in Yasmin Moll's studies of the internal workings of the Islamic TV channel Iqra. Moll shows that the preachers vary in their preaching style as well as personal and educational background, meaning that they make an effort to attract different audiences (Moll 2010, 2012). There are also disagreements and discussions among performers and producers regarding how to best use the TV medium in an Islamically appropriate way: how best to subtitle Arabic shows into English (Moll 2017), and how to use the visually entertaining possibilities of the TV medium, rather than simply showing the talking head of a preacher in minimalist style, which is often preferred by Salafi-oriented actors (Moll 2018). Uses of and reflections on various media formats for preaching purposes are an important field of inquiry.

Media can also offer people whose social freedoms are curtailed enhanced opportunities for communicating with larger audiences. The Saudi female preachers studied in Laila Makboul's chapter are well educated and articulate, yet there are limits to the ways in which they can act in public as Islamic scholars. Through their use of social media, however, they are able to connect with a large and varied number of people – women as well as men. This means that their voices – both literally and metaphorically – can be heard well beyond the confines of women's physical gatherings. Such a transgression of physically demarcated gendered spaces can allow these women to participate in public discourses in new ways; however, this also means that they become more exposed to public moral criticism as well as apparatuses of state repression. In addition, even though these women in some ways expand the frame of women's public roles, the religious messages they communicate are nevertheless socially conservative. A newfound media-based publicness is not necessarily used to challenge dominant discourses or advocate progressive values.

In Simon Stjernholm's chapter, a different kind of adaptation to the contemporary media environment is examined, namely preachers' production of short videos that are disseminated through social media. With everything simultaneously present for today's media users, some preachers try to attract an audience's attention in order to activate pious norms and influence young Muslims towards what is seen to be a more pious lifestyle. The societal context in this chapter is the minority context of Sweden, where non-Muslim norms and practices dominate public discourse. In ways comparable to the TV channel studied by Moll, but in a much more low-budget and do-it-yourself manner (Stjernholm 2019) and, crucially, with a self-imposed brevity, individual preachers combine audio and visual modes of communication and try out various genres. When employed effectively, this type of preaching can achieve a different kind of rhetorical work than a regular lecture or sermon. Preachers who creatively combine genres and communicative modes, as well as adapt to the temporal economy of contemporary media practices, can thereby broaden their appeal and potential influence.

Identities

While preachers in general can be said to exhort their audiences towards being more observant of religious duties (*ʿibādāt*) and avoid sinful temptations in order to be rewarded rather than punished in the hereafter, there are also many issues regarding social and religious identities at play. Who are 'we' and 'they' in a given preacher's rhetoric? How do preachers articulate the rights, duties and status of different groups: men and women, children and parents, Muslims and non-Muslims, or various ethnic groups and nationalities? How are audiences encouraged to relate (or not) to the society in which they live? With whom should they identify, and why? These and similar issues are often central in preachers' discourses. Naming and addressing various groups have a long history in Islamic tradition. The Qurʾan itself addresses a number of different groups, often without defining them in detail, such as the believers (*al-muʾminūn*) and the people of the book (*ahl al-kitāb*). Muslim preachers throughout history have used various terms, often taken from the Qurʾan and other authoritative texts, to speak about groups of people. These terms are then filled with the semantic content best suited to the message a speaker is advocating, for example expressing sectarian and political conflicts through the use of terms like 'unbelievers' (*kuffār*) or 'hypocrites' (*munāfiqūn*).

With the development of the modern state, national identities have come to the fore also in various forms of preaching. This may be conveyed as authoritative statements in *khuṭab* or officially supervised *waʿẓ* oratory promoting the interests of the state or the dominant ethnic group. Such boosting of national identities in homiletic discourses is especially characteristic for Muslim majority countries, such as Turkey, Egypt and Jordan. The situation is different in Muslim-minority and/or migration contexts, where a particular political ideology may serve as an essential identity marker. In Susanne Olsson's chapter on the *daʿwa* videos of a puritan Salafi group in contemporary Sweden, she shows how their preachers take care to distinguish themselves from all violence, as well as being very concerned with the local environment in the socially troubled suburbs of Stockholm. To these local Salafi preachers, with an Islamic education from Saudi Arabia, it is essential to ground all their claims in scriptural 'proofs', thereby portraying themselves as true Muslims. From that self-understanding, they address what they see as social and religious ills, ranging from troublemakers and petty criminals in the suburbs to Islamic State sympathisers and jihadi foreign fighters. These preachers give 'advice' on the importance of not straying from what they see as the correct Islamic path, with reference to the pious forefathers.

Yet identities are not only relevant in public life and between groups of people distinguished by creed, religious practice or ideology. In a chapter focused on domestic life, in particular marriage and gender roles, Linda Jones analyses two very different instances of preaching: one pre-modern, the other contemporary; one from a Muslim majority context, the other from a minority context; one with a message of hyper-masculinity and wifely obedience, the other emphasising gender equality and marital harmony. Yet the analytical point is not to argue for a gradual general development from conservative to progressive Muslim interpretations of marriage. Rather, Jones is able to show a remarkable continuity in spite of the obvious discrepancies. The two preachers refer to the same texts and specific verses but render interpretations of them that are widely separated. This makes it exceptionally evident that the individual preacher on the one hand can be an outstandingly important character, if able to persuade the audience of the correctness of a particular interpretation and path of action, but on the other hand, an individual preacher is very much embedded in a social, political and cultural environment where certain discourses are dominant. In order to find a successful combination between the heritage of religious tradition, individual interpretation and the particular context of uttered speech with its specific audience, the preacher needs to strike a delicate balance.

As the varied cases in this book illustrate, Muslim preaching takes many forms. Though being a potentially vast field of research, this introduction has pointed to some entry points and analytical paths we see as useful. These can be relevant across cultural and historical differences, which brings us to another topic, namely studies of Muslim preaching in comparative perspective. Although most case studies in this volume are not explicitly comparative, the volume nevertheless creates a basis for viewing and understanding practices related to preaching in a comparative light. In particular, this volume brings together studies of both Muslim majority and minority contexts. It also includes analyses of both historical and contemporary material.

Since this combination of perspectives is not very common, we have wanted to bring what is usually treated as separate fields of research a little closer together. The aim is that this will generate new perspectives on the studied material, by providing it with a somewhat different context than the one commonly established by academic disciplines. In the volume's epilogue, we will briefly elaborate on possible further problematics and lines of inquiry that might prove useful in future research.

Notes

1. Notably, in her recent work on Arabic oration, Qutbuddin (2019: 16) writes that she utilises a 'multipronged approach in my analysis that combines methodologies from a large and eclectic package of disciplines, including orality, literary criticism, linguistics, communication theory, discourse analysis, anthropology, sociology, theology and religion, historiography, political science, jurisprudence, thematic and context analysis, music theory, gender and post-colonial studies, trauma studies, Qur'an exegesis, the Muslim prophetic tradition (hadith), biblical studies, philosophy, and studies of Classical Greece and Rome'.
2. However, for an overview of how the classical Islamic oratorical heritage is variously used and modified in different contemporary national environments, see Qutbuddin 2019: 432–84.
3. For an overview of religious authority and religious authorities in Muslim societies more generally, see Krämer and Schmidtke 2006.

Bibliography

Antoun, Richard T. (1989), *Muslim Preacher in the Modern World: A Jordanian Case Study in Comparative Perspective*, Princeton: Princeton University Press.

Armstrong, Lyall R. (2016), *The Quṣṣāṣ of Early Islam*, Leiden: Brill.

Asad, Talal (1986), *The Idea of an Anthropology of Islam*, Washington DC: Centre for Contemporary Arab Studies, Georgetown University.

Berkey, Jonathan P. (2001), *Popular Preaching and Religious Authority in the Medieval Islamic Near East*, Seattle: University of Washington Press.

Brinton, Jacquelene G. (2016), *Preaching Islamic Renewal: Religious Authority and Media in Contemporary Egypt*, Oakland: University of California Press.

Cook, Michael A. (2000), *Commanding Right and Forbidding Wrong in Islamic Thought*, Cambridge: Cambridge University Press.

Eickelman, Dale F. and James Piscatori (1996), *Muslim Politics*, Princeton: Princeton University Press.

Gaffney, Patrick D. (1994) *The Prophet's Pulpit: Islamic Preaching in Contemporary Egypt*, Berkeley: University of California Press.

Grimes, Ronald L. (2008), 'Performance Theory and the Study of Ritual', in P. Antes, A. W. Geertz and R. R. Warne (eds), *New Approaches to the Study of Religion, Volume 2: Textual, Comparative, Sociological, and Cognitive Approaches*, Berlin and New York: Walter de Gruyter, pp. 109–38.

Halldén, Philip (2001), *Islamisk predikan på ljudkassett: En studie i retorik och fonogramologi*, Lund: Almqvist & Wiksell International.

Halldén, Philip (2005), 'What Is Arab Islamic Rhetoric? Rethinking the History of Muslim Oratory Art and Homiletics', *International Journal of Middle East Studies* 37 (1): 19–38.

Hashem, Mazen (2010), 'The Ummah in the Khutba: A Religious Sermon or a Civil Discourse?', *Journal of Muslim Minority Affairs* 30 (1): 49–61.

Hirschkind, Charles (2006), *The Ethical Soundscape: Cassette Sermons and Islamic Counterpublics*, New York: Columbia University Press.

Hirschkind, Charles and Brian Larkin (2008), 'Introduction: Media and the Political Forms of Religion', *Social Text* 26 (3 (96)): 1–9.

Jones, Linda G. (2012), *The Power of Oratory in the Medieval Muslim World*, Cambridge: Cambridge University Press.

Kalmbach, Hilary (2015), 'Blurring Boundaries: Aesthetics, Performance, and the Transformation of Islamic Leadership', *Culture and Religion* 16 (2): 160–74.

Krämer, Gudrun and Sabine Schmidtke (2006), 'Introduction: Religious Authority and Religious Authorities in Muslim Societies: A Critical Overview', in *Speaking for Islam: Religious Authorities in Muslim Societies*, G. Krämer and S. Schmidtke (eds), Leiden and Boston: Brill, pp. 1–14.

Lincoln, Bruce (1994), *Authority: Construction and Corrosion*, Chicago: University of Chicago Press.

Lynch, Marc (ed.) (2017), *New Islamic Media*, POMEPS Studies 23, Institute for Middle East Studies, George Washington University, <https://pomeps.org/wp-content/uploads/2017/02/POMEPS_Studies_23_Media_Web-rev.pdf> (last accessed 10 November 2019).

Meyer, Birgit (2011), 'Mediation and Immediacy: Sensational Forms, Semiotic Ideologies and the Question of the Medium', *Social Anthropology/Anthropologie Sociale* 19 (1): 23–39.

Millie, Julian (2017), *Hearing Allah's Call: Preaching and Performance in Indonesian Islam*, Ithaca, NY: Cornell University Press.

Moll, Yasmin (2010), 'Islamic Televangelism: Religion, Media and Visuality in Contemporary Egypt', *Arab Media & Society* 10: 1–27.

Moll, Yasmin (2012), 'Storytelling, Sincerity, and Islamic Televangelism in Egypt', in P. Ninan Thomas and P. Lee (eds), *Global and Local Televangelism*, Basingstoke: Palgrave Macmillan, pp. 21–44.

Moll, Yasmin (2017), 'Subtitling Islam: Translation, Mediation, Critique', *Public Culture* 29 (2): 333–61.

Moll, Yasmin (2018), 'Television is Not Radio: Theologies of Mediation in the Egyptian Islamic Revival', *Cultural Anthropology* 33 (2): 233–65.

Qutbuddin, Tahera (2008), '*Khuṭba*: The Evolution of Early Arabic Oration', in W. Heinrichs, M. Cooperson and B. Greundler (eds), *Classical Arabic Humanities in Their Own Terms: Festschrift for Wolfhart Heinrichs on His 65th Birthday*, Leiden: Brill, pp. 176–273.

Qutbuddin, Tahera (2019), *Arabic Oration: Art and Function*, Leiden: Brill.

Samuri, Mohd Al Adib and Peter Hopkins (2017), 'Voices of Islamic Authorities: Friday Khutba in Malaysian Mosques', *Islam and Christian–Muslim Relations* 28 (1): 47–67.

Schulz, Dorothea (2012), 'Dis/Embodying Authority: Female Radio "Preachers" and the Ambivalences of Mass-mediated Speech in Mali', *International Journal of Middle East Studies* 44 (1): 23–43.

Starrett, Gregory (1998), *Putting Islam to Work: Education, Politics, and Religious Transformation in Egypt*, Berkeley: University of California Press.

Stjernholm, Simon (2019), 'DIY Preaching and Muslim Religious Authority', *Journal of Muslims in Europe* 8 (2): 197–215.

PART I

RITUAL AND PERFORMANCE

1

THE FRAMEWORK OF ISLAMIC RHETORIC: THE RITUAL OF THE *KHUṬBA* AND ITS ORIGIN

Jan Retsö

The *Khuṭba* Ritual

The word *khuṭba* means 'oration' and can be used in Arabic for any kind of public speech. To most people today, however, the word designates a special kind of public oration, namely the sermon in the mosque held at noon on Fridays. It is this kind of speech that will be dealt with in this chapter, since the Friday noon *khuṭba* is the main context of rhetoric in Islam. In many ways it can be seen as the Middle Eastern counterpart to the public political speech in Hellenistic antiquity – the mosques in Islam playing a similar role to that of the agora/forum in the Hellenistic-Roman world. To be sure, mosques are centres for religious activities like praying, study and discussion, but they also function as a general meeting place where a great variety of things can be discussed. The *khuṭba* ritual on Fridays, however, has a special status as one of the main rituals of Islam. It is also a unique Islamic institution, the origins of which are not completely known. This chapter offers an introduction to the historical aspects of that ritual.

The outline of the ritual practised for more than a millennium is as follows: after the call to prayer (*adhān*) from the minaret at noon when the congregation is assembled, the preacher (*khaṭīb*), often equipped with a stick, ascends the minbar or 'pulpit', and sits down. Then a second *adhān* is heard, this time not sung in the festive manner of the call to prayer from the minaret. The *khaṭīb* then rises, gives a *khuṭba*, often leaning on the stick, after which he sits down again. After a short silence he rises a second time and gives another *khuṭba*. Then he descends from the minbar while the *muʾadhdhin*, the person voicing the call to prayer, sounds a new *adhān* for prayer, the *iqāma*. The following *ṣalāt* prayer consists of two *rakʿāt* or prayer cycles, not four as is the religious obligation (*farḍ*) for the noon prayer on other weekdays (Wensinck 1986: 74–5; for a classic description of the ceremony including a specimen of a sermon, see Lane 1966: 85–92).

According to custom, the following elements should be present in a *khuṭba*:

1. *al-ḥamdallah*, the praise of God;
2. *ṣalāt al-nabī*, the prayer for the Prophet;
3. *al-waṣiyya*, the exhortation to piety;
4. *al-duʿāʾ*, the prayer for the believers;
5. *al-qirāʾa*, the reading from the Qurʾan.

There is some discussion in the different law schools about how to distribute these elements. Most agree that (1), (2) and (3) should occur in both sermons; (4) should occur only in the second. The position of the *qirāʾa* is debated. Most allow it to occur in both sermons, but it is preferable to have it in the first one. There is a tradition that in earlier times the reading from the Qurʾan could be quite long. The Prophet himself is said to have read *sūrat qāf* (Sura 50) in its entirety (Becker 2006: 51–74; originally published as Becker 1912). The custom today is to read one of the short suras at the end of the Qurʾan or just a few verses from one of the longer ones.

The Public Speech in the Age of the Prophet

The Friday *khuṭba* is not mentioned explicitly in the Qurʾan. The Friday service is mentioned only once (Q. 62:9): ‘O believers, when proclamation is made for prayer (*nūdiya li-ṣ-ṣalāti*) on the Day of Congregation (*yawmi l-jumuʿati*), hasten to God’s remembrance (*dhikri l-lāhi*) and leave trafficking (*bayʿ*) aside; that is better for you, did you but know’ (Arberry’s translation, 1964). The Qurʾan prescribes an unspecified number of daily prayers, but this passage singles out Friday as a day of specific ‘mentioning’ or ‘remembrance’ of God. The exact meaning of the term *dhikr* is not clear. The word *khuṭba* is not mentioned. It is not even said which of the daily prayers is intended.

There are features in the oral performance of the *khuṭba* which undoubtedly have pre-Islamic roots. Public speech in front of the majlis, the tribal council of elders, was most likely a well-established custom in Arabia and we have several specimens in early Arabic literature of speeches said to have been held in pre-Islamic times. Their genuineness can be doubted, but the linguistic form and style in these pseudepigraphic texts without doubt reflect an early rhetorical tradition in Arabia, for example the frequent use of rhymed prose, the continuous use of parallelism, chiasms and antitheses, as well as the dominating tone of moral instruction and, not least, the employment of the Arabiyya language (Dähne 2001: 171–210).[1] It is very likely that the Arabiyya was used in this context in pre-Islamic Arabia and that this was one of the main factors that made it a pan-Arabian medium which could be used all over Arabia without being the mother tongue of everybody – or anyone – in the audience. In fact, it can be argued that large parts of the Qurʾan itself, especially in the so-called Medinan suras, reflect this kind of rhetorical moral instruction.

Public speech in pre-Islamic Arabia took place on a spot singled out for that purpose, by a procedure called *ikhtiṭāṭ*. There is evidence that the place was marked by a fence and/or a fosse (*khandaq*), and a kind of sacredness like that of the *ḥimā* was attributed to it. The *ḥimā* was an area which stood under specific restrictions and taboos, among which were the prohibition of the killing of animals and bloodshed. Even from the Islamic sources we hear that one of the designations for this place was masjid, a word which is now also documented from pre-Islamic South Arabia, where it most probably refers to Jewish or Christian places for prayer (Lammens 1911: 242, nn. 1 and 4; Biella 1982: 327). Masjid and majlis seem to be used as synonyms even if the two words originally may refer to different things. Masjid could be derived from the Syriac root s-g-d, 'to perform prostration' (*proskynesis*), that is, a place for proskynesis. Proskynesis was practised in monastic environments independently of the Christian liturgy (Vööbus 1988: 167–9). This would point towards a milieu of asceticism and monastic life.

Muhammad's masjid in Yathrib was apparently a place where proskynesis was performed as well as nocturnal vigils with recitation of the holy text, elements deriving from Syriac monastic practices. But it was also a place of public meeting often mentioned in biographies of the Prophet Muhammad, the *sīra* literature. Even if it had a kind of sacredness, it was not primarily a place for religious cult in the conventional sense. In ancient Arabia, the majlis seems to have been mainly a neutral ground where people could meet and discuss matters of mutual concern, not least to solve conflicts. This is why the public speech, the *khuṭba*, belonged to it. The latter factor implied that it was often under the protection of a chief with acknowledged judicial authority, a most important function in conflict-ridden pre-Islamic Arabia. As far as the Prophet's majlis is concerned, this makes good sense: Muhammad's main function in Yathrib according to the Medina document, which is one of the very few contemporary documents we have about Muhammad's Medina, was that of an arbiter, a *fayṣal*, a mediator in conflicts (Wellhausen 1889: 67–73; Wensinck 1982: 52–71; Nagel 2008: 342–7; Donner 2010: 72–5, 227–32). In many ways the old Arabian majlis looks similar to the *thingvöll* in early medieval Scandinavia, which is especially well documented from Iceland, where it was a place for negotiations and conflict-solving, screened off from the surroundings and characterised by certain taboos (Byock 2001: 170–84). The parallel becomes even more interesting due to the many salient parallels between pre-Islamic Arabia and medieval Iceland, two societies in crisis. The use of both terms, masjid and majlis, for the house of the Prophet in Yathrib indicated that it combined two functions: a house of ceremonial ritual for the believers, and a rallying place for local visitors from the surroundings of Yathrib as well as the rest of Arabia.

The majlis/masjid was a meeting place for discussion, solving of conflicts and instruction which generated the rhetorical tradition that survived and was developed in Islamic tradition. The traditions about the Prophet show, however, that speeches of hortatory and instructive nature were not limited to the majlis in Yathrib. He is said to have delivered *khuṭab* in many places, sometimes even sitting on the back of a camel, such as the famous farewell speech delivered in 632 during the hajj, just before his death. But the main forum was obviously the majlis of his own house. So, a *khuṭba* could be delivered everywhere, not only in the majlis/masjid. It should, however, be remembered that none of these reported speeches show the characteristics of the present-day Friday *khuṭba*, as outlined above.

Origins of the Ceremony

In the early twentieth century, the islamologist Carl Becker (1912) suggested that the basic structure of Friday prayer, the *khuṭba* and the following *ṣalāt*, could be derived from the Christian liturgy. He pointed out that the obligation of reciting the Qurʾan, the hortatory *waṣiyya* (admonition) and the finishing *duʿāʾ* (supplication), are basic elements in the Christian pre-Eucharist: reading of scripture, sermon and intercession for the believers. He further claimed that the following *ṣalāt* was the equivalent to the Eucharist.

The following year, Becker's colleague Eugen Mittwoch (1913) criticised several of his conclusions. Instead he pointed to the parallels in the Jewish synagogal service on the Sabbath as a more obvious parallel. The Jewish morning service on the Sabbath contains the usual confession of the creed (the *shemaʿ*) followed by seven supplications, *berakhôt*. Then comes the ceremonial reading of the Torah during which the reader stands up. The scrolls are folded together by the reader or someone else sitting down. The reading of Torah is followed by reading from the Prophets (the *haftarah*), the function of which is said to be that of consolation and hope. The reader has to stand up again. After the ceremonial readings comes the intercession for the congregation. On sabbaths the readings are followed by a repetition of the seven supplications, the so-called *mûsaf*-prayer (Elbogen 1967 [1931]: 14–60, 112–17, 155–98). Mittwoch points out that the reciting of the seven supplications according to Talmudic tradition (Talmud Babli Berakhot 34b) originally contained prostrations during the first and last one. According to Mittwoch, the *adhān* before the *khuṭba* is a remnant of the recitation of the *shemaʿ*. The *khuṭba* itself corresponds to the two readings from Scripture and the finishing *ṣalāt* is derived from the *mûsaf*-prayer.

Mittwoch's arguments have much that speak in their favour. One could remark that the Talmudic tradition also mentions hortatory sermons in connection with the readings from Scripture. The question is, of course, how to understand the historical connection between the Jewish service and the assumed Islamic one. We are not certain that the classic structure of the Friday service was established in Medina during the Prophet's lifetime. Goitein has quite convincingly argued that the reason for choosing Friday was the fact that this day was a market day in Medina. The *khuṭba* was held at noon because that was the hour when the transactions at the market were finished (Goitein 1966: 111–25) What is fairly certain is that the Friday ritual was established in Medina, not in Mecca (Nagel 2008: 273–6). It is interesting to note that according to the Medina Constitution, some of the members of the community of the Prophet were Jewish clans (Donner 2010: 72–4). One should also keep in mind that the Jewish Torah-reading and the Christian pre-Eucharist have a common (Jewish) root which is obvious from the many parallels between them. It raises the question about the connections between early Islam and the other two Abrahamic religions. The difference between Christianity and Judaism in Arabia at this time should not be dramatised. It is often forgotten that there was something called Judaeo-Christianity and the religion found in the Qurʾan is very close to this movement (Donner 2010: 214–15).

The Minbar

It is said that in the beginning Muhammad used to lean on a palm trunk when speaking. But we also hear about the Prophet's minbar. According to the descriptions it was a wooden construction of two low steps on which a primitive chair was placed. The chair indicates that the speaker delivered his speech sitting down. The sources claim that this device was introduced during the last years of the Prophet's life (Becker 1906; see, for example, al-Ṭabarī I: 1591).

The tradition about the minbar indicates a special function. The sitting down shows that here we have something else than the *khuṭba* as described above. The use of a seat is namely connected with court procedures and judgement. This use was widespread in the ancient Middle East and is often mentioned also in texts referring to pre-Islamic Arabia. It is difficult to judge if the mentioning of the Prophet delivering a *khuṭba* from this minbar is genuine. It could, of course, very well reflect the usage of later times. But there is no doubt that the chair is connected with the authority of a judge or a ruler. Muhammad's role as a mediator in the Medina Constitution goes well with the idea of a minbar and this could be a hard-core historical memory.

The word minbar is obviously a borrowed word from an Ethiosemitic language. The normal verb for 'to sit' in Geez is *nabara*, and *mənbar* or *manbar* means 'place of sitting', that is 'chair', 'seat', 'throne'. It is also remarkable that the stone thrones, called the thrones of judges, standing today in the sacred precinct at Aksum, the holy city of Christian Ethiopia, very well fit the description of the Prophet's minbar (Krencker 1913: 45–69 and Tafeln XIII, XIV (also in Krencker)). Since they most likely are from the Aksumite period (300–600 CE), they shed unexpected light on the story of the Prophet's minbar. It can be suggested that this piece of furniture was introduced in Yathrib under the influence of Ethiopian tradition as is indicated by its very name. The connection between the early Muslim community and Ethiopia is a fact indicated in the sources. The most well known is the story of how a group of Muslims from Mecca, among them the future caliph ʿUthmān ibn ʿAffān (d. 656), sought refuge with the Ethiopian *negus* and stayed there for ten years (Ibn Hishām 1858: 208ff.).

That the minbar was seen as a throne is very well documented in early Islamic sources. When Abū Bakr (d. 634) was proclaimed the successor to Muhammad, he sat on a minbar in the masjid of the Prophet (Ibn Hishām 1858: 1017; al-Ṭabarī I: 1228). Muʿāwiya (d. 680) tried to bring this object to Damascus where it would serve as a throne. It is also said that the Umayyads had a practice of giving *khuṭab* sitting down on the minbar, not standing up, a practice rejected by later orthodoxy (al-Ṭabarī I: 2144, 2800, 3068).

The use of a chair as a sign of judicial authority is well known from Jewish tradition. In Matthew 23:2, Jesus says that the scribes and Pharisees sit on Moses' *kathedra*, that is 'seat', from where they impose rules on the people. At least one such seat has been found, the one in the synagogue at Korazin in Galilee. The custom continued in the throne of the bishop in early Christianity. We have samples of images of rulers in the Middle East sitting on a throne and, interestingly enough, equipped with a stick, for example the famous relief of Darius the Great from Persepolis (Porada 1985: fig. 23). The stick or rod is, of course, a very ancient representation of power and authority. The term for the rod of Moses or Aaron (*shebeṭ ʾelôhîm*, 'the divine rod', Exodus 4:20) shows that it originally was seen as more or less a separate deity and the stick of the present-day *khaṭīb* may thus have a venerable history behind it. In Christian art there are some representations of the enthroned Christ holding the cross which looks very much like the stick held by Darius the Great.

There are thus several indications that the minbar originally is a throne, the seat of a ruler that was used also in Arabia for men of authority. It was a place from which the ruler could speak with a special kind of authority. Today the Pope has a special authority when he speaks 'from the throne', *ex cathedra*. And we can still observe the concrete ceremony today, performed once every year at the State Opening of the UK Parliament, when the monarch delivers the throne speech. In Sweden it was also the custom until 1973 for the king to give the throne speech standing in front of the silver throne of Queen Christina. This practice is still upheld in the Norwegian Parliament.

The minbar is thus a throne upon which the ruler proclaims his judgements and laws. In Islamic tradition this custom is attributed to the Umayyads and is seen as yet another sign of their ungodliness and heresy. We do not know for sure if the uniting of the traditional pre-Islamic *khuṭba* with the ordinances of the ruler from the throne goes back to the Prophet himself. But for later *sharʿi*-minded circles, the usurpation of the *khuṭba* by the Umayyads met with strong opposition.[2] It looks as if the practice of standing up when delivering the *khuṭba* became a mark of anti-Umayyad opposition. We have seen that the standing up most likely comes from Jewish tradition. It would not be the only Jewish element in the *sharʿi* movement that became a major component in Islam after the Abbasid revolution and later became the foundation of Sunnite Islam. One fact should be pointed out: the specimens of public oration we have (compare with Dähne *loco citato*) do not exhibit the structure of the *khuṭba* as it is known today. If the connection with the Jewish Sabbath service is true, both the standing up and the structure of the *khuṭba* may be the result of applying Jewish (or Judaeo-Christian) elements in certain circles in the Umayyad period as a sign of opposition.

As regards the physical shape of the minbar today, we notice that it looks very different from the original one in Medina. Where does it come from? The earliest preserved specimen of a minbar of the type that became standard in Islam is the one still standing in the Great Mosque of Qayrawān, Tunisia. This piece was originally made in Samarra, Iraq, around 850 CE (Golmohammadi 1993: 76). This might not be a pure coincidence. In 1950, the Swedish scholar Geo Widengren started a series of studies on the traditions around kingship in the ancient Middle East and its afterlife in later ages. He points out that far back in time, already during the Sumerian age, that is 2000 BCE and earlier, the enthronement of the ruler of the city state can be shown to have consisted of a ritual ascension on a staircase to the main temple in the city state for an encounter with the main god(s). From there he received a written text, the Tablets of Destiny, on which the events of the coming year were written. Equipped with these he then appeared to the people and proclaimed the new year. We can quote a text emanating from Sippar, *c.*2000 BCE:

> Enmeduranki, the king of Sippar,
> The beloved of Anu, Enlil and Ea,
> Shamash into Ebarra caused him to enter,
> Shamash and Adad to their assembly called him
> Shamash and Adad on a great golden throne placed him,
> To inspect oil on water, the secret of Anu, Enlil and Ea they taught him,
> The tablets of gold, the bag with the mystery of heaven and earth,
> The cedar staff, the darling of the great gods, they caused his hand to seize.
> (Widengren 1950: 7–8)

It is, of course, a bold hypothesis that the whole set-up of the Islamic *khuṭba* is formed by memories of this ancient ceremony. But when looking at the material it is not unlikely. Traditions and customs from ancient Mesopotamia were very much alive and remembered not least in Iraq, adopted and transmitted by the Iranian dynasties who ruled large parts of the Middle East from the sixth century BCE until the rise of Islam. Many of these ancient traditions and ceremonies were then taken over by the Roman Empire. The throne ceremonies of Western European monarchies in fact show strong influences from the Middle East, both via imperial tradition from the Late Roman Empire into Byzantine times and direct influence during the early Middle Ages. Is it really only a coincidence that the physical shape of the minbar since the ninth century CE until today is reminiscent of the staircase of the Mesopotamian *ziqurrat*?

Notes

1. Specimens are found, for example, in the writings attributed to Wahb b. Munabbih: *Kitāb at-tījān* (1928). Several examples from the early Islamic period can be studied in Dähne 2001: 27–137; cf. ibid. 248. The term Arabiyya is

used as a cover term for the language of the early Arabic poetry, the Qur'an, the Medieval classical literature and Modern Standard Arabic. These represent different variants and periods of a language which, however, preserves its main characteristics during the ages. The term Classical Arabic is not quite adequate as a cover term and should be reserved for the linguistic system established by the medieval grammarians, which is a further variant of the Arabiyya and remains a grammatical ideal, a kind of grammatical shariʿa.

2. For the concept of the *sharʿi* movement, see Hodgson 1974: 315–58.

Bibliography

Arberry, Arthur J. (1964), *The Koran Interpreted*, London: Oxford University Press.

Becker, Carl H. (1906), 'Die Kanzel im Kultus des alten Islam', in C. Bezold (ed.), *Orientalische Studien Theodor Nöldeke zum siebzigsten Geburtstag (2 März 1906) gewidmet von Freunden und Schülern*, Vol. 1, Gieszen: Alfred Töpelmann, pp. 331–51.

Becker, Carl H. (1912), 'Zur Geschichte des islamischen Kultus', *Der Islam* 3, 74–99.

Becker, Carl H. (2006), 'On the History of Muslim Worship', in G. Hawting (ed.), *The Development of Islamic Ritual*, London: Routledge, pp. 51–74.

Biella, Joan C. (1982), *Dictionary of Old South Arabic Sabaean Dialect*, Chico, CA: Scholars Press.

Byock, Jesse (2001), *Viking Age Iceland*, London: Penguin.

Dähne, Stefan (2001), *Reden der Araber: Die politische huṭba in der klassischen arabischen Literatur*, Frankfurt am Main: Peter Lang.

Donner, Fred M. (2010), *Muhammad and the Believers: At the Origins of Islam*, Cambridge, MA: Belknap Press.

Elbogen, Ismar (1967 [1931]), *Der jüdische Gottesdienst in seiner geschichtlichen Entwicklung*, 3 Aufl., Berlin; repr. Hildesheim 1967: Olms.

Goitein, Shlomo D. (1966), *Studies in Islamic History and Institutions*, Leiden: Brill.

Golmohammadi, Javad (1993), 'Minbar', *The Encyclopaedia of Islam*, 2nd ed., Vol. 7, Leiden: Brill, p. 76.

Hodgson, Marshall G. S. (1974), *The Venture of Islam, Vol. 1: The Classical Age of Islam*, Chicago and London: The University of Chicago Press.

Ibn Hishām (1858), *Das Leben Muhammed's nach Ibn Ishâk bearbeitet von Abd el-Malik Ibn Hischâm*, Vol. 1, hrsg. F. Wüstenfeld, Göttingen; repr. 1961 Frankfurt am Main: Minerva.

Krencker, Daniel (1913), *Deutsche Aksum-Expedition Bd. II: Ältere Denkmäler in Nordabessinien*, Berlin: Georg Reimer.

Lammens, Henri (1911), 'Ziād ibn Abīhi, vice-roi de l'Iraq, lieutenant de Moʿāwia I', *Rivista degli studi orientali* 4, 1–45.

Lane, Edward William [1860] (1966), *The Manners and Customs of the Modern Egyptians*, London: Dent & Dutton.

Mittwoch, Eugen (1913), *Zur Entstehungsgeschichte des islamischen Gebet und Kultus*, Abhandlungen der Königlichen Preussischen Akademie der Wissenschaften Jahrgang 1913 Phil.-Hist. Classe Nr. 2, Berlin: 3–42.

Nagel, Tilman (2008), *Mohammed: Leben und Legende*, Munich: Oldenburg.

Al-Ṭabarī (1879–1901), *Annales quos scripsit Abu Djafar Mohanmmed ibn Djarir at-Tabari*, I–III, J. Barth, Th. Nöldeke, P. de Jong, E. Prym, H. Thornbacke, I. Fraenkel, I. Guidi, D. M. Müller, M. J. de Goeje, S. Guyard. M. Th. Houtsma and V. Rasen (eds), Leiden: Brill.

Porada, Edith (1985) 'Classical Achaemenian Architecture and Sculpture', in I. Gershevitch (ed.), *Cambridge History of Iran, Vol. 2: The Median and Achaemanian Periods*, Cambridge: Cambridge University Press, pp. 793–827.

Vööbus, Arthur (1988), *History of Asceticism in the Syrian Orient: A Contribution to the History of Culture in the Near East* (CSCO 500), Louvain: Peeters.

Wahb ibn Munabbih (1928), *Kitāb al-tījān ʿan Wahb b. Munabbih riwāyata Abī Muḥmmad ʿAbd allāh b. Hishām*, ed. Zayn al-ʿĀbidīn al-Mūsawī, Haidarabad: Dāʾirat al-maʿārif al-ʿuthmāniyya.

Wellhausen, Julius (1889), 'Muhammads Gemeindeordnung von Medina', *Skizzen und Vorarbeiten* IV, Berlin: Georg Reimer, pp. 67–73.

Wensinck, Arent J. (1982), *Muhammad and the Jews of Medina*, 2nd ed., W. H. Behn (trans.), Berlin: Adyok.

Wensinck, Arent J. (1986), 'Khuṭba', *The Encyclopaedia of Islam*, 2nd ed., Leiden: Brill, pp. 74–5.

Widengren, Geo (1950), 'The Ascension of the Apostle and the Heavenly Book (King and Saviour III)', *Uppsala Universitets Årsskrift* 7, pp. 7–8.

2

THE *KHUṬBA* SCENE IN ARAB RELIGIOUS FILMS AND TV DRAMAS

Jakob Skovgaard-Petersen

The growing body of scholarship on ʿulamaʾ in the twentieth century tends to focus on the rise of their institutions, the development of their teaching, their relationship to the state and their international linkages.[1] There has also been some interest in how they began to use the media, in particular print. However, the depiction of ʿulamaʾ in modern fiction has received little scholarly attention. This is unfortunate, as it might yield insights into the changing role and status of the *ʿālim* in modern Muslim societies. As vehicles of mass culture, film and later television are interesting, not just for their mass culture appeal, but also for their capacity to create identifiable images and stereotypical roles. This chapter explores the changing perceptions of the role of the ʿulamaʾ by focusing on one particular activity of theirs, the delivery of the Friday sermon, and on how the films and TV dramas relate them to their audiences.

Analysing a specific scene can be fruitful. Film narrative is composed in edited scenes of light and sound. Specific locations, acts or characters evoke particular responses in audiences, often supported by standard shots or sounds. For instance, a scene of a muezzin's call to prayer, with a panoramic shot of a rural landscape and village, is a staple of Egyptian films. This scene connotes the tranquil, peaceful rhythm of daily life as it once was, and perhaps ought to be (Qasim 1997: 67). Films rarely depict the call to prayer in a busy, modern Cairo district – although it takes place there as often – but the meaning would be much less clear and identifiable to cinema audiences.

The scene of the Friday *khuṭba* is well known to most Muslim men in the Arab world. Loudspeakers, radio and television have familiarised other groups in Arab society with sermon content, and they readily recognise the scene. The use of the word minbar (pulpit) as the title of Islamic periodicals and TV programmes testifies to the association of the *khuṭba* with authoritative religious address in contemporary Arab public imagery. It is an instance of communication and of collective attention, and thus eminently suited to narratives of social engagement and action, of communal life and of religious inspiration as the mover of men. Hence, it makes for an attractive scene in a film.

The question, then, is how this scene is shot, and what it conveys. What kind of authority (if any at all) does the preacher embody? What are the messages of his sermonising? Does it have an impact? What is the relationship between the audience and the preacher? As we shall see, there is a great variety here, but there are also some developments. My main argument is that, with time, the authoritarian quality of the classical *khuṭba* scene makes it more apt to depict fire-and-brimstone preachers – or good preachers speaking up against rulers or the West – than to characterise the harmonious relationship between the model religious authority and his flock.

This preliminary exploration is far from exhaustive, given the volume of fictional media production. The main directory of Egyptian films lists over 4,000 works produced in the country since 1923 (Qasim 2008). No figures are available for the number of TV serials produced in the Arab world, but in later years over 100 serials, each of thirty episodes, have been produced for the month of Ramadan, mainly in Egypt, Syria and the United Arab Emirates. This is obviously much more than anyone can watch. To identify scenes of *khuṭab*, I rely on two recent Egyptian studies of religion in films (which do not specifically study scenes of the *khuṭba*) and on discussions and interviews with film producers and religious figures in Egypt, Syria, Tunisia and Qatar, as well as on my own ongoing work on the portrayal of ʿulamaʾ in the contemporary Arab TV serial.

The Role of ʿUlamaʾ in Film

The treatment of religion in films varies tremendously. There are works designed to propagate a religion or a religious truth. Among these are the great epic films about events in mythical time, easily recognisable across the various religions because of their numerous set formulas: deep, sonorous narrative voices in a slow, portentous style, long shots, big skies with clouds and lights, and miracles in the form of special effects (Grace 2009: 1). Other films seek to convey a sense of the numinous by evoking the emotional life of an individual believer. More commonly, films include religious references, deal with religious motives or depict religious institutions as part of a broader narrative. It is mainly this latter type of film, which may introduce clergy among its characters, that is analysed here. In European and American films, Christian priests and ministers appear in a variety of roles. There is an anti-clerical tradition of ridiculing priests and ministers as moral hypocrites, or as powerful guardians of an unjust social order. But there are also works depicting the priest as social worker, helping the poor, understanding his flock's social and moral predicaments, and leading the community in times of crisis (in treatments of the resistance during World War II, for instance). On occasion, he is portrayed as a quintessentially modern figure, tormented by doubt, reflecting on existence and striving to behave morally (Butler 1969: 55ff.).

The role of the *ʿālim* in Arab films is considerably less varied. The reason for this, I believe, is that the Egyptian film industry has operated with strict limits on depictions of Islam and Christianity. An early controversy transpired in 1927, when Yusuf Wahby announced his intention to play Muhammad in a French-produced film, and a prohibition against depicting Muhammad in film ensued. In 1931, this proscription was formalised in an industry regulation banning the depiction of the age of the Prophet, or the roles of contemporary men of religion, in films (Shafiq 1998: 48–9). In the growing commercial cinema of Egypt before 1950, the scholar appears only in peripheral roles, such as the judge in a court scene.

This taboo was finally broken in 1951 with the film *Zuhur al-islam* ('The appearance of Islam'). Its director, Ibrahim ʿIzz al-Din, succeeded in enlisting two ministers (his uncle, the new foreign minister Muhammad Salah al-Din Bey, and minister of education Taha Hussein whose novel *Waʿd al-haqq*

('The divine promise') was the basis of the manuscript) to overcome the initial resistance to the project (Salah al-Din 1998: 14–18). *Zuhur al-islam* opened in April 1952 to an enthusiastic reception from both critics and audiences. Faced with the torments and persecution of the first Muslim community (the Prophet Muhammad did not appear in person himself), viewers cried *Allahu akbar!* in the theatres (Salah al-Din 1998: 23–7). *Zuhur al-islam* was a commercial success in Egypt and did well in the wider Arab and Muslim worlds (Salah al-Din 1998: 19–23). Over the next twenty years, a dozen films with religious themes were produced.[2] Ironically, this religious trend 'stopped abruptly at the end of the Nasser era', as Viola Shafiq observes (Shafiq 1998: 170). To these Egyptian films may be added the Syrian Mustafa al-ʿAqqad's famous *al-Risala* ('The message', 1976) which was the first attempt at depicting the life of Muhammad himself (Bakker 2006). *Al-Risala* encountered fierce resistance from King Faysal of Saudi Arabia and was eventually financed and shot in Libya, whose leader, Muammar Ghaddafi, was at odds with the Saudi monarchy. It seems that the difficulty of raising funds in spite of opposition from some (wealthy Gulf) religious quarters, and the rise of television, combined to end this first wave of religious films. When religion reappeared as a theme in Egyptian films in the 1990s, these works were aimed at countering the rise of militant Islamism (Armbrust 2002). The 2000s saw the emergence of 'clean cinema' (*sīnimā naẓīfa*), produced by people from within the Islamic awakening (van Nieuwkerk 2011). Both these tendencies are mirrored in the TV dramas, as we shall see.

Almost all the religious films of the 1950s to 1970s were set in seventh-century Mecca but, respecting the ban against showing the Prophet and his family, centred on peripheral figures in Islamic piety (Shafiq 1998: 170–3). Only two works portrayed later religious figures, namely the Sufis Ahmad al-Badawi (d. 1276), whose shrine in Tanta still attracts huge numbers of Egyptian visitors, and Rabiʿa al-ʿAdawiyya (d. 801), perhaps the most well-known female Sufi. Meanwhile, there was a steady production of historical films, and new attempts at art films and social realism created a space for the introduction of religious characters, including ʿulamaʾ. As a rule, the character of the *ʿālim* continued to be a fairly minor role, and the use of a limited number of actors to play this role (notably Yahya Shahin) ensured that audiences learnt what to expect from it (Qasim 1997: 104–11). The stereotypical ʿālim was a fairly old man, dressed in *galabiyya*, with a red and white turban (ʿ*imāma*) on his head, and often a generation older than the hero. His marital status and private life were rarely revealed. He was a public man, taking part in public discussions, and often expressing public sentiments and positions. But there are also a few more elaborate portraits of ʿulamaʾ. An early one is *Shaykh Hassan* (1954) by Ismail Sidqi, about a young shaykh who converts a Christian girl (Qasim 2008: 229). Another complex portrait is the famous film *al-ʿArd* ('The land', 1969, based on a novel by Abd al-Rahman al-Sharqawi) by Youssef Chahine, about a village that has stood up against the British in 1919, but suffers defeat when the local landlord has a road constructed over some of its land. Here the Azhari Shaykh Hassuna returns from Cairo and tries to mobilise his erstwhile revolutionary brethren who end up on both sides of the conflict. In line with the historical role of the ʿulamaʾ, Shaykh Hassuna commands the prestige and standing to call on the big landowner and the planning office, while also conspiring with the peasants at night. The film depicts the ʿ*ālim* as both an actor and a witness to the event, understanding what is going on, but ultimately powerless in the face of a new kind of brutal capitalism. The cleric is typically leading the peasants against colonial powers, local rulers or capitalists.[3]

Negative portrayals of ʿulamaʾ akin to the European anti-clerical tradition are very rare. A few films from the 1960s show an ʿ*ālim* allied to the corrupt and powerful against the good and humble. This is the case in *al-Zawja al-thāniyya* ('The second wife', Salah Abu Saif, 1967), where the shaykh helps the village chief (ʿ*umda*) by declaring valid his marriage to a beautiful woman, after first having forced one of the village peasants to divorce her (Qasim 1997: 72). *Kahraman* (1958) is the only film portraying the shaykh as sinner, falling in love with the dancing girl who has infatuated his brother. Tellingly, it is based on a European novel, *Taïs*, by Anatole France.

The *Khuṭba* in Films

Khuṭab rarely appear in films. Historical epics set in the early days of Islam obey the prohibition on showing the Prophet Muhammad and have little interest, of course, in showing others preaching. Nevertheless, his teachings are often treated obliquely. In the early religious film *Bilal, muʾadhdhan al-rasul* ('Bilal, the Prophet's muezzin', 1953) by Ahmad al-Tukhi, Bilal has attended the Prophet's sermons and refers to them. At the end of the film, however, Muhammad has died, and Bilal himself addresses the believers in Syria in a *khuṭba*, explaining the prescription for jihad.

A special case is Muhammad's farewell sermon, the *khuṭbat al-waddā'*, considered to be of great importance in the twentieth century as the foundation of an Islamic humanism addressed to all mankind. The most famous of all Arab religious films, Mustafa al-'Aqqad's *al-Risala* ('The message', 1976), is known for using subjective camera to overcome the prohibition against showing Muhammad, in effect situating the camera inside his eyes in a few scenes (Bakker 2006: 83). This feature is employed elegantly and powerfully in the final scenes, where the narrator explains that Muhammad, knowing his death was near, summoned people to his last pilgrimage and addressed them for the last time. When Muhammad speaks, the narrative moves to direct address of the audience, as if this is now Muhammad's own voice. The camera pans over the faces of the believers, not as an undistinguished mass, but as individual representatives of mankind: men and women, young and old, of dark and light complexion, all in deep concentration and emotion, relishing the historical moment when, for the last time, man will receive the direct speech of a prophet of God. Muhammad addresses the downtrodden men and women who will now live in freedom and through them humankind in its future totality: men and women, all equal in the eyes of God. The scene lasts several minutes and continues with the narrator's voice describing Muhammad's death and the community that grew forward after his death. This device, of focusing on the sermon audience as a group of unfortunates, each with his or her own history of hardship and suffering, who are now given new hope, has also been used in socialist films interpreting religious awakenings in the Christian tradition (Walinsky-Kiehl 2006: 47–8).

The *khuṭba* appears occasionally in more contemporary settings in Egyptian films. A typical scene shows the good *'ālim* trying to mobilise the believers for a political goal. The classic case is the events of March 1919, when Egypt rose against the British exiling of leading nationalist Saad Zaghlul. In the films of the 1990s and 2000s, a negative variant appears, namely the fanatic preacher inciting impressionable young men to his radical goals. In *'Imārat Ya'qūbiān* ('The Yacoubian building', Marwan Hamed, 2006), the *khuṭba* of the radical preacher, an absolute authority to the young men in his flock, is at the same time used to denounce the Egyptian government as authoritarian.

An interesting variant of the mobilising *khuṭba* is the symbolic counter-position of Muslim and Christian sermons as a comment on Muslim–Christian relations. In Shadi Abd al-Salam's *Bayna 'l-qaṣrayn* ('Palace walk', 1962, based on the novel of Naguib Mahfouz) it is not merely the preacher, nor the faces of the audience, nor the content of the *khuṭba*, which is depicted, but the show of unity of the nation as a whole. Singing the national anthem, the crowd marches into al-Azhar Mosque and listens to the sermon of a Coptic priest on the minbar, proceeding afterwards to the Coptic cathedral where it is addressed by a Muslim shaykh – a twist on the *khuṭba* expectations of the audience. In this famous scene there is no contrast between the preacher and the audience; they, like all Egyptians – Muslims and Christians – are united as an organic nation, the classical interpretation of 1919 (Gershoni and Jankowski 1986: 40–54). In what must be a deliberate reference to this famous scene, the film *Ḥassan wa Murquṣ* ('Hassan and Morqos', Rami Imam, 2008, the title of a pun on a 1950s comedy) crosscuts a Christian and a Muslim cleric preaching hate against the other community. The two preachers are inciting their flocks to fight each other in the streets of Alexandria (while the two heroes and their families survive an attempted arson and walk through the mayhem, embodying national and inter-communal solidarity despite the violent times).

The mobilisation *khuṭba* scenes are examples of a *mise-en-scéne* where the preacher agitates his audience and makes them do his bidding. The camera either focuses on the preacher or cuts back and forth to demonstrate his impact on the audience. A very different type of *khuṭba* appears at the climax of the film *al-Ḥadaq yafham* ('The clever guy will understand', Ahmad Fuad, 1986). An outlaw, Jaber, steals the clothes of a shaykh, ʿAshur, and enters the village to get the funds the shaykh was collecting. Jaber plays the role well, but becomes emotionally involved with the good-hearted villagers, and is moved to help them. At the end of the film, with the police closing in on him, he is asked by the ʿ*umda* (village chief) to deliver a *khuṭba* in the small village mosque. Standing on the minbar and about to begin his fake *khuṭba* he reads the word 'Allah' on the wall, instantly repents, and reveals his true identity. Here it is the lack of communication from the preacher, the tellingly pious expectations of the audience, and the writing on the wall that the camera captures in a rare instance of interest in the inner life of the preacher (who is, however, a fraud). Conversely, in the Algerian film *Bab al-Ouad City*, we see the individual emotional response of a listener to a *khuṭba*: the hero Buʿallam is so annoyed with having to listen to the preacher over a loudspeaker on his roof that he climbs up, tears it down and throws it into the sea (Hafez 1995: 72). In the first case the *khuṭba* is seen as representing religion as such, and the hero's response is indicative of his acceptance of its demands and his reintegration into the religiously defined social order. By contrast, in the Algerian case the *khuṭba* is part of a disciplining process, and Buʿallam's response exposes him to the bullying of a group of vigilantes.

The Religious TV Dramas

The production of Egyptian films peaked in the 1980s with a total of 562 for the whole decade, but the disappearance of cinemas, the spread of the video cassette, pirating and the migration of advertising to television has led to a gradual decrease in production numbers (Qasim 2008: 639–813). By contrast, Arab television serials (*musalsalāt*) have grown significantly since the 1980s, and especially after the increase in channels that followed the introduction of satellite broadcasting in the 1990s. Once again, Egypt has been the dominant producer, although since the mid-1990s, and particularly with the rise of satellite television and Gulf television financing, Syria has become a major competitor. The standard format of an Arab TV serial is thirty episodes (of forty-five minutes), allowing it to run during the fasting month of Ramadan.

The length of the serials, and their much lower cost-per-hour, means that the story is much more protracted, and set scenes and standard shots are common. Accordingly, the *khuṭba* is bound to appear, not just as a short indication or symbol, but as a scene where a sermon (or part of it) is actually delivered. A good illustration of this is the above-mentioned adaption of the novel *The Yacoubian Building*. In the film, the *khaṭīb* criticises the lack of democracy, as his listeners are watched by the police. Yet the *musalsal* based on the same book has much more time at its disposal, letting the preacher talk for a full two minutes on the benefits of jihad as a personal duty. Eventually, it moves on to a back-stage discussion between the shaykh and several named adepts about how they should avoid drawing too much attention from the police whilst they build up their strength ('The Yacoubian building', 2007, Ahmad Saqr, episode 16).[4]

In the dominant genre of 'social serials' (*musalsalāt ijtimāʿiyya*), religion was almost invisible until the early 1990s when, as Lila Abu-Lughod has demonstrated, the Egyptian state changed tactics and encouraged the insertion of religious themes and figures as a way of promoting politically acceptable forms of religiosity (Abu-Lughod 2005: 163–91). As mentioned, a similar tendency can be identified in Egyptian film production. The new serials had three priorities: discrediting the discourse of militant Islamists, stressing Coptic–Muslim brotherhood, and showing a locally rooted culture (primarily in upper-Egypt) that was non-violent (Abu-Lughod 2005: 163).

There is, however, also a specific genre of TV drama known as 'the religious serials' (*al-musalsalāt al-dīniyya*) which has, so far, received little scholarly attention. These again fall into sub-categories: (1) serials about the prophets; (2) serials about the time of the Prophet Muhammad; (3) serials about major historical religious personalities, such as the founders of the schools of Islamic jurisprudence, or caliphs; and (4) serials about nineteenth- and twentieth-century religious figures, such as major reformers or scholars. The typical religious serial, then, is a biography.

The most popular serials about the prophets are Iranian and shot in Persian but dubbed for the Arab TV market: *Maryām al-Muqaddasa* ('The Holy Mary', 2003), *Yūsuf al-Ṣaddīq* ('The Righteous Joseph', 2008). The prophets actually appear in these serials, and they preach, but not in the formal setting of a *khuṭba*. It would, of course, have been rather strange to place the later developed Islamic *khuṭba* speech in these pre-Muhammadan peoples' lives. The same is true for the serials set in the era of the Prophet. In the dramas about major figures of Islamic history, preaching occasionally occurs, and is sometimes delivered formally from the minbar. The most salient aspect of these historical dramas is their use of the *khuṭba* as the political address to the Muslims by the caliph. When the *khuṭba* is delivered by ʿulamaʾ, there are also some notable features. In the successful Syrian serial about the Mamluk sultan Baybars (*al-Zahir Baybars*, Muhammad al-ʿAziziyya, 2005, episode 16), the theme of the mentioning of the (legitimate) ruler is exploited when the general Faris al-Din persuades the leading ʿulamaʾ of Cairo to mention in the *khuṭba* the name of Qutuz as a statement of their acceptance of a change of sultan. In *Saqf al-ʿAlam* ('Roof of the world', Najdat Anzour, 2007, episode 19), the Prophet's farewell sermon is quoted at length when the traveller Ahmad ibn Fadlan preaches about Muhammad to the Vikings.

A novelty in the TV drama, with no equivalent in Arab film, is the *musalsal* about a nineteenth- or twentieth-century *ʿālim*. Naturally, this genre places preaching and the *khuṭba* at the centre of its attention. An early forerunner was the serial on Jamal al-Din al-Afghani from 1981. Not being formally an *ʿālim*, but more a politico-religious orator, al-Afghani (1839–97) spoke to Muslim audiences on countless occasions. In the serial al-Afghani generally teaches more than he preaches, but in Cairo in the early 1870s he delivers a long *khuṭba* to an audience of impressionable Egyptians, among them Muhammad Abduh. The scene serves to sum up his message, display his passion and show how his preaching enabled young Egyptian nationalists to adopt a more modernist understanding of Islam (*Jamāl al-Dīn al-Afghānī*, Jamal Ghunaim, 1981, episode 12).

In three long *musalsalāt* from 2002 to 2007, the Egyptian director Hassan Yusuf portrayed some leading Egyptian ʿulamaʾ of the twentieth century. A former actor, Yusuf went through a personal religious awakening. Since then he has dedicated his work as a director and producer to religious dramas that support and direct the Islamic reorientation of Egyptian society. His wife, the actress Shams al-Barudi, withdrew from acting, and he believes that this decision was decisive in making many Egyptian women don the veil (van Nieuwkerk 2007: 187).

Two of the serials are about ʿulamaʾ who obtained the highest and most prestigious position for Islamic scholars in Egypt, the Shaykh al-Azhar. These are historical characters whose lives have been fictionalised. We see their early years as students at al-Azhar University, finding their mentors. The favourite scene, then, is the *dars*, where the teacher sits at a pillar in al-Azhar Mosque with the students in a circle around him.

In the serial about ʿAbd al-Halim Mahmud (1910–78) there is a *khuṭba* by a young local shaykh, Islam, which the young student ʿAbd al-Halim attends in the first row. Drawing on the Qurʾan, Shaykh Islam talks about the world of the unseen (*ʿālam al-ghayb*) that we must not believe that we shall see (*al-ʿArif bi Allah ʿAbd al-Halim Mahmud*, 'ʿAbd al-Halim Mahmud, the God-knowing', Hassan Yusuf, 2008, episode 7).[5] This is a criticism aimed at some of the village Sufi practices, but the viewer will recall that seeing the unseen world was precisely what ʿAbd al-Halim had set out to do as a young boy, and the serial grants him the capacity for mystical experience. It can thus be seen as a defence of a Sufi worldview against the claims of the sermon.

In the earlier serial about Mustafa al-Maraghi (1881–1945), the hero's mentor Muhammad Abduh prefers to give classes in a modern classroom, and we do not see him on the minbar. Later in the serial, al-Maraghi himself appears on the minbar on a few occasions: working as a judge in the Sudan in 1912, al-Maraghi is fighting superstitions and fatalism in the Sufi-dominated Sudanese Islam. Here he gives a sermon on fate and divine decree (*al-qaḍā wa 'l-qadar*), stressing the demand on the Muslim to be useful to his community. As is generally the case in the episodes set in the Sudan, the Sudanese are portrayed as a mass – good-hearted, but ignorant of their faith and prey to superstitions and manipulations by religious leaders (*Imām al-Marāghī*, Hassan Yusuf, 2006, episode 13). This scene depicts the preacher as a fatherly educator. It contrasts with a number of scenes with peasants in a village in the Egyptian Delta where ʿAbd al-Munʿaim, al-Maraghi's friend from their student days, preaches harshly to the people about their unforgivably sinful life. Initially shocked, the peasants gradually begin to mobilise against this fire-and-brimstone preacher, and after a while actively oppose him (episodes 10 and 11).

At the end of the serial, when al-Maraghi has become the Shaykh al-Azhar, we see yet another type of *khuṭba* scene. It is actually a short series of scenes that serve to characterise the relationship between al-Maraghi and the young King Farouk. In the first *khuṭba*, al-Maraghi is happy that the king has come to al-Azhar, and optimistically he talks of youth and faith (episode 25). Al-Maraghi believes in the religious conscience of the king and dismisses rumours of his debauchery. When he realises that much of the hearsay is true, he uses his weekly sermon (now held in one of the royal mosques) to speak on the subject of marriage and virtue. The king considers this an intentional insult. Shortly afterwards al-Maraghi delivers another *khuṭba* denouncing the Nazi ideology of race as contradictory to Islam (although he knows that the king sympathises with the Germans) (episodes 27 and 28). In delivering these speeches, al-Maraghi is living up to a well-known hadith that 'the best jihad is speaking the truth to an unjust ruler' (Sunan Abu Dawud 2040). During all three sermons, the camera moves between the faces of a calm and convinced al-Maraghi and an increasingly angry and frustrated King Farouk, thus using the scene of the *khuṭba* to portray an evolving conflict between two persons, and between worldly and religious authority.

'The First among Preachers'

The first and most successful of the new musalsalāt about ʿulamaʾ is *Imām al-duʿā* ('The first among preachers', Hassan Yusuf, 2002), no doubt due to the popularity of its subject, Shaykh al-Shaʿrawi (1911–98) who had died only a few years before its airing and was vivid in the memory of all Egyptians. Al-Shaʿrawi had been minister of religious endowments during the era of Anwar al-Sadat (1976–8), but, as the title of the drama indicates, more than anything else he was a pre-eminent preacher who had gained fame first over the radio and later on television where he had his own regular performances for decades. Yves Gonzalez-Quijano (2000) has analysed the subtle ways in which 'Uncle al-Shaʿrawi' was enshrined in the Egyptian public imagination as the traditional and good-hearted but also morally censorious shaykh. Karin van Nieuwkerk (2011: 54) has pointed to his success in making several famous actresses 'repent' and withdraw from acting – some of whom reappear in this very *musalsal* about his life. More controversially, a recent monograph by Jacquelene G. Brinton covers his long media history and argues that he represents a renewal, also in his interpretation of Islam (Brinton 2015).

'The First among preachers', then, is both the life story of a gifted preacher, and a history of preaching and the media in modern Egypt. In almost every episode we see al-Shaʿrawi preaching; in the village mosque, among fellow students in the Azhari school, in mosques at home and abroad, on the radio and on television.

In one episode, al-Shaʿrawi dreams of a Sufi shaykh (whom he later meets in Algeria) who tells him that preaching in the media is his vocation in life. Waking up, al-Shaʿrawi realises the truth of these words. He energetically sets out to produce a series of TV lessons 'defending Islam' against secularism (episode 17). We also follow how he manages to convert a young man, Islam, to Islamic living through his radio preaching (episode 9). When in 1977 his fellow shaykh Muhammad al-Dhahabi is assassinated by jihadists, al-Shaʿrawi preaches on television against terrorist interpretations of Islam. We see villagers, urban café-dwellers, political figures and his own family sitting and watching, thus demonstrating how the nation as a whole was listening to him and taking his message to heart (episode 24). This is the preacher as the voice of the nation.

In another notable episode, al-Shaʿrawi is scheduled to preach in his village when a difficult situation arises over the simultaneous celebrations of a Coptic and a Muslim festival. Contrary to the local shaykh, who is suspicious of the Copts, al-Shaʿrawi allows for the Muslims to listen to a talk by the Coptic bishop. In his own ensuing sermon, al-Shaʿrawi stresses that Copts and Muslims are brothers, that Muslims respect the prophets of the Bible and the Virgin Mary, and that Christians have always lived as a protected community (*dhimma*) under Muslim rule (episode 13). The benevolent paternalism evinced by al-Shaʿrawi in his speech is a far cry from the complete subordination of religion to national identity in *Bayna 'l-Qaṣrayn*, or the defiant civic egalitarianism in *Ḥassan wa Murquṣ*, both of which were discussed earlier. The fact that *Imam al-duʿā* and the other ʿulamaʾ serials are produced and broadcast by Egyptian state television is evidence of a major reappraisal of the acceptable public role of Islam that took place in Egyptian cultural production in the later years of the Mubarak era. The tenor of these works is pro-Islamist in the sense of demonstrating that the Egyptian identity is, at heart, religious, and that Islam provides viable solutions to the problems of the modern age by establishing legal, moral and social norms for a healthy society. This turn is reflected in the serial by its approving treatment of the scandal that al-Shaʿrawi caused in 1967 when he interpreted the military defeat to Israel as a grace from God – meaning that this would be the death-knell of atheist politics in Egypt. The following episodes show him preaching to Egyptian soldiers at the Suez Canal, thus casting the 1973 recapture of the Sinai Peninsula as a war in the name of Islam (episodes 19 and 20).

Only a few of al-Shaʿrawi's media appearances are recognisably sermons; even when he speaks in the village mosque, it is not from the minbar, but in a circle (*ḥalqa*) in front of the minbar, and always answering questions posed by the devout and good people who have come to listen. It is also true that al-Shaʿrawi preferred the informal *ḥalqa* to the formal *khuṭba* (Gonzalez-Quijano 2000: 248). When in the serial he actually appears on the minbar, it is to speak beyond his audience; giving *khuṭab* on a tour of cities in Europe and North America, these talks are not aimed at his immediate audience, but at the Western world (episode 21). Finally, in 1975 or 1976 he gives the sermon of the pilgrimage (*khuṭbat ʿArafāt*) to millions of pilgrims outside Mecca. This *khuṭba* is depicted in a long scene where his voice is heard through loudspeakers reciting the set formulas of the sermon, while close-ups of his face, in deep emotion, flow into panoramas of pilgrims praying, giving the sense of a stream of consciousness where ordinary time has been suspended (episode 22). The aim of the scene is to show the emotional culmination of a life of preaching – the most gratifying experience, but for its immensity, and ritual and formulaic dimensions rather than for its message; on the hajj no *daʿwa* is needed.

Conclusions

In *The Prophet's Pulpit*, Patrick Gaffney (1994: 35–8) introduces three Weberian types of contemporary preachers: the affirmer of traditional authority, the advocate of religiously inspired modernity and the apologist for the ideology of Islamic fundamentalism. The first ideal type uses a formulaic language that employs Qurʾanic references in a quantity bordering on circularity. Gaffney observes that this may be a political stratagem in an age of aggressive Islamisation (Gaffney 1994: 198). This formulaic *khuṭba* is practically absent from the films and *musalsalāt*, only appearing perhaps as examples of staid preaching and teaching at al-Azhar in the al-Maraghi serial, or in the *khuṭbat ʿArafāt*, as mentioned above. The preacher as advocate of modernity, on the other hand, is quite common in nationalist films and serials, such as *Jamāl al-Dīn al-Afghānī* and *Imām al-Marāghī*, where he mobilises against superstitions, but also against the colonisers. Apart from these, most films and TV serials depict the last type, the preacher as a representative of a sociopolitical Islamic revival in society. That trend may, however, be variously interpreted and depicted. Earlier serials tend to depict the preacher as a manipulator of young ardent believers, but by the 2000s, there are also serials supporting the Islamic revival and thus portraying the sermon in a much more positive light.

Given the ubiquity of the *khuṭba* in Arab societies, and the significance of Islam, especially in contemporary Arab film and TV drama, *khuṭba* scenes are remarkably rare. The prohibition against depicting prophets certainly explains this absence when it comes to dramas set at the time of the Prophet Muhammad. Likewise, the early prohibition against showing ʿulamaʾ is just as important when it comes to films before 1950. Apart from a few films with an anti-clerical agenda, one may surmise that this apprehension endures; even if you want to depict a shaykh negatively, you may choose not to do that on the pulpit. By contrast, there are examples (the robber in *al-Ḥadaq yafham*, al-Shaʿrawi delivering the *khuṭbat ʿArafāt*) where the act of preaching itself is depicted as a religious experience of great force, reaching into the conscience and emotional depth of the preacher. As a means of communication, however, the scene of the *khuṭba* seems to be shunned by the directors of Arab film and TV drama.

The reason may be found in its use. As we have seen, apart from some examples of display of national unity, *khuṭba* scenes are employed to show the preacher mobilising the flock for national or social goals. When the audience of the sermon is depicted, they appear impressionable and willing to act. In the earlier films, this may be for laudable national purposes, but since the 1990s, *khuṭba* scenes are often used to depict mobilisation for violence. This top-down communication, once considered natural and admirable, is now used to depict social agitation and abuse of power. In recent *musalsalāt* about ʿulamaʾ, *khuṭba* scenes are employed when the preacher is teaching (naïve Sudanese), defending Islam (against the Western world), or courageously speaking up against the political power (al-Maraghi against King Farouk). That is, he is not speaking to the ordinary Egyptian conscientious Muslim. These are no longer addressed top-down from the pulpit, but in a more levelled manner, in a *dars* or *ḥalqa*, and often as a response to a question or a statement. Top-down *khuṭab* were acceptable in the 1960s, in an age of paternalism (modernist or other), but seem less attractive today where, in turn, some of the most popular films are mocking the political speech in parliament (also known as *khuṭba*) as pompous and self-serving. To appear fully legitimate in the eyes of the contemporary Arab television audience, the preaching must no longer appear authoritarian. Even the most famous preacher, Shaykh al-Shaʿrawi, is shown preaching in schools, universities, halls, tents, mosques and even the desert, but very rarely from the top of the minbar. The depiction of his preaching in radio and television provides new possibilities of showing the audience as the nation itself. While he preaches, we can see people in homes and cafés all over the country listening, commenting and approving. This is a new way of making the point that the religious message is not just delivered to the listeners, but that the audience actively and conscientiously receive and reflect on it. The ideal remains the dialogue, as we see it in the village mosque when the peasants are seated in the *ḥalqa* (circle) and al-Shaʿrawi answers their questions. Al-Shaʿrawi is the 'first of the preachers', but the preacher of this and other TV dramas and films has now become the *dāʿī*, and no longer the *khaṭīb*.

Notes

1. On the development of ʿulamaʾ institutions in the twentieth century generally, see Zaman 2002; Krämer and Schmidtke 2006; Hatina 2008. On ʿulamaʾ institutions related to the state in Egypt, see, for example, Eccel 1984; Zeghal 1996; Skovgaard-Petersen 1997.
2. These are: *Intisar al-islam* ('Victory of Islam', 1952); *Bilal muʾadhdhan al-rasul* ('Bilal, the Prophet's muezzin', 1953); *al-Sayyid Ahmad al-Badawi* ('Sayyid Ahmad al-Badawi', 1953); *Bait Allah al-haram* ('Allah's Kaʿba', 1957); *Khalid ibn al-Walid* (1958); *Allahu akbar* (1959); *Shahid al-hubb al-ilahi* ('Martyr of divine love', 1962); *Rabiʿa al-ʿAdawiyya* (1963); *Hijrat al-rasul* ('The Prophet's migration', 1964); *Fajr al-islam* ('The dawn of Islam', 1971); and *al-Shaymaʾ ukht al-rasul* ('Shayma, the Prophet's sister', 1972).
3. Shaykh Ibrahim in *Shayʾ min al-khauf* ('Something of anger', Hussein Kamil, 1969) is a case in point.
4. The published manuscript: Ahmad Ra'if, *Jamal al-Din al-Afghani* (Cairo, al-Zahraʾ, 1988), 219–21.
5. Such *khuṭab* are found in, for instance, 'The Yacoubian building' (Marwan Hamed, 2006) and *Morgan Ahmad Morgan* (ʿAli Idris, 2007).

Bibliography

Abu-Lughod, Lila (2005), *Dramas of Nationhood: The Politics of Television in Egypt*, Cairo: American University in Cairo Press.

Armbrust, Walter (2002), 'Islamists in Egyptian Cinema', *American Anthropologist*, new series, 104, 922–31.

Bakker, Freek (2006), 'The Image of Muhammad in The Message, the First and Only Film about the Prophet of Islam', *Islam and Christian–Muslim Relations* 17 (1): 77–92.

Brinton, Jacquelene G. (2015), *Preaching Islamic Renewal: Religious Authority and Media in Contemporary Egypt*, Berkeley: University of California Press.

Butler, Ivan (1969), *Religion in the Cinema*, New York: A. S. Barnes.

Eccel, Chris (1984), *Egypt, Islam and Social Change: Al-Azhar in Conflict and Accommodation*, Berlin: Klaus Schwarz.

Gaffney, Patrick (1994), *The Prophet's Pulpit: Islamic Preaching in Contemporary Egypt*, Berkeley: University of California Press.

Gershoni, Israel and James Jankowski (1986), *Egypt, Islam and the Arabs*, Oxford: Oxford University Press.

Gonzalez-Quijano, Yves (2000), 'Cheikh Shaarawi, star de l'«islam électronique»', *Réseaux* 18 (1): 239–53.

Grace, Pamela (2009), *The Religious Film*, Chichester: Wiley-Blackwell.

Hafez, Sabry (1995), 'Shifting Identities in Maghrebi Cinema: The Algerian Experience', *Alif* 15: 39–80.

Hatina, Meir (ed.) (2008), *Guardians of Faith in Modern Times: ʿUlamaʾ in the Middle East*, Leiden: Brill.

Krämer, Gudrun and Sabine Schmidtke (eds) (2006), *Speaking for Islam: Religious Authorities in Muslim Societies*, Leiden: Brill.

van Nieuwkerk, Karin (2007), 'From Repentance to Pious Performance', *ISIM Review* 20: 54–5.

van Nieuwkerk, Karin (2011), 'Of Morals, Missions and the Market: New Religiosity and "Art with a Mission" in Egypt', in K. van Nieuwkerk (ed.), *Muslim Rap, Halal Soaps, and Revolutionary Theater: Artistic Developments in the Muslim World*, Austin: University of Texas Press, pp. 177–205.

Qasim, Mahmud (1997), *Surat al-adyan fi al-sinima al-misriyya* [The image of religions in the Egyptian cinema], Cairo: Wizarat al-Thaqafa.

Qasim, Mahmud (2008), *Dalil al-aflam fi al-qarn al-ʿashrin fi misr wa al-ʿalam al-ʿarabi* [A guide to twentieth-century films in Egypt and the Arab world], Cairo: Maktabat Madbuli.

Salah al-Din, Muhammad (1998), *Al-Din wa 'l-ʿaqida fi al-sinima al-misriyya* [Religion and creed in Egyptian cinema], Cairo: Madbuli.

Shafiq, Viola (1998), *Arab Cinema*, Cairo: American University in Cairo Press.

Skovgaard-Petersen, Jakob (1997), *Defining Islam for the Egyptian State: Muftis and Fatwas of the Dār al-Iftā*, Leiden: Brill.

Walinsky-Kiehl, Robert (2006), 'History, Politics and East German Film: The Thomas Müntzer (1956) Socialist Epic', *Central European History* 39 (1): 30–55.

Zaman, Muhammad Qasim (2002), *The Ulama in Contemporary Islam: Custodians of Change*, Princeton: Princeton University Press.
Zeghal, Malika (1996), *Gardiens de l'Islam: Les oulémas d'al-Azhar dans l'Egypte contemporaine*, Paris: Presses des Sciences Po.

3

INSTRUCTIVE SPEECH AMONG BOSNIAN MUSLIM WOMEN: SERMONS, LESSONS OR GUIDANCE?

Catharina Raudvere

In the study of Islamic devotional activities, the ethical instructions, explications of canonical texts and comments on Islamic history embedded in such rituals have often been disconnected from the world of Islamic learning and not regarded as modes of knowledge production – especially if the executors happen to be women. However, in recent decades a more inclusive way to approach to the study of Islamic knowledge production has developed, mostly influenced by anthropological studies with special emphasis on religion as practised in local environments. Likewise, seminal contributions on Muslim women's instruction practices and interpretive authority have been published over the last two decades.[1] This development has been a productive challenge for the study of religion at large. More attention has been paid to the interface between words and deeds, the uses of scriptural traditions in local Islamic practice, and the role of agents and agency in relation to Muslim interpretive practices (Krämer and Schmidtke 2006; Schielke and Debevec 2012).

Following the work of Bowen (1993), Lambek (1993) and van Bruinessen (2011), this chapter provides a discussion about the relationship between choice of oratory and ritual genres, access to spaces and claims of authoritative religious knowledge. Hence, my consideration of theology extends beyond the conventional understanding of 'systematic theology', such as *kalam*, *ilahiyat* and *fiqh*, which omits many other modes of interpretation and communication. Instead, I apply a broader definition that emphasises local actors' ambitions to teach and transmit systematised knowledge of the Islamic faith within their communities. Through such an understanding, there are alternative perspectives on those who claim authority, explicitly or implicitly, by making use of their access to scriptural sources and their training in formulating educative guidance in varying environments. Such an approach to what theology and knowledge production can be requires the identification of other spaces, speakers, genres and means of communication than are conventional in the study of Islam and Muslims. When contemporary studies of Islam and Muslims raise questions about knowledge production, they are as much about who and where, as about which ritual practices can be regarded as instructive.

Qur'an Recitations during Ramadan: A Time for Learning and Reflection

The empirical material for the following discussion is taken from teaching traditions among Muslim women in Bosnia. Of special interest is how local Islamic knowledge is transmitted among women embedded in ritual practices such as prayer, recitation, singing and teaching, exemplified by a case of a Sarajevan women's gathering at the end of Ramadan which included prayers, Qur'an recitation and instructive speech of some length.[2] During the month of fasting, it is a common practice all over the Muslim world to attend recitations where the whole of the Qur'an is recited after dividing the text into thirty parts (sing. *juz*): one per day. A gathering of this kind is known in Bosnia as a *mukabela*. The core element is the structured recitation, which is most often combined with some form of instruction or preaching to conclude the event. In mosques all over the country, men and women gather to listen to the male *hafiz*s and imams, placing themselves according to the local customs of gender-divided spaces, with women mostly sitting on the balcony or at the back of the mosque.

Some mosques in Sarajevo are known to organise special *mukabela*s conducted by women during Ramadan; women attending these gatherings repeatedly emphasised that they identified themselves as part of a long Sarajevan tradition of having well-trained women as reciters and in charge of firmly structured rituals. In the case selected for this chapter, the reciters were young and all had diplomas accrediting them with the title of *hafiza* (the female form for an officially certified Qur'an reciter). There were about thirty women attending, representing various age groups, but mostly elderly and younger women; middle-aged women seemed to be busy with professional and domestic commitments. The institutional framework was clearly indicated on a billboard outside the mosque in the wording of an invitation extended to women by the Islamic Community (*Islamske Zajednica*) to attend a *ženska mukabela* (women's *mukabela*) held by its local congregation (*Medžlis Islamske Zajednice Sarajevo*). The gathering was the last in a series of *mukabela*s held in the mosque throughout Ramadan, at which the women who had participated regularly had encountered several different reciters and speakers. The location was an old downtown mosque with many wooden details, not one of those which have been recently erected or heavily restored.[3] The traditional style, according to some of the participating women, added to the atmosphere and feeling of being part of something with a long history that was specifically Sarajevan. Attendance, it was argued among the participants, was a statement pointing to loyalty to tradition, a position opposing both contemporary indifference to religion as well as Arabised influences that scorn local customs.

The initial Qur'an recitation, which defined the ritual event, took about forty-five minutes. The ensuing sermon took about the same length of time and was equally appreciated by the attending women. As a whole, however, the gathering was even longer. It began with arrivals and greetings, along with individual preparations in terms of prayer and concentration; then six young women placed themselves in front of the *kibla*, which indicated the direction of Mecca, and took turns to recite from the last part of the Qur'an, as Ramadan was coming to an end in a few days' time. The young woman who gave the sermon that followed was not among the reciters and was somewhat older; she also had stronger educational credentials.

Identifying alternative agents, spaces and ritual contexts is not the same as locating theological interpretations in opposition to the dominating Islamic institutions. Women do not necessarily produce alternative or critical discourses in situations such as this, where the proceedings are part of a conventional mode of speaking and reiterating traditional themes. Nevertheless, women in command of rituals can, by the mere fact of their visibility be provocative, possibly impinging on the validity of teaching outside women's circles.

Spaces for Islamic Teaching and Knowledge Production

This chapter primarily discusses how teaching and sermon practices can constitute parts of local production of Islamic theology. The term theology is used here for discursive practices in two very different domains: Islamic theology is, of course, mainly produced within a framework of institutional learning, but it is also part of local initiatives for teaching and learning. The *mukabela*, an example of the latter, indicates some different ways of defining the research area: identifying the making of Islamic theology; contextualising knowledge production; and exploring the means by which to capture the voices of the agents.

To the participants in such gatherings, as well as to the broader Muslim community in the city, the women's *mukabela* activities represent the transmission of a regionally established repertoire of devotional practices, which many Bosnian Muslims also recognise as part of a national legacy. After the Yugoslav period and the war in the 1990s, local ritual traditions were (among all denominations of the country) linked to conceptions of belonging and self-definition. The identification of spaces and genres of communication other than those customary among male instructors (imams, teachers at *medresas*, and Sufi *šejhs*, to mention some of the roles accessible to men with Islamic education) is therefore an important point of departure when making local instruction visible.

The visibility of previously unrecognised, and to some extent altogether new, agents whose voices are being heard in alternative spaces is by no means a unique development in the Muslim world. To a great extent, most features that are highlighted here in order to characterise Bosnian Muslim life are relevant for religious life in the contemporary world at large. Individuals and groups are connected through social media beyond the immediate locus of activities, meaning that it is easy to encounter a multitude of varying positions taken on what constitutes authentic tradition and who can serve as a legitimate interlocutor. As these more general developments and the Bosnian case discussed here suggest, when studying local Islamic teaching and its ritual context, it is relevant to ask where it takes place and, moreover, to recognise that women's involvement in it has a long history. Furthermore, conditions under which the gatherings are organised are not only a question of gender; authority in the immediate community is built around education and legitimacy (which do not necessarily go hand in hand), along with social position, and are embedded in local networks far beyond religious circles.

Sermons and Ethical Instruction: Genres and Gender, Education and Authority

Before analysing the instructions given as the final part of this specific *mukabela* in Sarajevo, some aspects of the genre and the ritual form of the gathering should be considered. Recitation is thought of as generally an honorary duty during various kinds of ritual gatherings and can be distributed to women with the required qualifications: training in Arabic and rhetorical performance, but not necessarily a degree from an Islamic faculty. Informally, but unquestionably, the aesthetic dimension also plays a decisive role in the estimation of the reciter: a beautiful voice and training in *kirat*, Qur'an recitation and *mekam* (melodic system). The characteristic feature for the Sarajevan gatherings is the educational level of the women engaged in Qur'an recitation and instruction during the *mevlud* gatherings. Almost all those who appear as reciters in the mosques in the city during Ramadan are formally recognised as *hafiza*. They are familiar with public recitations and some of them are well acquainted with giving public addresses. In the context of the present volume, it raises the question as to when and where instructive speech is recognised as a sermon.

A sermon is by definition instructive and disciplining in both form and content; it inevitably embodies hierarchical relations (speaker and recipients), and local tradition gives the speaker and listeners specific roles in terms of active participation and decorum. Local conceptions of legitimacy and authority are based on schooling and reputation, as well as on the speaking person's assertion to present religion in its authentic form. Religious authority mostly works in combination with claims of authenticity. A key rhetorical feature is, therefore, how the speaker connects the Medina model of the textual worlds of the hadith literature to contemporary life and its challenges. The success of transmission of the teaching is linked to certain expectations from the audience concerning not only the religious message, but also the solemnity of the speaker. A woman who takes on a teaching commitment has to guard herself from scorn and criticism. By instructing through role modelling, preaching ideals and condemning misconduct, her behaviour must reflect the norms she wants to implement.

The traditional Muslim sermon is very much linked to the formal speech directed to men during the Friday noon prayer (*hutba*) in a mosque, which has strong connotations in Islamic tradition to Muhammad as the role model, and to the sermons he delivered to the first Muslim community in Medina. The formal title of a man who delivers a *hutba* is a *hatib*, and it is usually the imam of a mosque who takes on this duty.[4] As well as the *hutba*, there are other types of formalised speech with instructive ambitions that could be included as a variant of the concept of sermon. In mosques all over the Muslim world there are a number of teaching activities inside the mosque building itself. Teaching can also be offered in (the often nearby) *medresa* or by a shaykh in a Sufi lodge that, in terms of speech genres, can be described as sermons, homilies, lessons, consultancy, prayer or recitation; other important arenas include youth clubs, student organisations, welfare societies and – most obviously – the worldwide reach of the Internet and social media. Even if these instructive traditions are not part of women's history to any great extent, there have always been channels for women to educate other women. Throughout history this has mostly been performed in domestic or semi-public spaces, but Muslim women in Bosnia had access to *medresa* education as early as the 1930s, although with long disruptions during the Yugoslav period (Giomi 2015a, 2015b; Raudvere 2012).

In today's Sarajevo, the women who spoke at the *mukabela* gatherings referred to their discourses as lectures or lessons (sing. *ders*). In terms of style, structure and content, though, it would perhaps be more adequate to discuss them as sermons or homilies (*vaz*), that is, short discourses on spiritual or moral matters. *Vaz* is also the term used by the attending women who referred to the speaker as a *vaiza*. This title is generally given to female preachers at women's gatherings in mosques outside prayer hours or at ritual events in private homes.

The speaker who presented the instruction after the recitation in the case discussed here was only slightly older than the reciters, and definitively younger than several of the participants. This indicates that the younger women take responsibility for the practical side when *mukabela*s are arranged (making sure that there is a schedule and that it is followed), although the Islamic Community is the formal organiser. Approval from the Islamic Community is needed in order to arrange a *mukabela* in one of the mosques.

Speaking to the Sisters

The performance of the instructive speech was part of individual and collective Ramadan celebrations. The participants underlined that the regular recitation was intimately connected with a sense of belonging along with and sharing an Ottoman heritage that constitutes a vital part of the city's history. After a very short break at the end of the Qur'an recitation, the reciters gave place to a new woman in charge of the instructive talk. The beginning of the sermon was more distinctly marked as an opening of a second part of the *mukabela* gathering, rather than the words at the very end closing the event. The opening was preceded by a blessing (*bismillah*), a prayer (*dova*) and blessings for the Prophet (*salavat*) that the women said together, bringing the congregation together to focus on spiritual matters. It was now time for the *vaiza* to take the floor, and she did so with an invocation directed to the participants as a greeting. Although the sermon had an informal character, it had distinct sections of different kinds of speech and marks of shifts, starting with a formal invocation of respectful phrases addressing the women, especially the older participants: 'Dear mothers and respected sisters, our dear youngsters, *assalamu alaikum*.' Greeting the audience also included phrases that situated the ritual event in the calendar of Islamic holidays, despite this being the last *mukabela* before the upcoming *bajram*, the feast at the end of Ramadan. The *vaiza* articulated her hope: 'We can share this joy today and then continue next Ramadan.' Even the current Ramadan celebrations were inscribed in a larger cycle of holidays and rituals this and coming years. This was also the first example of the *vaiza*'s use of shifting temporalities, giving the present a depth by connecting to the past and the future.

Like all good speakers, the *vaiza* began by presenting the main themes to be expected in the sermon, also referencing the previous sermon by a different *vaiza* that had been interrupted by a wedding ceremony in the mosque. This comment connected the ritual events over the month as a series, as well as indicating that these women's gatherings sometimes have to make way for other events arranged in the mosque by the local imam. The location was definitely provided for, but at the same time at risk of not being prioritised.

The *vaiza* referred to her talk as a *ders*, assigning herself a humble position among those who should continue to strive to complete the duties of a good Muslim: 'My aim is to encourage myself and you to continue with our worship (*ibadet*) and our journey on the straight path (*istikamet*).' Throughout the sermon, she balanced between positioning herself as a humble Muslim among others and marking her role as a teacher. It is debatable how much weight should be given to the fact that *vaiza* called the talk a *ders* while her audience referred to it as a *vaz*. Certainly, her voice in what followed was demanding and challenging, and the rhetorical function of repeating the term for the speech genre was not necessarily to diminish its value, but, rather, to emphasise its seriousness. She also demanded the attention of her audience by stating that the last part of the *mukabela* was a lesson, a term also used for the instructive speech of imams.

From the beginning of the sermon, two main themes were raised by using Arabic phrasing, immediately followed by explanations in Bosnian: *istikamet*, the straight path (and how to keep to it), and *ibadet*, worship (and the correct way of fulfilling the ritual requirements). These two concepts, which occupied the *vaiza* during the next forty-five minutes, appeared to be generally known to the audience in their Arabic form, but the use of Arabic added something more than a precise definition of what topics to expect. Together with the references to the Qur'an and the hadith that followed immediately after, it confirmed the *vaiza* as a trustworthy *muallima*, a teacher with access to the classical narratives and images of authentic Muslim life in the canonical scriptures.

Some of the references to the Qur'an in the sermon were direct quotations that required explication, while others were paraphrases, often an integrated part of an ongoing narrative. On the whole, the sermon was structured around a number of short narratives, each ending in a moral conclusion that led into the next narrative. The structure was mostly a combination of paraphrases of stories from the hadith literature and glimpses of the *vaiza*'s own moral outlook, embedded in a contemporary Bosnian context.

The interspersed stories the *vaiza* introduced from contemporary life were presented as didactic examples. Problems were identified and situated in a distinguishable scene with agents in marked positions, usually in some kind of dispute or clash of interests. The moral stances were easy to identify, and the narratives mostly presented the constructed issue as a choice between two viewpoints. Meanwhile, the repeated references to the Prophet and his era included in the narrative added to a sense of timelessness wherein the conduct of the Prophet constitutes the everlasting moral point of comparison. This method of juxtaposing today's issues with both history and eternity is hardly advanced sermon rhetoric, but nevertheless it functioned as a forceful rhetorical strategy; moving between ideals and the identified problems of present times made it possible for the audience to follow the speaker and identify with the suggested solutions. In short, the narratives included in the sermon served as morality tales that maintained it as a coherent whole. The time perspective shifted between that of Muhammad and his early followers, contemporary times and the Day of Judgement: a long-term approach to the moral message of the sermon that provided a sense of unbroken continuity in which the fundamental problems remained the same, furnishing a cosmology where Heaven and Hell are sites as real as Medina and Sarajevo.

A sermon is by definition a monologic form of speech that presupposes a receiving audience that has trust in the speaker. Nonetheless, in the midst of a presentation of an example embedded in a narrative, a woman raised a question directly to the *vaiza*, asking for an expansion of the theme. She wanted clarification regarding appropriate behaviour during *namaz* (the mandatory daily prayers), and whether there is a duty to correct other people one thinks are misbehaving. Such an interruption would be unthinkable during a Friday *hutba*. The *vaiza* immediately took the opportunity to elaborate further on the issue, however, and a short dialogue developed in which she showed no signs of being disturbed by the interaction: quite the opposite, she encouraged it. It created liveliness in the communication and strengthened the *vaiza*'s position as a good speaker and an engaging teacher, ready to address any concerns among the attending women. Ultimately, the woman's questions resolved the issue and the problems discussed were taken to the more profound level of moral codes and ideals in relation to life as lived. While the *vaiza* said that it is the duty of all to correct and inform in their everyday life, by integrating the normative literature she took the opportunity to deal with general matters. Then, after trying to answer the queries so that they had relevance to the larger audience, the *vaiza* skilfully navigated back to her own narrative line. Instead of being an interruption, this interplay added to the picture that the message of the sermon was embedded in the everyday concerns of the women in the audience. In terms of performance, this monologic genre was enacted as a partly dialogic event. It was not only the direct questions from the concerned woman, it was also the body language of the speaker – gestures, making eye contact – that marked the concord in the crowd.

The major theological theme of the sermon concerned religious and social duties, and the difficulties humans face when trying to live up to the Islamic code of conduct. The ultimate point of reference was obviously the Prophet himself and the moral codes that were stipulated for his followers; even if concepts like *istikamet* and *ibadet* have apparent ritual aspects, it was still the dogmatic side of religion that dominated the sermon. At the same time, there were also references to a kind of Muhammad-orientated piety well known from Bosnian *mevlud* and *zikr* traditions that combine blessings, narrative poems about the Prophet, repetition of Allah's names and formulaic prayers. The *vaiza* encouraged the audience to perform:

> *zikrullah*, remembering Allah, reciting *zikr*, as we call it. However, I'll just briefly mention, *subhanallahi we bihamdihi, subhanallahi-l-azim*. The Messenger (PBUH) said that reciting it one hundred times a day destroys sins, or erases them, even if you have as many sins as there are bubbles of foam in the sea.

In a characteristic way, this instruction by the *vaiza* alternated between devout personal piety and a more mechanical side of the rituals where prayers are counted as restitution for failure and mistakes. Although some of the prayers during the *mukabela* were intense and emotional, they did not develop into a *zikr* proper, a longer repetition of Allah's names. Such piety practices are apparently reserved for other kinds of prayer meetings and made the centre of a ritual gathering.

The cosmology sketched in the sermon constituted the space and framework within which the *vaiza*'s theological discourse was explicated. The time perspectives brought out a duality between a period when the ideals were possible to achieve (especially in the representations of the Prophet and his companions in the hadith literature) and our time, when so many things distract, tempt and deceive. Shifting between different temporalities gave the *vaiza* a tool for keeping a line in her discourse, while giving space for urgent matters in the audience. Such concerns are not necessarily of theological or moral character. Stress, family matters and generational conflicts were addressed in a frank mode, but with pious answers to soothe. Praying was not said to immediately solve the issues, but to give strength to cope with them. In this way, the ritual event as a whole, with its prayers, recitation and instruction, constituted a pocket of time for spiritual and social companionship for the participants.

The speaker did not use any manuscript or notes; nonetheless, it was a well-prepared sermon. Rather than being an exegesis of the earlier quotations from the Qur᾿an, the *vaiza* took advantage of the ritual's point of departure in the religious calendar; the fact that Ramadan is a period when many people try to lead a better and more structured religious life constitutes an obvious opportunity for a preacher. The dominant themes were therefore morals in a broad sense, purity and doing what is right in the small things of life. The *vaiza*'s narrative, with its several short morality tales, uncomplicated histories and rhetorical questions, was addressed directly to the women, frequent mosque attenders or not.

The rhetorical structure of this long *ders*, from its initial invocation to the concluding well-wishes and blessings, was at the same time well structured and improvised. The core elements were Qur᾿an quotations, allusions to the holy book, and paraphrases of hadith narratives which interpolated the discourse, along with blessings and prayers in combination with moral dicta and invocations for moral improvement.

Authoritative Islamic Knowledge: Genres, Spaces and Speakers

It is questionable whether traditional theological positions would recognise the kind of sermon and instruction presented here as a contribution to Islamic knowledge. It would probably be considered a *dava*, an invitation to return to the proper faith, but not as intellectual contribution in any significant sense. The women engaged in the organisation of this series of *mukabelas* do not regard themselves as theologians – a concept which they associate with interpretive spaces and institutions to which they do not have any immediate access. Yet, they are proud to be part of local knowledge production that informs and forms lives in the immediate vicinity, although aware that their engagement also can be a source of conflict.

The theme of this volume on Muslim homiletics addresses a conspicuous challenge: the identification and analysis of interpretive domains in local religious communities. By asking who the rightful speaker is, an identification of previously not-so-visible actors – with their attendant choice of speech and communication genres – is unavoidable, along with the issue of accessible spaces and how a temporal ritual room is constructed within a building defined by its conventional features. Arenas where Islamic knowledge is produced and negotiated are many and various, and can readily be pointed out, yet many of the difficult questions about where theology takes place are left unanswered.

Individual agency and the autonomous character of local activities should not be over-emphasised; they are also inscribed in larger patterns of power and hierarchy. As the case presented in this article has indicated, the official Islamic authorities exert influence on both form and content – not necessarily as direct control, but in terms of governance – and the link between grassroots actors and the public authorities is ambiguous. On the local level, however, the delivery of the sermon in this Sarajevan case took place in a mosque that belongs to the Islamic Community that thereby gave legitimacy to the ritual events as well as exerting control.

Muslim women in charge of prayer events, devotional rituals and reciting are frequently also in command of talks at the sort of gatherings discussed above, whether formal sermons, instruction or counselling on social and moral matters. This has been the case throughout Islamic history. The types of communication regarded as suitable for these kinds of speech events thereby fulfil the criteria stipulated at the beginning of this chapter for a wider view on what religious instruction can be, as they provide structured presentations of the Muslim faith and claim to deliver trustworthy interpretations of the holy scriptures and thereby authentic imagery of early Islamic history. A producer of theology, however, is not necessarily a theologian. As the case discussed in this chapter has indicated, even women with formal Islamic education from a *medresa*, or who even have studied at the Islamic Faculty, find it hard to be accepted as a *muallima* in a general sense. Bosnian women's contributions to the teaching of Islam are not to be sought in the institutions, but elsewhere, a fact that also is of importance to the local debate – or lack thereof – about the basis of religious authority. This does not only apply to discursive instruction through the sermon; it also relates to how decorum is maintained in social practice.

A genre like a sermon in its conventional form has a processual character; that is to say, it is inscribed in a ritual interactive context from which it cannot be removed. If the focal point of analysis is shifted from the ritual event as such, to include the larger context of knowledge production and the structural power relations it represents, the Bosnian case, in all its particularities, indicates perspectives on contemporary homiletics that takes both discursive and ritual aspects into consideration.

The *vaiza* underlines the adage, 'None of us is perfect, we know who is perfect', but also notes that it is the duty of every believer to try, meanwhile arguing strongly in favour of everyone's obligation to correct and instruct: 'We all have the duty to say it [point out the lapses and misunderstandings] to others.' Thus, the role of the speaker is flexible throughout the sermon. On the one hand she is the teacher of the assembled women, with access to tradition and learning; her seating in the room also marks her special role. On the other hand, she emphasises at several points during the sermon that the fundamental contrast lies between the perfect world of Allah's intentions and Muhammad's behaviour, and the shortcomings of people in our time.

Sermons, as a genre, are instructive and disciplining, making statements about religious truths and opening up a focus on hierarchical relations and ethical verdicts. Today, there are so many channels for communicating messages of this kind, but traditionally – in Judaism, Christianity and Islam alike – communal instruction is associated with the main weekly service. However, Islamic history has rich traditions of additional sermons and other forms of instructive speech that have constituted an important arena for the local production of Islamic knowledge and Islamic theology, and here women have played a part. The present case has indicated the importance of identifying the actors, the space(s) available, the form of speech (that is, the sermon as a genre), as well as the embeddedness in a ritual event. In Sarajevo, the premises were granted by the Islamic Community which added to the legitimacy of the gathering, but each individual speaker in the *mukabela* series had to catch the attention of her audience and mostly did so by shifting temporalities throughout the sermon: connecting a normative model of the past with life here and now.

Guidance and Governance

The sermon connected to the *mukabela* discussed here was part of a larger ritual event that, in its turn, is a vital part of the Sarajevan Ramadan celebrations. The participants take pride in the city's legacy of women trained to recite well, learned women who are both able to instruct with reference to the Qur'an and the hadith, and who also possess a sense of contemporary issues that are difficult to deal with for a practising Muslim. Seen from this perspective, these preaching women are producers of theology in that they offer interpretations of normative texts and ethical conventions to an audience that accepts their authority as teachers, while maintaining these presentations as coherent performances.

Contemporary studies of Islamic theology do not only discuss conceptual matters. From a humanities perspective, this opens up the sphere to interdisciplinary work enhancing rhetoric and communication analyses, ethnography and the aesthetic disciplines, to mention but a few academic fields that are necessary to provide more complex conceptions of the area. This broader definition of theology implies methodological challenges for the academic studies of Islam that approach local knowledge claims as their analytical subject matter. If identifying alternative actors is one undertaking (with implications for the sort of empirical material to use), further methodological development is another. The last few decades have seen anthropological theory exerting a vital influence on the study of religions, along with reflective approaches to the objects of study. This trend, accompanied by a steadily growing interest in religion in practice, has had a profound impact on how comparative religion is studied.

The focus on speakers, spaces and power structures, also at the core of many ethnographic studies, would nevertheless benefit from a greater emphasis on content: intellectual contributions to local theology and a conceptual history of what terms for homiletics and instruction can connote, from which women's contributions are not disconnected. Furthermore, agents other than conventional preachers and teachers are certainly not only women. In an age of transnational religious communication across denominations, social media are opening up spaces that can parry political and religious attempts to silence, not only in terms of alternative interpretations of religion, but also new modes of interpretation.

In Sarajevo, attending the recitations is a cherished way of celebrating Ramadan, marking the fast as a spiritual training and making the space of the mosque a social meeting ground. This *ders* does not differ substantially from a Friday *hutba* when it comes to formal content. It is full of corrective advice and references to canonical literature. Yet it is not formal speech in the strict sense of the concept; the tone is rather informal, and the space for the *ders* is arranged quite differently from the *hutba*. The young *vaiza* sits in front of the mihrab and constitutes the focal point of the circle of assembled women, but she does not enter the *minber*, the nexus for the authority of the *hutba*. The study of Islamic teaching and learning is an emerging academic field and we can expect forthcoming studies of all parts of the Muslim world, analysing decisive features in these processes such as gender, social status, formal and informal education, and governance.

Notes

1. To mention but a few: Gade 2004; Deeb 2006; van Doorn-Harder 2006; Rasmussen 2010; Hassan 2011; Hafez 2011; Bano and Kalmbach 2012; Basarudin 2015; Kalmbach 2015; Bano 2017.
2. The specific gathering at the Hadžijska Mosque discussed in this chapter was documented on film in August 2012 as part of the larger collection of material for the educational film *Bosnian Muslim Women's Rituals: Bulas Singing, Reciting and Teaching in Sarajevo* (2016) by Catharina Raudvere and Zilka Spahić-Šiljak. It presents the elaborate Sarajevan traditions of women arranging and performing *mevlud* ceremonies and teaching (with special references to women's formal and informal Islamic education) that are included in such gatherings. The film is available at <https://modernity.ku.dk/documentary/> (last accessed 31 January 2020). The overall documentation is based on fieldwork conducted as part of my project at the research centre, 'The Many Roads in Modernity: The Transformation of South-East Europe 1870 to the 21st Century', at the University of Copenhagen,<www.modernity.ku.dk> (last accessed 31 January 2020). The research centre is generously funded by the Carlsberg Foundation.
3. After the war in the 1990s, many demolished and damaged mosques were rebuilt

or pervasively restored with the support of foreign Islamic aid funding, in designs unfamiliar to Bosnian architecture. This did not only affect the aesthetics of the mosques, but also how space was organised.

4. *Hatib* can refer to a preacher in a mosque in general, but the term is commonly understood to refer to the leader of and the preacher at Friday prayers (although these two tasks can sometimes be divided between two men).

Bibliography

Bano, Masooda (2017), *Female Islamic Education Movements: The Re-democratisation of Islamic Knowledge*, Cambridge: Cambridge University Press.

Bano, Masooda and Hilary Kalmbach (eds) (2012), *Women, Leadership, and Mosques: Changes in Contemporary Islamic Authority*, Leiden: Brill.

Basarudin, Azza (2015), *Humanizing the Sacred: Sisters in Islam and the Struggle for Gender Justice in Malaysia*, Seattle: University of Washington Press.

Bowen, John (1993), *Muslims through Discourse: Religion and Ritual in Gayo Society*, Princeton: Princeton University Press.

van Bruinessen, Martin and Stefano Allievi (2011), *Producing Islamic Knowledge: Transmission and Dissemination in Western Europe*, London: Routledge.

Deeb, Laura (2006), *An Enchanted Modern: Gender and Public Piety in Shiʿi Lebanon*, Princeton: Princeton University Press.

van Doorn-Harder, Pieternella (2006), *Women Shaping Islam: Indonesian Women Reading the Qurʾan*, Urbana: University of Illinois Press.

Gade, Anna M. (2004), *Perfection makes Practice: Learning, Emotion, and the Recited Qurʾān in Indonesia*, Honolulu: University of Hawai'i Press.

Giomi, Fabio (2015a), 'Daughters of Two Empires: Muslim Women and Public Writing in Habsburg Bosnia and Herzegovina (1878–1918)', *Aspasia* 9 (1): 1–18.

Giomi, Fabio (2015b), 'Forging Habsburg Muslim Girls: Gender, Education and Empire in Bosnia and Herzegovina (1878–1918)', *History of Education: Journal of the History of Education Society* 44 (3): 274–92.

Hafez, Sherine (2011), *An Islam of Her Own: Reconsidering Religion and Secularism in Women's Islamic Movements*, New York: New York University Press.

Hassan, Mona (2011), 'Women Preaching for the Secular State: Official Preachers (*bayam vaiziler*) in Contemporary Turkey', *International Journal of Middle East Studies* 43: 451–73.

Hassan, Mona (2012), 'Reshaping Religious Authority in Contemporary Turkey: State-Sponsored Female Preachers', in M. Bano and H. Kalmbach (eds),

Women, Leadership, and Mosques: Changes in Contemporary Islamic Authority, Leiden: Brill, pp. 85–104.

Kalmbach, Hilary (2015), 'Blurring Boundaries: Aesthetics, Performance, and the Transformation of Islamic leadership', *Culture and Religion* 16 (2): 160–74.

Krämer, Gudrun and Sabine Schmidtke (eds) (2006), *Speaking for Islam: Religious Authorities in Muslim Societies*, Leiden: Brill.

Lambek, Michael (1993), *Knowledge and Practice in Mayotte: Local Discourses of Islam, Sorcery and Spirit Possession*, Toronto: University of Toronto Press.

Rasmussen, Anne K. (2010), *Women, the Recited Qur'an, and Islamic Music in Indonesia*, Berkeley: University of California Press.

Raudvere, Catharina (2002), *The Book and the Roses: Sufi Women, Visibility, and Zikir in Contemporary Istanbul*, London: I.B. Tauris.

Raudvere, Catharina (2012) 'Textual and Ritual Command: Muslim Women as Keepers and Transmitters of Interpretive Domains in Contemporary Bosnia and Herzegovina', in M. Bano and H. Kalmbach (eds), *Women, Leadership, and Mosques: Changes in Contemporary Islamic Authority*, Leiden: Brill, pp. 259–78.

Raudvere, Catharina (2013) 'Women and Sufism: Contemporary Thought and Practice', in N. J. Delong-Bas (ed.), *The Oxford Encyclopedia of Islam and Women*, Oxford: Oxford University Press.

Schielke, Samuli and Liza Debevec (eds) (2012), *Ordinary Lives and Grand Schemes: An Anthropology of Everyday Religion*, Oxford: Berghahn.

PART II

POWER AND AUTHORITY

4

PREACHING AND THE PROBLEM OF RELIGIOUS AUTHORITY IN MEDIEVAL ISLAM

Jonathan P. Berkey

Preaching was central to the Muslim tradition and the Muslim experience from the very beginning. Muhammad is frequently depicted in the sources as preaching to his community – as, for example, in the famous 'Farewell Sermon', delivered shortly before his death, in which the Prophet is said to have communicated his final instructions to his followers. Muhammad did not, however, pioneer an entirely new genre of discourse. On the contrary, he and his contemporaries could draw on a long tradition of oratory and homiletics among the pre-Islamic Arabs (Serjeant 1983: 117–22).

Preaching became an important part of most Muslims' experience of their faith and has remained so down to the present day.[1] There are several reasons why this was the case. In the first place, Islam – like Christianity and especially Judaism – is an explicitly normative faith. Those who live in, or come from, the monotheistic traditions which emerged from the late antique Near East may take this for granted, but in fact not all religions are so keen on shaping the behaviour of their adherents. Judaism, as it emerged in the centuries before Christ, was constructed around a central paradigm: that God expects us to do (or not to do) certain things; and if we follow his will, we will be rewarded, and if we do not, we should expect punishment of some sort, either in this life or in the world to come. Christianity and then Islam followed the same paradigmatic structure. Islam especially became a religion of laws, expressed ultimately in the comprehensive shariʿa. But the impulse to shape the behaviour of its adherents is already deeply embedded in the Qur'an, with its repeated injunction to 'command what is good and forbid what is evil'. Islam is a normative faith, and so from the beginning a degree of exhortation, in which some Muslims would encourage other Muslims to behave in a certain way, was a part of the mix.

Islam is also a textual religion. This point should need no elaboration: without the Qur'an, without the hadith, there would be no Islam. It is significant that the closest thing to a clergy in the Muslim tradition is the 'ulama', 'those who know' – that is, specialists on the texts on which the religion rests. But one consequence of the tradition's textual basis was to reinforce the role of 'preaching' in Islam. This is because, from the very beginning, what the sources refer to as 'preaching' involved not only moral exhortation, the propagation of normative guidance, but the transmission of and elaboration upon the texts which were central to the tradition. This is, broadly, what is meant by *'ilm* (knowledge), and which defined the sphere of the 'ulama'.

And so, any contest over the nature of that knowledge, and over how it should be shared and by whom, was a contest over defining Islam itself. That is why the contest over preaching which lies at the heart of this chapter, as difficult as it is to define, was so important, and so divisive. Authority in the Islamic tradition is inherently problematic, and the tension over it was productive of much of the intellectual and social dynamism of pre-modern Islamic societies.

As has been recognised for many years, pre-modern Islam lacked a formal institutional structure through which the religious tradition was defined. There was nothing resembling an organised church, no formal institutional network of schools, no distinctive clerical class. But the absence of such a structure did not mean that religious authority was lacking, and in fact made questions regarding the nature and construction of that authority more critical. From a fairly early period, the large and amorphous group known as the 'ulama' established themselves as the principal arbiters of what constituted 'Islam'. This made them, by their own account, the 'heirs of the Prophet', those who, with the book of prophecy closed, held the responsibility to define the parameters of acceptable thought and action. They accomplished this by articulating and developing a series of discursive traditions, which collectively constituted the faith: Qur'anic exegesis, hadith commentary and especially jurisprudence. They also held the responsibility to transmit that collective knowledge to future generations, and to ensure that believers generally had sufficient access to it to enable them to live proper Muslim lives.

But who would be recognised as part of this authoritative group? Lacking a formal system of ordination or for the awarding of institutional degrees of the sort which marked off priests and professors in Europe, the pre-modern ʿulamaʾ developed less formal mechanisms for limiting access to that status. They sought to restrict individuals' ability to claim scholarly authority to those convincingly trained by earlier scholars – amounting, in effect, to an effort to replicate both their own social authority and their construction of what 'Islam' was. Over time, these mechanisms grew more formalised and restrictive. By the Islamic Middle Period, they included the spread of endowed institutions of learning, an increasingly sophisticated system of 'licenses' (*ijāza*s) identifying the bearer as a recognised scholar, and in some cases closer cooperation with political authorities. Eventually, under the Ottomans, an organised system defined and supported by the state regulated access to ʿulamaʾ status. But at least until then, the system remained stubbornly flexible and, to a certain degree, porous. And preaching in fact was one area of religious practice and discourse where the ʿulamaʾ's efforts to control access to the 'guild' were most frequently challenged.[2]

Preaching was a diverse phenomenon: it occurred at different levels and in radically different contexts. Medieval writers used a variety of terms to refer to homiletic oration. These terms, while reflecting a range of practices and purposes, were used in overlapping ways, and so developing a precise typology of Islamic preaching in the pre-modern period is difficult. (For a cogent summary, see Jones 2012: 15–20.) But generally, we can say that, at the top, was the delivery of the *khuṭba*, the oration delivered on a series of prescribed liturgical occasions, especially during noon prayers on Fridays. The fourteenth-century Egyptian scribe and encyclopedist al-Qalqashandī, enumerating all the various offices to which a scholar or a jurist might be appointed, called the position of *khaṭīb* (the individual who delivered the *khuṭba*) 'the grandest office' (al-Qalqashandī 1964: 4.39). Delivery of the *khuṭba* required the preacher to follow a precise array of formulae and conventions, many of them rooted in memories of the Prophet's own practice or that of his companions, with regard to the content of his sermon and to his comportment during delivery (Jones 2012: 38–86). The responsibility of delivering the Friday sermon in congregational mosques quickly grew into a formal office. Consequently, the position had, from the very beginning, an explicitly political dimension. Acknowledging the reigning caliph (or, later, sultan) in the course of the *khuṭba* became one of the markers of political legitimacy, and the failure to mention the ruler's name an act of rebellion. In the Islamic Middle Period, the political character of the *khaṭīb*'s office is reflected in the fact that many of them were appointed by the ruling political authorities – in Mamluk Cairo, for example, the reigning sultan.

The subject of this chapter constituted a different group – although defining the parameters of the group is rather difficult. The topic concerns those who routinely delivered homiletic exhortations outside of canonically prescribed occasions. Western historians have often referred to them collectively as 'popular preachers'. This is somewhat awkward and misleading, since it suggests a sharper distinction between them and those charged with delivery of the *khuṭba* than perhaps is warranted. The problem is compounded by the fact that there was no single term or phrase in Arabic by which these individuals were known. A fourteenth-century scholar named al-Subkī has left a typology of religious offices and occupations, and he identifies three separate terms by which the popular preachers were known: the *wāʿiẓ* (admonisher), a term frequently encountered in various forms; the *qāṣṣ* (storyteller); and the *qāriʾ al-kursī* (one who reads while sitting down) (al-Subkī 1908: 217–18). In fact, the sources employ a few other terms as well. The term *qāṣṣ* was especially prominent and problematic, and scholarly critique of the practice often focused on those labelled 'storytellers'. But the precise terms are not really important, because they were not used precisely or consistently by the medieval Muslims who wrote about these matters. By whatever term they were called, the individuals in question were those who embraced 'the task of transmitting basic religious knowledge to, instilling piety in, and encouraging pious behaviour among the common people'. And who were the 'common people'? They were 'that large body of Muslims who by nature, temperament, or profession were not clearly members of the ʿulamaʾ, the class of religious scholars, and those training to be such' (Berkey 2001: 14–15).

Those we will call 'popular preachers' did not constitute a separate and exclusive group. Since both moral exhortation and the transmission of textual knowledge were important religious activities, and since receiving religious and ethical guidance and becoming in some sense learned in the faith were valuable for all Muslims, many who preached and who were 'popular' with their audiences were themselves esteemed and reputable scholars – the members of the Bulqīnī family of Cairo, for example, who in the fourteenth and fifteenth centuries developed a reputation for teaching and preaching to the common people (Berkey 2001: 66). Ibn al-Jawzī (d. 1200) and Ibn Taymiyya (d. 1328), both of whom fiercely criticised some practices of popular preachers, nonetheless preached and acquired a broad following among the Muslim population of their home towns (Baghdad and Damascus, respectively).

Other preachers, however, did not have sterling reputations as scholars, and their activity effectively challenged the authority of the ʿulamaʾ. Reconstructing their history is difficult. The biographical dictionaries, which serve as perhaps the most important source for social historians of the medieval Islamic world, are of limited use. Aside from prominent scholars who also developed reputations for delivering sermons to the common people, most of the popular preachers were individuals of only minor academic accomplishment, and so the authors of the biographical dictionaries, who were especially interested in the leading scholars of the day, paid them scant notice. We know, however, that there was a significant and (at least to Muslims at the time) distinctive group of individuals who served as 'popular preachers'. We know of them because their activities generated a coherent and persistent strain of polemic. The most famous of these polemics was written by Ibn al-Jawzī. Ibn al-Jawzī's critique of the preachers is well known in part because it was edited and translated into English several decades ago (Ibn al-Jawzī 1986). But what is really significant about this text is that it was not unusual. Ibn al-Jawzī's *Kitāb al-quṣṣāṣ wa ʾl-mudhakkirīn* was only one of numerous similar works critical of the popular preachers.[3] This was a strain of criticism which reached back to the earliest years of Islamic history, and which continued in a remarkably consistent form down into the early modern period. Moreover, this polemic inspired a vigorous defence of the popular preachers by one of the leading Sufi mystics of fourteenth-century Cairo, a man named ʿAlī Wafā, the subject of an important study by Richard McGregor (McGregor 2004). This polemic and ʿAlī Wafā's defence of the popular preachers will figure prominently in what follows.

In a recent book, Lyall Armstrong has given a comprehensive account of the early history of popular preaching (Armstrong 2016). Armstrong focused on those identified in the sources as *quṣṣāṣ* (storytellers), but his study in fact demonstrates how from the beginning that term and others related to it were applied to a broad range of activities which combined the tasks of pious admonition and exhortation to proper behaviour with that of transmitting religious knowledge and texts to the Muslim faithful. While acknowledging a series of early reports that condemned admonitory storytelling (*qaṣaṣ*) as an improper innovation (*bidʿa*), Armstrong insists that most of those identified as *quṣṣāṣ* in the first Islamic century were reputable scholars – hadith transmitters, Qurʾanic exegetes, jurists and others. At some unidentified and unidentifiable point, however, the term came to be applied instead to a less reputable cast of figures – men (and sometimes women) with minimal training and dubious reputations as scholars whose preaching could not be trusted.

Nonetheless, by the Middle Period, what I am by default calling 'popular preaching' had become one of the principal channels for the transmission of religious knowledge to the broad Muslim populace. In a city such as Cairo, sessions headed by individuals identified as 'popular preachers' – as *quṣṣāṣ*, *wuʿʿāẓ* or other terms – were regularly held in a variety of spaces. Often, they took place in mosques, and certain mosques were widely understood to be popular with them and with their audiences. In a few mosques and madrasas, the institutional endowments provided a stipend for a scholar to preach to and instruct the common people – that is, people from the wider community, and not simply full-time students who were enrolled in more formal classes in *fiqh* or hadith. Cemeteries, too, such as the vast necropolis which surrounded Cairo to the south and east, provided a popular setting for the popular preachers – not surprisingly, perhaps, since these cemeteries provided a safe and convenient forum for a variety of religious practices beyond the control of the ʿulamaʾ (Taylor 1998), a point to which we will have occasion to return.

What exactly went on in these popular preaching circles? This is a difficult question to answer. The sessions themselves were by definition fleeting, and so have left little trace in the historical record. We have the complaints of the preachers' critics, who sometimes explain their concerns with reference to things that transpired in these sessions of which they did not approve – but one must be careful about letting the critics have the final say. Still, we can give at least an outline of an answer to the question.

In the first place, there was more than a passing similarity to more formal classes in religious subjects. Given the importance of the Qur'an for all Muslims, it is hardly surprising that Qur'anic exegesis should form one central focus of the popular preaching circles. This was true already in the earliest centuries of the Islamic era, when the figures identified as *quṣṣāṣ* included among their ranks a number of experts in *tafsīr* (Armstrong 2016: 80–111). Among the Qur'anic passages which were especially popular with the preachers and their audiences were those which concerned the pre-Islamic prophets – no doubt because those passages are among the most compelling narratives in the holy book. Stories about the earlier prophets in the Qur'an often appear in fragmentary, incomplete form, and so the popular preachers drew heavily on the body of tales known as the *qiṣaṣ al-anbiyā'*, or somewhat more pejoratively as the *isra'īliyyāt*, in expounding on them to their audiences. Although the *qiṣaṣ al-anbiyā'* were themselves closely related to the earliest historical layers of *tafsīr*, the 'ulama' grew increasingly sceptical of them over the course of the Middle Ages. Consequently, the popularity of these texts with the preachers and their audiences was one reason for the suspicion in which they were held by critics such as Ibn al-Jawzī.

Hadith, accounts of the words and deeds of the Prophet Muhammad and his companions, also formed a staple of the popular preaching sessions. This, too, is hardly surprising, given the centrality of hadith both in the education of the 'ulama', and in expressions of popular piety. We know that madrasas, mosques and other institutions in the medieval period routinely made provisions for the public recitation of the major compendia of hadith. Given the open character of educational institutions, and the persistently informal and personal channels through which the hadith collections were transmitted from one generation to the next, many Muslims (and not just full-time students) participated actively in reading and studying the prophetic traditions – and the popular preachers and their audiences were among them (Berkey 2001).

Despite their popularity, or perhaps because of it, popular preachers were looked upon by reputable scholars such as Ibn al-Jawzī and the polarising figure Ibn Taymiyya with suspicion. Why? What were the parameters of their concerns? In the first place, the critics perceived the popular preaching circles as loci of corruption, both moral and intellectual. Preachers were accused of manipulating their audiences' emotions for their own benefit. For example, they might weep copiously, to convince their listeners of their piety, when in fact they produced their tears by wiping their faces with handkerchiefs soaked in vinegar and mustard. If the critics are to be believed, preachers would sometimes stage occasions when an individual planted in the audience would suddenly burst into tears, apparently overcome by the power of the preacher's words – and thereby persuade the audience to leave a payment for the preacher, to thank him for his piety and eloquence. Moreover, according to their critics, popular preaching circles were the scene of the disruptive mixing of the sexes. A sixteenth-century Syrian critic condemned the apparently frequent occasions when men and women would gather in a mosque to hear a preacher with no barrier, no hijab, between them. Women, he said, attend these circles wearing their finest clothes and costly perfumes, all to attract the attention of men in the audience (al-Idrīsī fol. 60v). Some of these complaints about sexual improprieties sound rather formulaic, but it is striking how consistently the critics voiced concerns. Ibn al-Jawzī, for example, described female listeners in popular preaching circles becoming overwrought, losing control and shedding all decency. They will, he said, 'cry out like the crying of a pregnant woman at the time of her delivery. At times they even throw off their outer garments and stand up', exposing themselves to the lustful gazes of the men around them (Ibn al-Jawzī 1986: 117, Eng. trans. 130).

A much more serious problem, however, lay in the threat which the preachers posed to the integrity of the Islamic tradition itself – or in their ability to corrupt their audiences' understanding of the faith. Beyond the critics' suspicion of the *isra'īliyyāt,* their concerns focused on the hadith – the alleged hadith – which the preachers transmitted to their audiences. In the opinion of the critics, many of whom were prominent hadith transmitters themselves, false hadith formed the stock-in-trade of the preachers' texts. This was an old complaint. Sometimes the problem was simply that the preachers were not properly trained, and recited hadith without strong chains of authority. So, for instance, according to one oft-cited anecdote, a well-respected eighth-century hadith transmitter from Kufa named al-Aʿmash once encountered a popular preacher in Basra reciting hadith which he claimed to recite on the authority of al-Aʿmash himself. The scholar moved into the circle and began to pluck the hair out of his armpit. The preacher was horrified and called on al-Aʿmash to stop: 'Have you no shame?' he shouted. To which the scholar coolly replied:

> What I am doing is better than what you are doing, since what I am doing is sunna, whereas what you are doing is a lie and an innovation. I am al-Aʿmash, and I never recited to you what you have alleged! (al-Ṭurṭūshi 1990: 231–2; Armstrong 2016: 119)

Similarly, the prominent traditionist Aḥmad ibn Ḥanbal in the ninth century lumped religious storytellers along with beggars as the most untrustworthy people (Ibn al-Ḥājj 1929: 2.146).

But the problem was not simply one of falsely transmitting hadith; the larger danger was that the hadith the popular preachers transmitted were themselves false. This, in fact, was the principal concern of Ibn al-Jawzī and other medieval critics. The storytellers, said Ibn al-Jawzī, will recite false traditions to their audiences, who then pass them on to others, and justify doing so on the grounds that 'we heard [this hadith] recited on the authority of so-and-so'. In this way, he said, 'how many storytellers have misled others with false hadith?' (Ibn al-Jawzī 1983: 1:32). Indeed, Ibn Taymiyya in the early fourteenth century went to the trouble of writing a book cataloguing the traditions recited by the popular preachers (Ibn Taymiyya 1972). Some of them were well-attested hadith found in the standard compilations, such as the *Ṣaḥīḥ al-Bukhārī*. Others – for example, 'paradise lies at the feet of mothers' or 'the poor are [opportunities for] your acts of charity' – articulated ideas which were unobjectionable or were commensurate with prophetic principles, although the ever-vigilant Ibn Taymiyya naturally objected to the storytellers falsely ascribing words to Muhammad. But others, popular no doubt with the preachers and their audiences – for example, that the Prophet 'ordered women to flirt with their husbands during intercourse' – were in Ibn Taymiyya's view simply lies.

One source of the critics' anxiety lay in the enormous influence wielded by the popular preachers – who were indeed, it seems, extremely popular. The polemical discourse is full of anecdotes demonstrating that the preachers had many devoted followers among the common people. The fifteenth-century Egyptian jurist al-Suyūṭī, who authored one of the most original critiques of the popular preachers, begins his account by describing an incident when he upbraided a *qāṣṣ* for reciting false hadith, only to find himself threatened by the preacher's audience, who tried to stone him (al-Suyūṭī 1972: 4). Preachers were the rock stars of their day; the more successful of them could sway enormous audiences through the emotional force of their dramatic preaching, and the more venal could command significant sums of money as payment for delivering their sermons. No wonder the more disciplined scholars were concerned.

The power of the preachers is perhaps not surprising – not, at least, to anyone who has witnessed the effect that charismatic preachers can have on the congregations of contemporary American megachurches. But there was another, less-widely recognised dimension to the threat which popular preaching circles posed: namely, the impact which the audiences might have on what was preached to them. Audiences were not merely passive recipients of whatever the preachers said. The twelfth-century Spanish traveller Ibn Jubayr, during his visit to Baghdad, was struck by how those listening to sermons pelted the preachers with questions, forcing them to respond and address their concerns – one of the beleaguered preachers, in fact, being none other than Ibn al-Jawzī (Ibn Jubayr 1980: 195, 198). Given the nature of the sources, this aspect of the phenomenon is extremely difficult to measure, but our understanding of the challenge posed by popular preaching would be incomplete without at least acknowledging it.

As this observation might suggest, in the medieval period the problem of popular preaching was fundamentally a question of religious authority. The problem of authority resulted from the absence of anything resembling a church, a centralised institutional structure capable of defining the parameters of the tradition. To a medievalist, the situation in the modern world appears somewhat different, as the rise of the nation-state since the Ottoman period has created a pathway to the creation of a more institutionalised religious authority. But in the pre-modern Middle East, the situation was much less clear. Richard Bulliet has called the ʿulamaʾ an 'unappointed clergy' (Bulliet 1979: 40). The centrality of the shariʿa to Muslim identity cast the ʿulamaʾ, whose discourse defined the shariʿa, in the leading social and religious role.

But the absence of any institutionalised religious structure left the boundaries of their authority porous.

This instability in the ʿulamaʾ's authority lay behind one of the unspoken but dominant themes in medieval discourse among the religious scholars: their persistent attempts to narrow the scope of knowledge – *ʿilm* – recognised as legitimate, and also the circle of individuals with acknowledged authority over that knowledge. I have laid out the broad terms of this discourse elsewhere (Berkey 1995). Here I will simply note that the ʿulamaʾ's efforts took many different forms, including the growing popularity of textbooks designed to restrict the range of opinions embraced by the different schools of Sunni jurisprudence, and the proliferation of biographical dictionaries which aimed to achieve something similar (Fadel 1996; Jaques 2006). Central to their efforts was their increasingly strident, even frenzied opposition to *bidaʿ* (innovations), which threatened to lead Muslims astray from the path of the sunna. In these ways and more, the ʿulamaʾ sought to exert their control over an inherently flexible and polymorphous religious tradition.

The ʿulamaʾ's concerns about popular preaching fitted squarely into their larger worries over illicit innovations. The Egyptian jurist al-Suyūṭī began his treatise condemning these popular preachers by citing a well-known hadith in which the Prophet decried innovations, *bidaʿ* (al-Suyūṭī 1972: 3). The charge that the work of those identified in the sources as *quṣṣāṣ* (storytellers) was an innovation was, ironically, an old one: it goes back to the formative period of Islam. Despite some reports linking the practice to the Prophet himself, there are more which condemn it as a heretical innovation. The threat posed by the storytellers, in the eyes of their critics, was existential, even political. One consistent theme of the critics is that the practice threatened not just the individuals who practised it and those who listened to and relied upon them, but the coherence and identity of the Muslim community itself. Hence, for example, traditions which connect it with the rise of the Khariji movement and subsequent civil wars (Armstrong 2016: 190–232). Medieval commentators picked up on these themes and repeated and amplified them. Ibn al-Jawzī, for example, associated storytelling with the Kharijis, but also linked the practice to the destruction of the nation Banū Isrāʾīl (the Israelites of biblical times), implicitly warning his contemporaries that they risked a similar fate (Ibn al-Jawzī 1986: 127, Eng. trans. 211). The matter was deadly serious: 'waging jihad against [the storytellers] is more meritorious', said one critic, 'than doing so against the unbelievers of the House of War, as the evil they inflict is greater than that of the people of the House of War' (al-Idrīsī, fol. 64v).

These are rather astonishing remarks, and I do not think they can be summarily dismissed as mere rhetorical flourish. They suggest in fact a deeply rooted anxiety. What fuelled that anxiety among the ʿulamaʾ, I think, was the fear that popular preachers operated independently of the informal personal networks through which the ʿulamaʾ guaranteed the safe transmission of religious knowledge. It is not irrelevant that, at least according to their critics, many of the popular preachers operated in the enormous cemeteries which ringed medieval cities such as Cairo. These cemeteries more generally constituted a liminal space. In Cairo, for example, one of the most popular religious activities was the regular visits which Muslims paid to the tombs and shrines of saints and other revered figures, a practice which also gave rise to consternation on the part of the ʿulamaʾ because of the wild and disorderly celebrations they encouraged (Taylor 1998). Critics of the popular preachers envisioned them plying their trade in the cemeteries, well beyond the range of the ʿulamaʾ's limited powers of supervision and control. Even more remarkable is the fact that – again, at least according to the critics – some of the popular preachers were women. Not all of the female preachers were threatening: the biographical dictionaries contain reports about women who were 'reliable' and 'virtuous' who preached to audiences composed of other women. But the phenomenon posed an inherent danger, both because it threatened to overturn established social hierarchies (if the women preached to men), but more importantly because women operated even further outside the scholarly networks through which the ʿulamaʾ attempted to regulate the transmission of knowledge. Most of them, said one critic, have read little, and consequently transmit 'stories and tales' that are riddled with lies. His instincts were plainly misogynistic, but his concern was for the integrity of Islam, since such female preachers were 'crooked, root and branch', and therefore unable to distinguish the sound from the unsound (Ibn al-Ḥājj 1929: 2.12–14).

Whether the preachers were women, or simply improperly trained men, the critics thus perceived them to pose an existential threat to the survival of Islam as they understood it. The threat might come in the form of false hadith or dangerous ideas. It certainly came in the form of those operating outside the networks of personal authority by which the ʿulamaʾ regulated the transmission of knowledge – and which defined their own authority. Reliable knowledge of religious matters could only be acquired through those academic networks, as one of the critics of the popular preachers explicitly pronounced in the context of a public disagreement with the Egyptian Sufi defender of the preachers, ʿAlī Wafā (Wafā: fol. 29v–30r; Berkey 2001: 86). So, the conflict between the popular preachers and their critics was fundamentally a conflict over knowledge, and over the authority to determine what knowledge was legitimate.

It was precisely on those two grounds that ʿAlī Wafā chose to defend the popular preachers. If a preacher intended to lead his audience astray, or if he did indeed recite to them false hadith, then ʿAlī agreed that he (or she) was deserving of censure. But in general, he defended their right to preach, to guide their audiences, and to transmit to them texts and traditions which were supportive of the faith. He took a much more expansive view than did the ʿulamaʾ critics of how a preacher might acquire his knowledge. He accepted procedures for the transmission of texts, for example, which relied upon the simple reading of texts, rather than on the careful recitation of them in the presence of their authors or of scholars who have been authorised by previous scholars to do so. Drawing on the principles of Sufism, with its emphasis on intention, intuition and individual religious experience, he stressed the ability of those who were rightly guided to transmit and comment upon texts and to expound to others on matters of religious import (Berkey 2001: 70–80).

In particular, ʿAlī defended the ability of a rightly guided preacher to acquire the knowledge which he passed on to his audience through dreams – a dream, perhaps, in which the Prophet Muhammad spoke to them. This is not as unusual as it might sound to us, since many if not most medieval Muslims acknowledged the possibility of genuine communication from the Prophet, and even from God, in the form of a 'sound dream'. From the terms of the polemic against the popular preachers, it would appear that it was not unusual that they would claim that the Prophet had explicitly granted them permission to preach during the course of a dream. The critics, of course, worried that the popular preachers would invoke a vision of Muhammad to justify the transmission of unauthorised texts and ideas, and so corrupt the body of knowledge (*ʿilm*) which they understood to be Islam. But ʿAli would give the preachers considerably broader licence. 'If one sees a good dream,' he said, 'spread the news.' He went further: any message a preacher might receive through a vision which did not contradict the consensus (*ijmāʿ*) of the community must, he said, be considered 'correct' (*ṣaḥīḥa*) (Berkey 2001: 80–7).

ʿAlī Wafā's defence of the popular preachers amounts to a vigorous defence of the openness of Islam and of the tradition's willingness to let a broad range of believers contribute to its ongoing construction. It flew in the face of efforts by the medieval critics of popular preaching, and of the ʿulamaʾ more generally, to constrict the circle of those permitted to define the tradition. It is hard to tell how successful ʿAlī was. Certainly, the critics of the popular preachers were many, and their polemics constituted a distinct and persistent strand within medieval Muslim discourse. ʿAlī's voice was, by contrast, a lonely one: I am not aware of any other explicit, focused defence of the popular preachers from the medieval Muslim world. On the other hand, the contribution of the popular preachers to the common people's understanding of Islam may have been more significant than we would otherwise think; indeed, their potential impact is precisely what concerned the critics. As Ibn al-Jawzī himself said, 'the preacher brings to God a great number of people', far more than those who claimed the title of *ʿālim* (scholar) (Ibn al-Jawzī 1986: 20–1, 230, Eng. trans. 107, 144). In part through the efforts of these preachers, the tradition of Islam remained porous, contingent and flexible right through the medieval period.

Notes

1. Jones (2012) is an outstanding study of preaching in a particular pre-modern Muslim society. For representative studies of preaching in modern contexts, see Antoun 1989; Gaffney 1994; and Hirschkind 2006, as well as the studies in the present volume. Tahera Qutbuddin's monumental account of the origin and early evolution of Arabic oration and preaching, *Arabic Oration: Art and Function* (2019), arrived too late to be taken into account in this study.
2. The question of authority permeates most scholarship on the religious history of pre-modern Islam. For one example of the debate over the mechanisms of

the ʿulamaʾ to reinforce and replicate their authority, compare George Makdisi (1981) with Berkey (1992) and Chamberlain (1994).

3. Other works in this genre include *Tahdhīr al-khawāṣṣ min akādhīb al-quṣṣāṣ*, by Jalāl al-Dīn al-Suyūṭī (d. 1505); *Bayān ghurbat al-islām bi-wāsiṭat ṣinfay al-mutafaqqiha wa ʾl-mutafaqqira min ahl miṣr wa ʾl-shām wa mā yalīhima min bilād al-aʿjām*, by the sixteenth-century Sufi ʿAlī b. Maymūn al-Idrīsī; and a treatise by Zayn al-Dīn al-ʿIrāqī (d. 1404) which provoked a response by the Sufi preacher ʿAlī Wafā, *al-Bāʿith ʿala ʾl-khalāṣ min suʾ al-ẓann bi ʾl-khawāṣ*.

Bibliography

Antoun, Richard (1989), *Muslim Preacher in the Modern World*, Princeton: Princeton University Press.

Armstrong, Lyall (2016), *The Quṣṣāṣ of Early Islam*, Leiden: Brill.

Berkey, Jonathan P. (1992), *The Transmission of Knowledge in Medieval Cairo: A Social History of Islamic Education*, Princeton: Princeton University Press.

Berkey, Jonathan P. (1995), 'Tradition, Innovation, and the Social Construction of Knowledge in the Medieval Islamic Near East', *Past and Present* 146 (1): 38–65.

Berkey, Jonathan P. (2001), *Popular Preaching and Religious Authority in the Medieval Islamic Near East*, Seattle: University of Washington Press.

Bulliet, Richard (1979), *Conversion to Islam in the Medieval Period*, Cambridge, MA: Harvard University Press.

Chamberlain, Michael (1994), *Knowledge and Social Practice in Medieval Damascus, 1190–1350*, Cambridge: Cambridge University Press.

Fadel, Mohammed (1996), 'The Social Logic of *Taqlīd* and the Rise of the *Mukhtaṣar*', *Islamic Law and Society* 3 (2): 193–233.

Gaffney, Patrick D. (1994), *The Prophet's Pulpit: Islamic Preaching in Contemporary Egypt*, Berkeley: University of California Press.

Hirschkind, Charles (2006), *The Ethical Soundscape: Cassette Sermons and Islamic Counterpublics*, New York: Columbia University Press.

Ibn al-Ḥājj (1929), *Madkhal al-sharʿ al-sharīf*, 4 vols, Cairo: al-Maṭbaʿa al-Miṣrīya.

Ibn al-Jawzī, ʿAbd al-Raḥmān b. ʿAlī (1986), *Kitāb al-quṣṣāṣ wa ʾl-mudhakkirīn*, Merlin Swartz (ed. and trans.), Beirut: Dār al-Mashriq.

Ibn Jubayr, Muḥammad b. Aḥmad (1980), *Rihla*, Beirut: Dār Ṣādir.

Ibn Taymiyya, Aḥmad (1972), *Aḥadīth al-quṣṣāṣ*, Beirut: al-Maktab al-Islāmī.

al-Idrīsī, ʿAlī b. Maymūn, *Bayān ghurbat al-islām bi-wāsiṭat ṣinfay al-mutafaqqiha wa ʾl-mutafaqqira min ahl miṣr wa ʾl-shām wa mā yalīhima min bilād al-aʿjām*, Princeton Garret Ms. 828H.

Jaques, Kevin (2006), *Authority, Conflict, and the Transmission of Diversity in Medieval Islamic Law*, Leiden: Brill.

Jones, Linda Gale (2012), *The Power of Oratory in the Medieval Muslim World*, Cambridge: Cambridge University Press.

McGregor, Richard (2004), *Sanctity and Mysticism in Medieval Egypt: The Wafāʾ Sufi Order and the Legacy of Ibn ʿArabī*, Albany: SUNY Press.

Makdisi, George (1981), *The Rise of Colleges: Institutions of Learning in Islam and the West*, Edinburgh: Edinburgh University Press.

al-Qalqashandī, Aḥmad b. ʿAlī (1964), *Ṣubḥ al-aʿshā fī ṣinaʿat al-inshāʾ*, 14 vols, Cairo: al-Muʿassasa al-Miṣriyah al-ʿāmmah lil-taʿlīf wa ʾl-tarjama wa-al-ṭibāʿa wa ʾl-nashr.

Qutubuddin, Tahera (2019), *Arabic Oration: Art and Function*, Leiden: Brill.

Serjeant, R. B. (1983), 'Early Arabic Prose', in A. F. L. Beeston, T. M. Johnstone, R. B. Serjeant and G. R. Smith (eds), *Arabic Literature to the End of the Umayyad Period*, Cambridge: Cambridge University Press, pp. 114–53.

al-Subkī, Tāj al-Dīn ʿAbd al-Wahhāb (1908), *Muʿīd al-niʿam wa mubīd al-niqam*, D. W. Myhrman (ed.), Leiden: Brill.

al-Suyūṭī, Jalāl al-Dīn (1972), *Tahdhīr al-khawāṣṣ min akādhīb al-quṣṣāṣ*, Beirut: al-Maktab al-Islāmī.

Taylor, Christopher S. (1998), *In the Vicinity of the Righteous: Ziyāra and the Veneration of Muslim Saints in Late Medieval Egypt*, Leiden: Brill.

al-Ṭurṭūshi, Abū Bakr Muḥammad (1990), *Kitāb al-ḥawādith wa ʾl-bidaʿ*, Beirut: Dār al-Gharb al-Islāmī.

Wafā, ʿAlī, *al-Bāʿith ʿala ʾl-khalāṣ min suʾ al-ẓann bi ʾl-khawāṣ*, B.L. Or. Ms. 4275.

5

FRIDAY SERMONS IN A SECULAR STATE: RELIGIOUS INSTITUTION-BUILDING IN MODERN TURKEY

Elisabeth Özdalga[1]

Turkey holds a unique place in the Muslim world when it comes to centralisation and state control of religious life. This is closely connected to its rigid implementation of secularism, or laicism, which since 1928 has been written into the Turkish constitution (Article 2). Less secular-oriented states, such as Egypt and Jordan, have over the years entered a similar path, but at a more gradual and hesitant pace. In the less centralised, federal-like states of South East Asia, Indonesia and Malaysia, where the population is ethnically and religiously more heterogeneous (still, Indonesia is home to the world's largest Muslim population), the Islamic upswing gaining momentum during the 1980s has been carried by organised 'civil Islam', rather than by the state (Hefner 2000; Hoesterey 2016). The ambition of the official authorities in these countries has been to control, but not to organise, religious life. So, compared to many other Muslim countries Turkey offers a precursory example of the social and political dynamics – and predicaments – involved in having religion organised by a strictly secular and centralised state. The fact that the pro-Islamic Justice and Development Party (Adalet ve Kalkınma Partisi, AKP) assumed office in 2002, and has gradually turned increasingly Islam-oriented and authoritarian, did not alter the state's centralistic and, as far as the constitution goes, secular character.[2]

This chapter offers an outline of Turkey's century-long experience of official Islam with special emphasis on Friday sermons. It does so by focusing on the Directorate of Religious Affairs, Diyanet, the institution entrusted to implement such a programme; the media used for the distribution of official *hutbes*; and the conveyed messages, that is, the textual (discursive) aspects of this particular kind of Muslim homiletics. I will discuss these issues in reverse order, starting with a sermon from 1977, which illustrates the leading mood – not only of that particular time, but of the republic as a whole – of official Turkish homiletic discourse, based as it has been on an amalgam of official secularist and religious values.

May Day 1977: A Short Flashback

In spite of significant social and economic progress, Turkey's modern history has also been marked by severe setbacks. Seen in that perspective, the decade spanning the military interventions of 1971 and 1980 has gone down to history as one of unusual political turbulence. Increasingly violent clashes dominated the political landscape: on the left stood radical activists, including Marxist–Leninist, Maoist and other revolutionary factions, some of which advocated armed guerrilla warfare; on the right, various anti-communist and ultra-nationalist groups, who organised paramilitary training in order to conquer streets and university campuses. In 1977, in the midst of this escalating violence, the leftist labour confederation DISK organised a huge May Day meeting on Taksim Square in Istanbul, which ended in panic caused by gunfire from a nearby building and a tragic stampede resulting in thirty-nine people dead (Zürcher 1994: 276). The verdict over organisers – for their heedlessness – and official authorities – for their lack of responsibility and due security – was harsh and kept the newspapers busy for several weeks. In the aftermath of this terrifying event, the following text, in the form of a Friday sermon (*hutbe*), could be read in the fortnightly paper *Diyanet Gazetesi*, issued on 15 May (1977).[3]

> Fraternity in Islam
>
> Honourable community!
>
> Believe Allah the exalted and his Messenger that all believers that gather under the flag of unity in Islam are like siblings born from one mother and father; this fraternity in Islam is not a temporary fraternity but rather everlasting (*Ebussuud Tefsiri* 5:90).[4] One of the duties of a Muslim to

other Muslims is that in quarrelling and fighting that arises between two Muslims, he should reconcile and make peace between the two Muslims. Thus, on this topic it is stated in one noble verse:

'The believers are but brothers, so make settlement between your brothers. And fear Allah that you may receive mercy' (The Qur'an, The Chambers [49]:10). Our beloved prophet also states in a hadith: 'A believer is another believer's (religious) brother' (*Meşârık ul-Envâr*, İbn-i Melek, Vol. 2, s: 111).[5]

Honourable Muslims!

Our noble religion commands the fraternity of Muslims and living fraternally, and to live within unity and togetherness. For believers are to one another like the parts of one body. In another hadith our Prophet (peace be upon him) states, 'Believers love one another, have compassion for one another, and preserve one another like they are one body. If any part of the body becomes troubled, the other parts for this reason come down with sickness and insomnia' (*Câmi'uş-Şağîr, Azîziye Şerhi*, Vol. 3: 278).[6] Wherever he may be in the world, when one Muslim meets with a disaster, all Muslims feel sadness. Muslims are very compassionate towards one another. For compassion is the actual brother of love. Our religion informs that the life, property, honour and virtue of one Muslim are forbidden to another Muslim. When our Prophet, who is an example for us in all respects, gestured toward the Muslims who emigrated from Mecca to Medina and stated, 'Oh people of Medina! These immigrants are your brothers', the noble companion Saad Bin Rebîa (may God bless him) took his immigrant brother to his house, showed him his property, and said, 'Look, my brother, half of these possessions are yours.' Responding to this favour, his holiness Abdurrahman İbni Avf (may God bless him) was moved to the utmost and said, 'My brother, thank God for all of your possessions. You just show me the road that goes to the marketplace and leave the rest to me,' and he sold the bit of milk and cheese that he had bought from the marketplace and returned to his home in the evening (*Asrı Saadet*, Vol. 1: 307–9, old print).[7] With this in mind, today for the temporary benefits of this world we see no harm in strangling and killing each other. As such we become weak against our enemies. One incidence of anarchy that was caused by a few people disturbs the nation as a whole.

> Honourable Muslims!
> In conclusion, let us avoid all types of activities that break the bonds of fraternity between Muslims. Let's know that the best people are those who do favours for others. Let's not forget that our language, our book and our *qibla* are one (*El-Müfredât fi-Garîb-ül-Kur'an*, Rağıb-ı-Isfehânî: 13).[8] Let's know that consenting to evil is equal to doing evil and stay far from all types of actions that break peace.
> Let us also not be helpers to those who seek to cause unrest. Let us never forget that we are each other's brothers. (Author: Kamil Şahin)[9]

Against the background of the agitated and indignant feelings aroused by the day-by-day mounting political violence of which the May Day massacre became an alarming reminder, the tone of the quoted sermon is surprisingly subdued. Instead of stirring pronouncements of outrage and disappointment, the text contains repeated exhortations to remain calm, self-restrained and unified – a unity visualised as a body or a kinship (family) group, against an alleged threat of social disintegration.

This restraining position is characteristic of official sermons in modern Turkey. The text is set on damping, rather than inciting moral and political indignation. This should be seen in the light of the reduced and subordinated role assigned to Islam after the establishment of the republic in 1923. What was left of Islamic traditions after the abolition of shariʿa in 1924/5 was a set of beliefs (*itikat*) and ethical rules (*ahlak*). In secular Turkey, religion should not meddle with law and jurisprudence. However, it could well deal with fostering loyal citizens, but then in an unobtrusive manner. An essential aim of the republican leaders was to forge locally scattered communities of believers into one community of Turkish nationals. For this purpose, public school and military training, history writing, and various official ceremonies and celebrations were not enough. The authorities also needed the support of imams and preachers (*hatips*). Good Muslims were regarded as good citizens, and vice versa. The people/nation should be united as patriotic Turks and pious Muslims under the auspices of their political – and religious – leaders, but this should not be done with bulky movements and high-pitched voices. That sermonising should keep a low, undistinguished profile, that is, that it should not excite strong feelings, was not only a question of ideology, it was also a result of the formal institutionalisation of religious activities within Diyanet.

Diyanet: Institutional Consolidation

Diyanet was established on 3 March 1924, the same day the caliphate was abolished (Jäschke 1972: 21, 57). However, for several decades the religious institution remained in the shadow of other governmental agencies. It was not until the 1960s (especially with the implementation of Law 633 in 1965, see below) that Diyanet grew into becoming a more integral part of the increasingly complex and centralistic Turkish state system. This was no easy process. It brought with it different kinds of uncomfortable frictions between prominent representatives of the secular state such as the military, the upper echelons of the civil bureaucracy, including the judiciary and the academia, on the one hand, and more liberal-minded business circles, media groups and political parties, on the other. A whole range of opinionated actors on both sides of the divide between secularists and the devout wanted to have a say. Against such interventionist attempts stood groups of religious professionals and their sympathisers, who promoted a more autonomous and politically neutral organisation. No doubt, Diyanet functioned as a mediator or filter between various hegemonic interest groups and popular sentiments. However, it also acted on its own behalf, for example in the name of those religious bureaucrats who filled its office rooms and corridors.

When the future Director of Diyanet, Tayyar Altıkulaç, took up the post as deputy director in July 1971, he was shocked by the lack of order and discipline within the organisation. It became his task to infuse fresh life into the new legal structure of 1965 (Law 633). Altıkulaç started as deputy director of Diyanet on 15 July 1971, four months after the military intervention of 12 March, when the sitting government, unable to deal with mounting social and political unrest, was forced from power and replaced with an above-party cabinet of technocrats.[10]

As a manifestation of the junta's concerns for a secular and West-oriented Turkey, the government had had the then deputy director of Diyanet, Yaşar Tunagür, dismissed. This purge was occasioned by Tunagür's alleged connections to the Nurcu movement and other anti-secular Islamist networks.[11] There was thus an urgent need to replace Tunagür with a supposedly more reliable staff member and it seems that the responsible minister, Mehmet Özgüneş, had found Altıkulaç to be a suitable person for that position. Among these appointments, in August 1972, the Director of Diyanet since 1968, Lütfü Doğan, a cleric of simple origin, lacking formal academic education, was replaced with a theologian with a doctoral degree, coincidentally going by the same name, thus Dr Lütfü Doğan.

In spite of his relatively young age, Altıkulaç was, according to his own account, already known as a cleric especially proficient in reciting/chanting the Qur'an (*tilavet*), which had occasioned him to take part in several recordings for radio broadcasting.[12] He was known as a dependable secular-minded nationalist, who did not associate with Islamist circles. On the contrary, he kept a clear distance to Islamist party politics. As related in his autobiography, Altıkulaç had been approached by leading figures from the pro-Islamic National Order Party (Milli Nizam Partisi, MNP), formed in 1969. This happened when he was serving as imam in the eastern Tunceli province during his military service. The MNP people handed him a request to set up a district organisation on behalf of their party. They seemed to mean that, as imam, he would be especially suitable for such a mission. Altıkulaç rejected their appeal in straightforward terms, saying that to run a political party as if it were a religious community or movement could do nothing but harm to religion itself. He emphatically declared that by no means would he participate in that kind of undertaking (Altıkulaç 2011: 162–3).[13]

The government also appointed a teacher with a colonel's degree from the War College, Ahmet Okutan, as a second deputy director. The turnabout in having the allegedly Nurcu-affiliated Tunagür exchanged for two more secular-minded deputy directors – one of them from the military ranks – is a good illustration of the kind of showdowns that arose and the deals that were struck between state and government, on the one hand, and religious groups and communities on the other. However, that Altıkulaç, on merit of his secular-mindedness, was chosen for this post does not mean that he was a man of the Establishment. Deeming from the way in which administrative reforms were carried out under his leadership, he, in fact, managed to strike a balance, which bolstered the autonomy of Diyanet. This independence was realised through a momentum generated in the course of a number of reforms initiated under his management, with important implications also for Friday sermons.

Administrative Reforms

Altıkulaç has described Diyanet as being in a state of wreckage (Altıkulaç 2011: 183).[14] First of all, the corridors were overcrowded. The reason for this agonising situation was that in order to have an appointment settled – as imam, muezzin, *hatip*, or any other position – people would have to busy themselves personally. Otherwise, their tasks risked remaining undealt with for months. In addition, employees and their dependants would come from near and far to take care of personal problems also outside of the jurisdiction of Diyanet. People would bring up any issue related to health, education, family relationships and supply problems. The mere fact that Diyanet was an official institution situated in the capital attracted people to go there for all kinds of problems. Parliamentarians would come and go at their own discretion in order to have their own and their supporters' affairs solved. True, the problem with congested offices was not limited to Diyanet. The situation was similar all over the public sector. Still, it might have been that Diyanet was under heavier pressure because people expected a more sincere and generous reception there thanks to the religious glow and folksy character of this institution.[15]

The second problem pointed out by Altıkulaç was the lack of proper archives. In order to find a requested dossier, the official in charge may have to search for days. In addition, personal security was inadequate. Dossiers containing confidential information were sometimes passed around without proper caution or protection.

A third problem was what Altıkulaç identified as hidden unemployment. Women busy with knitting or crocheting during office hours has become a legendary synonym for low work output. This was also the expression used by Altıkulaç in his description of the lack of work discipline in Diyanet. He linked this problem to the fact that office rooms were small, which made it difficult to implement control and supervision. A fourth, and even more serious problem, was the lack of discipline in the chain of command. Decisions taken by the central authority were left to the discretion of the muftis at the provincial and/or district levels. 'Especially this situation made me very frustrated,' complains Altıkulaç (Altıkulaç 2011: 184).

Altıkulaç was eager to do something about these problems. In order to cope with the low production of work or services – 'hidden unemployment'

– Altıkulaç ventured to intervene into the very architectural design of the office building. As an alternative to the small office spaces, he introduced the idea of office landscape. Walls were torn down and three larger halls were constructed based on an already existing division of labour between employment records (dossiers or files), rosters of permanent staff and appointments (*sicil*, *kadro*, *tayin*). In this way, two aims were met: a more well-arranged and rational organisation was reached, and a stricter supervision, thus work discipline, was achieved. However, as it turned out, it was not an altogether easy task to have this plan realised. Lütfü Doğan, the then director of Diyanet, was generally passive and unwilling to implement any kind of change and had repeatedly tried to postpone Altıkulaç's proposals until a later date. The opportunity to carry out the reconstructions came when Doğan went on a few days' trip to Istanbul. Altıkulaç tells vividly how he made the preparations by begging for material support (financing and manpower) from a more well-to-do friend from his own home district and how he, on the day of departure, escorted his superior to the airport and then rushed back in order to finish the construction within a few days. On his return, the director did not say anything encouraging, but neither did he actively oppose the new open-plan arrangements (Altıkulaç 2011: 187).

With respect to archives, there were around 50,000 personnel files in pressing need of systematisation. With the purpose of finding a useful and effective model, Altıkulaç applied to the General Staff (High Military Command), the Ministry of Justice and the Ministry of Education. The General Staff provided the best model and the Ministry of Education the poorest, which is why he went for the former. What colleagues in Diyanet estimated would amount to a couple of years' work was finished in a couple of months. However, this was not reached without what Altıkulaç describes as tough measures concerning work pace and discipline (Altıkulaç 2011: 188–9).

Concerning the need to clear the offices from crowds, Altıkulaç decreed a prohibition against outside visitors. However, outside visitors could not just be dismissed and were instead advised to see the heads of divisions or the deputy directors. The aim was to provide the personnel at the lower levels peace and quiet. In addition, Altıkulaç also expended efforts in teaching the staff how to write official letters in order to raise the general quality of the produced services (Altıkulaç 2011: 189–91).

A reform that especially deserves mentioning concerned the way in which appointments of imams, *hatips* and muezzins around the country were carried out. To begin with, there was the basic problem related to the scarcity of personnel; the available personnel were not enough to cover the needs of all the mosques in the country.[16] In addition, the available personnel were unevenly distributed. From a survey arranged by Altıkulaç it became apparent that imams, muftis and other religious personnel too often got their appointments based on the power of certain politically influential parties or personalities. For example, in Isparta, which was the home province of Süleyman Demirel, a long-standing leader in Turkish politics, offices were filled to 100 per cent. In some less well-off provinces, on the other hand, the covering went down to 20 per cent. In order to avoid this kind of injustice, Altıkulaç introduced a statute (*tüzük*) in seven articles, stating which criteria to follow when distributing available cadres. Preparations were made in silence, without being displayed to the public. Thanks to these procedures, powerful political groups were kept at a distance, which meant that Diyanet was able to maintain a certain amount of independence or autonomy. When confronted with visitors, even if those were parliamentarians or other influential people, the personnel at Diyanet were now able to decline their requests by referring to existing regulations. In 1979, the government, a shaky cabinet led by Bülent Ecevit, leader of the Republican People's Party (Cumhuriyet Halk Partisi, CHP), with the support of eleven independent deputies, tried to change these regulations, which had been accepted only four years before, but Altıkulaç did not give in to the pressures. He asserted his own line in a formal report. What lent substance to that report was that it was signed not only by himself, but also by the members of Diyanet's High Committee for Religious Affairs (Din Işleri Yüksek Kurulu, DIYK), a situation that requires special explanation and clarification (Altıkulaç 2011: 194–8).

It was by force of the High Committee that the director was able to withstand the pressures imposed from various political circles in and around the central government and local administrative bodies. The committee thus constituted an important instrument for any front-runner or leading group within Diyanet, who strived to maintain and strengthen the independence or autonomy of the directorate. The strategic significance of the committee was also linked to the far-reaching authorities assigned to the director, especially concerning appointments of the personnel. In this sense, Diyanet had – or was able to claim – a more autonomous status than many other official institutions (Altıkulaç 2011: 692). These regulations were based in Law 633 from 1965, which also defined the legal framework of the High Committee.[17]

Law 633 thus offered the underpinnings of a relatively strong clerical independence. However, until Altıkulaç was appointed director of Diyanet in February 1978, this committee had not yet succeeded in constituting itself. The reasons were lack of enough candidates with the required qualifications, and interference in the appointment process by political groups, especially the pro-Islamic National Salvation Party (Milli Selamet Partisi, MSP), who picked candidates according to Islamist leanings, rather than professional qualifications.[18] It seems that Altıkulaç's predecessors were not as concerned about the significance of the committee for the maintenance of institutional autonomy, or the kind of political manipulations they might be exposed to. For Altıkulaç, however, it became a priority to make sure that the High Committee was formed and activated. It was by virtue of this board that he was able to maintain relative integrity and independence for Diyanet. In what comes out of his autobiography, this was not easy to accomplish, but the formation of the High Committee represented an important take-off for his own mission as director 1978–86 (Altıkulaç 2011: 343–6). After having obtained a degree of control over Diyanet, Altıkulaç could concentrate on certain critical issues. These included: strengthening Diyanet's representations abroad, especially in Germany; improving the organisation of pilgrimage (*hac*); raising the level of education for imams and other religious personnel; strengthening the control of various 'free' religious communities and increasingly obtrusive Islamist party interests; establishing the correct time to start fasting during Ramadan; and to supply the finishing touch of a comprehensive reform package, improving the quality of the Friday sermons (Altıkulaç 2011: 336).

New Regulations Concerning the Friday Sermons

*Hutbe*s represented a field of worship that was in need of reform, according to Altıkulaç. The weekly religious addresses were especially important, since it was by means of the Friday sermon that the people could be reached in larger numbers for religious education and enlightenment. Therefore, it was particularly regretful for a leading cleric like Altıkulaç to notice that the level of education of those delivering the homilies was so poor. In the early 1970s, the great majority of practising imams and *hatips* had but a primary school diploma. Those with higher education were so few that they could be counted on one's fingers (Altıkulaç 2011: 413). This reflected the general level of education in Turkey. In 1970, almost half of the population was still illiterate.[19]

When describing how Friday sermonising was carried out in Turkey, Altıkulaç distinguishes between four different styles:

1. *hutbe*s selected from various collections available in the book market or in libraries;
2. *hutbe*s chosen from texts produced and delivered by Diyanet in Ankara, especially through the fortnightly (or monthly) published magazine *Diyanet Gazetesi* (see below);
3. *hutbe*s written by the imam/*hatip* himself;
4. *hutbe*s delivered extempore. (Altıkulaç 2011: 413)

Altıkulaç was especially concerned about *hutbe*s delivered extempore, since they allowed for more emotional and politically seasoned addresses and therefore were regarded by him as particularly problematic. Such alleged 'misuses' of the minbar, for example propagating a particular political party, was from time to time reported by members of the congregations to the local mufti, who in his turn could – but by no means always did – forward such complaints to Diyanet in Ankara.[20] It even happened that imams were applauded because of an expressive sermon. Altıkulaç saw this as aberrations and signs of insufficient and inadequate education.[21] Poor quality in the art of sermonising was for him first and foremost a problem of inadequate education. Here was, in his evaluation, a field in need of reform, regulation and discipline.

The issue was delegated to the High Committee for Religious Affairs. However, since several members of the committee were absent during the initial round, Altıkulaç, displeased with the performance, returned the first proposal. The seriousness of the issue required, he decided, that every member was present during the deliberations. When finalised, the new regulations were distributed to all muftis on district as well as provincial levels. The document comprised the following principles:

1. *Hutbe*s should be read from a previously prepared text (not extempore).
2. Certain exceptions were allowed from the general ruling against extempore sermonising, namely for persons specially appointed by the central Diyanet organisation, muftis serving on district and/or provincial levels, and/or imams with special permission from officially appointed muftis.
3. Priority should be given to *hutbe*s that had either been published, or carefully examined and approved by Diyanet. Special permission from the district/provincial mufti was required for imams, who preferred to make use of existing *hutbe* collections, or, who wanted to write their own *hutbe*s.
4. Each *müftülük* – Diyanet's office on the provincial level – was required to set up a programme for the Friday sermons that aimed at conveying religious knowledge to the audiences. The aim was to sermon on the same topic in all mosques in the same province. (Altıkulaç 2011: 414–15)[22]

In order to further underline the seriousness of Diyanet's measures, Altıkulaç issued a ruling making it obligatory for each of the personnel working within the organisation to subscribe to *Diyanet Gazetesi*. This fortnightly magazine usually contained two *hutbe*s, ready to be used by the local imams and *hatip*s during the Friday noon service.[23] This obligatory subscription, imposed by Altıkulaç, had already started in March 1980 and was therefore not related to the dictates of the military regime of September 1980, even if voices critical of Altıkulaç's demanding style wanted to describe the forced subscription that way (Altıkulaç 2011: 428–30). For several decades, until the Internet at around the turn of the millennium considerably facilitated the distribution of *hutbe*s, *Diyanet Gazetesi* served as the main forum for authorised *hutbe*s.

Distribution of Official *Hutbes*: The Case of *Diyanet Gazetesi*

Due to scarce resources, Diyanet did not publish any periodicals of its own during the first decades of the republic. Short of the means to reach the common people through such media, the religious institution issued other types of publications, mainly books, addressing its own personnel. Among twenty-three editions published during the years 1924–50 were translations of hadith and commentary on the Qur'an (*tefsir*), books explaining the principles of Islam (*ilmihal*), and two *hutbe* collections written by Ahmed Hamdi Akseki (1887–1951), head of Diyanet from 1947 until his death (Akseki [1927]1928; Akseki 1936; Bulut 2015: 13–14).

The first periodical issued by Diyanet appeared in 1956. It was planned as a sixty-four-page yearly publication, but it took another five years for the next issue to appear and then in the format of a yearbook (1960–1) (Büyüker 2015: 22–3). A more regular periodical publication did not get on its way until November 1968. However, to start with, this sixteen-page, fortnightly 'newspaper' (*Diyanet Gazetesi*), appeared more sporadically with a longer break of one and a half years between April 1969 and October 1970. After this staggering beginning, the publication continued to appear on a regular basis until 1991, when it was reshaped into a monthly, more expensive, professionally laid-out and comprehensive 'magazine' called *Diyanet Aylık Dergi*. In the wake of the breakdown of the Soviet Union and, as a result of that, the social and political changes in the region, government representatives as well as leaders within Diyanet, felt a need to strengthen the profile of the country's religious institution, not only inwards but also towards the outside world. That initiative was also meant to bolster the image of Turkey in the newly opened-up Central Asian, Turkic republics.[24]

The model sermons of the previous, officially authorised *hutbe* collections (published in 1927 and 1936 respectively) offered imams and *hatip*s around the country a publication from which they could pick and choose – and expound – according to their own discretion. Official control was exerted more in the negative than the positive, meaning that rather than demanding or commanding a certain given text, warnings, or in the worst case, dismissals, would occur in case the preacher challenged the borders set by the secularist laws or regulations. However, with the regularly issued publications the character of the official voice changed. It did so in two respects. First, the visibility of the centre increased in the periphery, implying a stronger sense of supervision from above. To this was added the compulsory character of *Diyanet Gazetesi*, as every imam/*hatip* was obliged to subscribe to the publication. Second, even if the published *hutbe*s, for several years also referred to as 'Address from the pulpit' (*Minberden sesleniş*), did not have to be followed to the letter, they provided the guiding principle for the exhortations delivered by individual imams and *hatips* all over the country. This inevitably led to the strengthening of a nationwide sermonising discourse.

The consequence, however, of having the same texts distributed to every corner of the country was that it put a damper on the preaching act itself, both concerning its contents and its potential to spur emotional excitement. The first was related to the inconvenience involved in conveying the same message to people coming from very different geographical areas, and cultural, ethnic and educational backgrounds.[25] This problem – closely linked to the magnitude of the country – was, as a matter of fact, widely recognised by officials who, from time to time, complained about the difficulties in finding relevant topics. In an interview focusing on *hutbe* practices in modern Turkey, a senior lecturer at one of the country's many (105 in 2019) faculties of theology and also a former member of Diyanet's High Committee for Religious Affairs, voiced the following critical words:

> Let's say the *hutbe* is about traffic. This means traffic and traffic regulations are brought up on the [Friday sermon] agenda also in [the poor and old-time] villages in the south-east, where there are neither roads, nor vehicles. That's absurd![26]

To this, the interviewee added the problem of repetitiveness: *hutbe*s dealing with the same topics, even identical texts, were sent from the centre to the provinces over and over again. And the effects?

> Let's say you ask the people coming out from a mosque what the *hutbe* was about and just very few of them are able to remember, that would mean that either the topic of the sermon, or the way it was delivered, was too weak and lifeless. . . . Our sermons were dead, if I may put it that way.

*Hutbe*s were also devoid of enthusiasm and inspiration. A text written by officially employed clerics and academics, or Islamic oriented intellectuals at safe distance from the daily realities of local congregations, would hardly catch and respond to the sentiments of actual mosque-goers. However, that was not the only problem.

> Let's say we prepared a really good text and sent it out from Ankara. Unfortunately, our *hocas* really didn't know how to read it. They simply didn't have the diction.

Several times during the interview, this scholar, sermon-writer and preacher resentfully compared Turkey to Egypt and Jordan. In these countries, which he had visited repeatedly, preachers were freer to act in their own right, meaning they were able to bring up topics they themselves conceived to be of public concern. Under such conditions, there was also more space for oratory and eloquence.

In Turkey, however, Friday preaching had turned into a question of finding the lowest common denominator, a register that suited all and did not offend anyone.[27] Diyanet was obviously facing a dilemma: the stronger and more all-encompassing it became as an institution, the weaker and more insignificant the power of its official homiletics, especially when considered in relation to the raised expectations of increasingly better educated and politically tuned audiences. The cited interview reveals the frustration in official religious circles about this predicament. The remedies were looked for in various reorganisations, like encouraging the setting up of committees for sermon-writing on the provincial levels, at closer distance to problems and agendas of the local audiences, a system that was inaugurated in 2006. However, the problem with what the interviewee aptly named 'offside' *hutbe*s, meaning sermons based on topics of no or very little relevance for particular mosque audiences, was not so easily solved, since the state – even if it from time to time allowed for more openness and freedom – never really gave up on its hold over the organisation of religion in general, and *hutbe* sermonising in particular.

Concluding Words

By the end of the 1970s, Diyanet had reached a new level in its development as a governmental authority with a certain amount of autonomy. This was, as a matter of fact, the result of its leadership's efforts to keep both official secularism, most markedly held in control by the military, and political actors with a radical Islamist agenda, at arm's length. A balance was struck between an overall secular or laic political order and a religious institution fending for itself as long as it remained within certain restrained (centrally controlled) borders. However, during the following couple of decades, a more broad-minded and enlightened (less fanatically laic) atmosphere thrived – a situation favouring a softening of state–religion relationships, which in its turn allowed for more public space to religious-mindedness. The self-critical ideas brought forth in the above interview were an expression of this more liberal atmosphere. AKP entered the political stage and consolidated its power under these less restricted conditions. However, as the party's grip on power became stronger and more authoritarian, especially after its third straight election victory in 2011, Diyanet was also drawn closer into the orbit of the party and the state. Under AKP, the religious institution was considerably strengthened, both in terms of economic allocations and increase in number of personnel, abroad (especially Germany) as well as at home. However, this enlargement was not implemented for the benefits of the wider society, but for the particular interests of the ruling party and its leaders. An indication of this state of affairs was the way in which Diyanet was immersed into social media. Parallel to – and often in coordination with – the ruling party's monopolisation of the public media, Diyanet spent massive efforts in reaching out to the Turkish people with various propaganda-like educational campaigns. This was implemented both through Diyanet's own TV channel (TRT Diyanet) and various Internet platforms.[28] Concerning the Friday *hutbe*s, however, they seem to have remained largely untouched by these developments, an important reason being their embeddedness in longstanding liturgical traditions – a recurring theme in several chapters in this book.

Notes

1. The author wishes to thank the Foundation for Research in the Humanities and Social Sciences (Riksbankens Jubileumsfond) in Stockholm for generously supporting the research underlying this chapter.
2. Even if laicism has remained a fundamental article in the Turkish constitution, the balance between its basic institutional and societal components – state, religion and society – has certainly shifted along the century long road of deep-going social and political transformations (Gözaydın 2009; Kuru 2009; Lord 2018; Kaya 2018). During the period especially focused on in this chapter – the

1970s – religion gained ground, both as a political force with roots in various religious brotherhoods and other networks, and, in opposition to that, as a more assertive governmental and/or administrative force through the Directorate of Religious Affairs, Diyanet.

3. Translation by Allison Kanner.
4. Mehmed Ebussuud Efendi (also known as Hoca Çelebi, 1490–1574) (Ar. Muhammad Abu al-Suʿud) was an Ottoman jurist of the Hanafi School and Qurʾanic exegete, who, from 1545 until his death, was the Grand Mufti (*sheikh ül-Islam*) of Süleyman the Magnificent (entitled *kanuni*, 'the lawgiver') (1494–1566). *Tefsir* means commentary on the Qurʾan, often collected in a book (*EI2*, Vol. 1: 152).
5. İbn-i Melek (d. after 1418), scholar of jurisprudence, author of hadith commentaries. The work cited here is a commentary on an earlier scholar, Radıyyüddin Sagani's (b. Lahore 1181, Baghdad d. 1252), collection of hadith (TDV *Islam Ansiklopedisi*, Vol. 20: 175–6, Vol. 35: 487–9).
6. *Câmi'uş-Şağîr* is a collection of hadith authored by the famous Egyptian scholar al-Suyūṭī (1445–1505). The work referred to here is a three-volume commentary on al-Suyūṭī's vast collection by Ali bin Ahmet el-Bulaki, printed in Cairo several times between 1870 and 1895 (*EI2*, Vol. 9: 913–16; TDV *Islam Ansiklopedisi*, Vol. 7: 112).
7. *Asrı Saadet* refers to the lifetime of the Prophet, literally the 'Age of happiness'. There are several works with that title. The one referred to here is most probably an often cited six-volume publication, written by Mevlana Şibli (d. 1914) and his pupil Süleyman Nedvi (d. 1953) (TDV *Islam Ansiklopedisi*, Vol. 1: 501–2).
8. Rağıb-ı-Isfehânî (Ar. al-Raghib al-Isfahani) was a scholar of religion, moral philosophy and Arabic literature, who died at the beginning of the eleventh century, and who is said to have had some influence on al-Ghazali (d. 1111) and other later figures. The work referred to is an alphabetical lexicon of Qurʾanic vocabulary. A translation to Turkish by Abdülbaki Güneş and Mehmet Yolcu was published in Istanbul 2006–7 (*EI2*, Vol. 13: 389–90; TDV *Islam Ansiklopedisi*, Vol. 34: 398–401).
9. Authors of *hutbes*, mostly identified with name and title, were persons active within or otherwise attached to Diyanet. *Hutbes* were also, but very rarely, signed with an anonymous 'Diyanet'. Kamil Şahin (b. 1939) was a *hafiz* (a person who knows the Qurʾan by heart) with Imam-Hatip education. He served as mufti of Trabzon and chairman of Diyanet's High Committee of Religious

Affairs (more on this administrative unit below). (Source: Kamil Şahin summarises his biography and recites the Qur'an on YouTube, available at: <https://www.youtube.com/watch?v=OyqO6zyQjRU>, last accessed 7 June 2019).

10. Tayyar Altıkulaç was deputy director between July 1971 and September 1976, and later director between February 1978 and November 1986. For developments related to the military ultimatum of 12 March 1971, see Zürcher 1994: 271–6.
11. The Nurcu movement was a Sufi-like network initiated by the religious revivalist Bediüzzaman Said Nursi (1876–1960) from Bitlis in south-east Turkey. Nursi, who was of Kurdish origin, was arrested and tried several times between 1935 and 1953, accused of using religion for political purposes (Zürcher 1994: 201; Mardin 1989). Ceren Lord (2018: 111) describes Yaşar Tunagür as a person with connections in a broad range of Islamist networks such as the Muslim Brotherhood, Rabıta (Saudi Arabia), the Gülen movement and ultra-nationalist groups like the Turkish Hearth (Türk Ocağı).
12. The following section is based on Professor Tayyar Altıkulaç's testimony about his years as deputy director (1971–6) and director (1978–86) of Diyanet (Altıkulaç 2011), supplemented with a longer interview I had with him on 19 May 2014. Instead of dismissing Professor Altıkulaç's own account as an expression of pure subjectivity, I have wanted to give prominence to the fact that he has offered a rare inside account of this important period in Diyanet's and Turkey's modern history. As author, Tayyar Altıkulaç keeps a critical distance from events and personalities, including himself, but at the same time he manages to convey a strong sense of what it takes to press for reforms, including sacrifice and compromise. The book was well received in different political and academic circles, including being recommended as reading for students of religion and religious personnel (Mert 2011; Küçükkılınç 2011; Sürgeç 2011).
13. Tayyar Altıkulaç was also critical of the Islamist Süleymancı community (*cemaat*), a group named after its founder Süleyman Hilmi Tunahan (d. 1959). This network was especially engaged in Qur'an courses and Imam-Hatip education and fell out with Diyanet over who was to be responsible for the organisation of religious education. The rivalry between the religious brotherhood and Diyanet regarding religious education grew during the 1970s and was more openly articulated through the journal *Nesil Dergisi* (1976–80), which promoted a modernist and Diyanet-friendly organisation of religious life against more provincially based, traditionalist, Sufi-like brotherhoods. Tayyar Altıkulaç (2011: 715–83) devotes a whole chapter in his autobiography to his relations with such

communities, especially the '*Süleymancılar*'. For an interesting analysis of *Nesil Dergisi*, see Inal and Alagöz 2016.

14. The chaotic situation is also reflected in Gözaydın's analysis of the many uncertainties related to overlapping and temporary laws and regulations during this period (Gözaydın 2009: 88–94).
15. The folksy character of Diyanet was also reflected in the living conditions of its director, Lütfü Doğan (1968–72), who resided in a *gecekondu* area (squatter-town), and had meals, according to old traditions, sitting on the floor (Altıkulaç 2011: 183).
16. The lack of imams and other religious personnel is widely testified. See, for example, Lord 2018: 98, fig. 4.
17. Concerning the duties enjoined by DIYK, see Kaya 2018: 99–100, and Gözaydın 2009: 118.
18. MSP representatives insisted that appointments should be based on how many votes any particular imam or mufti could expect to acquire for their own religious party, MSP. They were also of the opinion that the lion's share of any sermon should be reserved for the promulgation of MSP's mission (*dava*) (Altıkulaç 2011: 483–4).
19. The exact number was 54.7 per cent (Turkey State Institute of Statistics 1977: 43).
20. The sensitivity of this question increased after Necmettin Erbakan had formed MSP. If the imam said, 'Let's stay with justice' (*adaletten ayrılmıyalım*), that meant support for Süleyman Demirel, leader of the Justice Party (Adalet Partisi); if he said, 'May Allah render salvation' (*Allah selamet versin*), this would be interpreted as alluding to Necmettin Erbakan and the National Salvation Party (Milli Selamet Partisi) (Altıkulaç 2011: 413–14).
21. A different colour is added to these statements, when regarding the disagreement between Altıkulaç and some religious communities, especially the *Süleymancılar*, over the organisation of religious education. It was not only a question of simple educational statistics, but also one of religio-political controversy. This conflict is only indirectly visible in Altıkulaç's own account. For more information on this issue, see Inal and Alagöz 2016.
22. These principles were confirmed by DIYK and signed by Altıkulaç on 1 December 1981 (Altıkulaç 2011: 415).
23. The *hutbe* quoted in the beginning of this chapter appeared in the 15 May 1977 issue of *Diyanet Gazetesi*.
24. Diyanet started to issue a magazine for children in 1979 (*Diyanet Çocuk Dergisi*),

and in 2013 a supplement featuring family questions was added to the *Diyanet Aylık Dergi* (Görgülü 2015: 26; Arslan 2015: 38–9).

25. For a clear description of the widely recognised social and cultural heterogeneity of Turkish society, see Kaya 2018: 42ff.
26. This interview by the author was conducted in June 2014.
27. In his study of oratory in modern Indonesia, Julian Millie discusses a similar problem, namely how the potential for division within an audience sets limits as to what a preacher can and cannot say (Millie 2017: 141).
28. Diyanet TV first appeared in 2009 under the name TRT Anadolu (Turkish Radio and Television Anatolia). In 2012 the name was changed to TRT Diyanet.

Bibliography

Akseki, Ahmet Hamdi (1928 [1927]), *Türkçe Hutbeler* [Turkish Friday sermons], n.p.

Akseki, Ahmet Hamdi (1936), *Yeni Hutbelerim* [My new sermons], 2 vols, Istanbul: Cumhuriyet Matbaası.

Altıkulaç, Tayyar (2011), *Zorlukları Asarken* [Overcoming the difficulties], 3 vols, Istanbul: Ufuk Yayınları.

Arslan, Elif (2015), 'Mütevazi Bir Aile Mektebi: Diyanet Aile Dergisi [A modest family school: Diyanet's family magazine]', *Diyanet Aylık Dergi*, Nr 300, pp. 38–41.

Bulut, Mehmet (2015), 'Kuruluş Yıllarında Diyanet Işleri Başkanlığının Yayın Hizmetleri [Publication activities of the Directorate of Religious Affair during its founding years]', *Diyanet Aylık Dergi*, Nr 300, pp. 12–17.

Büyüker, Kamil (2015), 'Mecmua'dan Dergi'ye. Sırat-ı Müstakim'den Diyanet'e Süreli Islami Yayıncılığa Dair Notlar [From journal to magazine. Notes on periodical Islamic publications: from The Straight Path to Diyanet]', *Diyanet Aylık Dergi*, Nr 300, pp. 18–23.

Geoffroy, Éric (1997), 'al-Suyūṭī', *The Encyclopaedia of Islam*, 2nd ed., Vol. 9, Leiden: Brill, pp. 913–16.

Görgülü, Faruk (2015), *Dini Dergicilik ve Süreli Yayınlarımız* [Religious magazines and our periodical publications]', *Diyanet Aylık Dergi*, Nr 300, pp. 24–7.

Gözaydın, Iştar (2009), *Diyanet. Türkiye Cumhuriyeti'nde Dinin Tanzimi* [Diyanet: the organisation of religion in the Turkish republic]', Istanbul: Iletişim.

Hefner, Robert W. (2000), *Civil Islam: Muslims and Democratization in Indonesia*, Princeton: Princeton University Press.

Hoesterey, James Bourk (2016), *Rebranding Islam: Piety, Prosperity, and a Self-Help Guru*, Stanford: Stanford University Press.

Inal, Ibrahim Hakkı and Alagöz Muhammed Nurullah (2016), '1970'ler Türkiye'sinde Dinde Reform Tartışmaları: Nesil Dergisi Çevresi Örneği [Religious discussions in Turkey of the 1970s: the example of the Nesil Magazine Group]', *Harran Üniversitesi Ilahiyat Fakültesi Dergisi* 35 (35): 28–52.

Islam Ansiklopedisi [Islam Encyclopedia] (2013), Istanbul: Türkiye Diyanet Vakfı.

Jäschke, Gotthard (1972), *Yeni Türkiy'de Islamlık* [Islam in the new Turkey], Ankara: Bilgi Yayınevi.

Kaya, Emir (2018), *Secularism and State Religion in Modern Turkey: Law, Policy-Making and the Diyanet*, London: I.B. Tauris.

Küçükkılınç, Ismail ([2011] 2018), 'Tayyar Altıkulaç: Sövülecek, Dövülecek ve Öldürülecek Adam [A man to be railed, beaten and killed]', *Haksöz Haber*, 20 December, <https://www.haksozhaber.net/tayyar-altikulacin-hatirati-110546h.htm> (last accessed 24 January 2020).

Kuru, Ahmet T. (2009), *Secularism and State Policies toward Religion: The United States, France and Turkey*, Cambridge: Cambridge University Press.

Lord, Ceren (2018), *Religious Politics in Turkey: From the Birth of the Republic to the AKP*, Cambridge: Cambridge University Press.

Mardin, Şerif (1989), *Religion and Social Change in Modern Turkey: The Case of Bediüzzaman Said Nursi*, New York: SUNY Press.

Mert, Hamdi (2011), 'Tayyar Altıkulaç Zorlukları Aşarken [Tayyar Altıkulaç overcoming the difficulties]', *www.aygazete.com*, 18 November, <https://studylibtr.com/doc/3711939/tayyar-alt%C4%B1kula%C3%A7-zorluklar%C4%B1-a%C5%9Farken> (last accessed 24 January 2020).

Millie, Julian (2017), *Hearing Allah's Call: Preaching and Performance in Indonesian Islam*, Ithaca, NY: Cornell University Press.

Rowson, Everett K. (1995), 'al-Rāghib al-Iṣfahānī', *The Encyclopaedia of Islam*, 2nd ed., Vol. 8, Leiden: Brill, pp. 389–90.

Schacht, Joseph (1986), 'Abu 'l-Suʿūd', *The Encyclopaedia of Islam*, 2nd ed., Vol. 1, Leiden: Brill, p. 152.

Sürgeç, Celal (2011), 'Zorlukları Aşarken [Overcoming the difficulties]', <https://docplayer.biz.tr/3938267-Zorluklari-asarken-zorluklari-asarken-dr-tayyar-altikulac-in-ufuk-yayinlari-nda-cikan-uc-ciltlik-kitabinin-adidir.html> (last accessed 24 January 2020).

Turkey State Institute of Statistics (1977), *1977 Statistical Yearbook of Turkey*, Ankara: Turkey State Institute of Statistics.

Zürcher, Erik J. (1994), *Turkey: A Modern History*, London: I.B. Tauris.

PART III

MEDIATION

6

GOING ONLINE: SAUDI FEMALE INTELLECTUAL PREACHERS IN THE NEW MEDIA

Laila Makboul

In a BBC report featuring Saudi Arabia's most popular Twitter accounts, a woman, Nawal al-ʿId (b. 1977), appears among three male clerics as the 'superstars' of social media with millions of followers.[1] While the names of the male clerics are followed with illustrative characterisations, such as the 'Brad Pitt' preacher (Muhammad al-ʿArifi), the 'cool' preacher (Ahmad al-Shugayr) and the 'former radical' preacher (Salman al-ʿAwda), al-ʿId is simply described as the 'female preacher'. It appears as if the very fact that she is a woman and a preacher is both an anomaly among the typology of popular tweeters and the reason for her being popular. Yet, al-ʿId is not the only known female preacher online. Although she is the unrivalled social media star among women in Saudi Arabia, with more than four million followers,[2] al-ʿId is joined by hundreds of other female preachers on social media who use Twitter, YouTube and other web-based platforms on a daily basis.[3] Having the most-followed Twitter accounts among women in Saudi Arabia, the category of preachers known as intellectual female preachers (*dāʿiyāt muthaqqafāt*) are known for disseminating their thoughts on a range of topics, including religious, social and, to a circumstantial extent, political.[4] Who are these women, and how can we understand their presence in the new media?[5]

This chapter examines the phenomenon of female intellectual preachers through an analysis of for what reasons and purposes they have made use of new media to participate in the public sphere.[6] To understand their encounter with the new media, the first part situates the phenomenon of female intellectual preachers within the wider historical context of Saudi Arabia and women's role in the society. This will give an insight into the religious, social and political factors that made way for the emergence of *dāʿiyāt muthaqqafāt* – a highly educated network of female preachers who intervene in the public sphere as both preachers and intellectuals. Having their public participation conditioned on preserving strict physical gender segregation, the next part looks at the different ways the new media have unprecedentedly facilitated the engagement and presence of the *dāʿiyāt muthaqqafāt* in the wider public. Analysing literature written by *dāʿiyāt*, this chapter argues that their participation in the new media has been advocated for mainly three reasons: representing the voice of so-called conservative women in the public sphere; facilitating and coordinating religious, social and by implication political activities; and performing the doctrinal obligation of commanding right and forbidding wrong, *iḥtisāb*. In the final part of the chapter, I examine how the new media pose new challenges in terms of transgressions of constructed gender norms and exposure to increased public criticism and political vulnerability. Consequently, this chapter contends that although the new media have been utilised to permeate the public sphere and, in many ways, have revolutionised their public presence, they have also altered the engagement of the *dāʿiyāt muthaqqafāt* in profound ways and ultimately exposed them to greater vulnerability.

The Phenomenon of *Dāʿiyāt Muthaqqafāt*

Women like Nawal al-ʿId belong to a category of highly educated Saudi women who in the name of religion and a specific expertise intervene in the public sphere. They describe themselves as *dāʿiyāt muthaqqafāt*, intellectual female preachers. To define what it means to be an intellectual female preacher is difficult, as it can have multiple and changing meanings depending on the context and the specific individual in question.[7] For example, Ruqayya al-Muharib (b. 1964), a highly renowned female intellectual preacher,[8] identifies the *muthaqqafa* on Twitter as a defensive shield against attempts to cut women off from Islamic values and principles,[9] as protectors of Saudi women,[10] and as active agents in the social, civil and cultural fields.[11] Accordingly, there is no clear understanding of what constitutes a *dāʿiya muthaqqafa*, as both *dāʿiya* and *muthaqqafa* are concepts with various connotations.

Nevertheless, based on the numerous answers I received during my fieldwork on the question of what the term *dāʿiya muthaqqafa* entails, recurring descriptions might help us distinguish some main features of the added epithet 'intellectual' of female preachers in contemporary Saudi Arabia.[12] First, *muthaqqafa* is mostly used for someone who has a formal higher education, primarily, but not limited to, religious sciences, and is therefore hierarchically distinguished from a self-proclaimed preacher who lacks academic credentials.[13] A second important characteristic is to have the skill to combine this religious knowledge with what many describe as social knowledge (*ʿilm al-ijtimāʿ*).[14] This is explained as having the ability to purposefully relate religious knowledge and Islamic theology to real life, to have an awareness of the contemporary context and what is occurring in the society and, consequently, to use that theological knowledge to engage in contemporary issues.

These preachers share some common features with a Foucauldian understanding of what constitutes an intellectual, which comprises: (1) being literate, (2) speaking to the broader public, (3) deriving one's merits from one's expertise and (4) engaging in a public power struggle in the name of a 'truth' (Foucault 1980).[15] Nevertheless, a *dāʿiya muthaqqafa* represents a localised version of what it means to be an intellectual, which is important to shed light on in order to grasp the importance of modern communication technologies in general, and the new media in particular, for their public engagement.

Dāʿiyāt muthaqqafāt began their careers in the Saudi educational system, first as students and later as academics at various local universities, typically combining Islamic sciences with disciplines within the humanities or social sciences.[16] When public mass education for girls was officially launched in 1960, it opened up the religious field to women beyond those who were descendants of well-known religious families.[17] Congruent with the nascent state's processes of institutionalising and co-opting religious centres since the early twentieth century, religious training was incorporated into higher educational institutions. Thus, when education for women was finally introduced, it gave women from a variety of backgrounds the chance to obtain formal religious training and become religious scholars (*ʿālimāt*) for the first time.

Saudi educational institutions had largely been developed by intellectuals from other Arab countries, in particular Salafi Muslim reformers during the first half of the twentieth century, followed by figures from the Muslim Brotherhood in the mid-1960s and early 1970s (Lacroix 2011; Farquhar 2017).[18] These figures and the ideologies they represented made way for the emergence of the Ṣaḥwa, a local intellectual, social and political movement that synthesised Wahhabi theology with modern Islamist thought and social activism.[19] One of their main trademarks was to counter any compartmentalisation of religious sciences into specialised disciplines, which they feared could secularise the educational system. Calling for an all-encompassing Islamic epistemology known as *shumūliyya*, they introduced religious teachings in other disciplines as well, such as education and social sciences. Consequently, it was only a matter of time before Islamic activists would emerge in the 1980s with the first batch of female university graduates who would advocate for *shumūliyya* also outside of the university campus.

According to Ruqayya al-Muharib, '[Ṣaḥwa] brought to fruition fervent cadres who were able to build an idea [*fikra*] and create [*tūjid*] a strong, conscious and efficacious movement [*tayyāran qawiyan wāʿiyan*] with a high level of religiosity' (al-Muharib 2006: 98–9). Encouraged by figures of the Ṣaḥwa, women gradually took a greater role in engaging in the broader public. To begin with, their activities were limited to religious themes in the field of *daʿwa* and to women-only spaces, such as on university campuses, where they set up gatherings for memorising the Qurʾan, and in women-only shopping centres, hospitals, female prisons and pilgrim groups making the hajj (al-Muharib, cited in al-Shuqayr 2017: 54).

Although arguing for the importance of women's participation in the realm of *daʿwa*, important figures belonging to the traditional Wahhabi establishment were relatively cautious of the role women should play in the broader public. While the former Grand Mufti ʿAbd al-ʿAziz bin Baz (1910–99) argued that the doctrinal justification of *daʿwa* in terms of commanding right and forbidding wrong (*iḥtisāb*) was equal for both men and women, he placed an additional requirement of preserving modesty (*ʿiffa*) and donning the hijab on women, and insisted that if a woman makes *daʿwa* to a man, she must avoid gender mixing (*ikhtilāṭ*) and observe seclusion (*khalwa*).[20] An even more restrictive opinion was held by the second most influential Wahhabi figure, Muhammad Salih al-ʿUthaymin (1929–2001), who limited women's engagement to women-only spaces and cautioned against women gathering in each other's homes for religious learning, unless they were neighbours or lived close to each other (al-ʿUthaymin 1998).[21] Yet, women would eventually engage in a broader public due to a number of concurring factors that included the increased influence of the Ṣaḥwa, the opening of the public literary field for women – and, importantly, technological advancements.

Following the rise of the Ṣaḥwa in the 1980s, the understanding of women's responsibility in the field of *daʿwa* was gradually expanded to include a broader public and a wider set of topics that primarily centred around women and family issues. The first women influenced by the Ṣaḥwa began their wider public engagement in the literary field, as it safeguarded women's physical segregation and provided a venue for secluded public participation. As an early example of Ṣaḥwi women, Suhayla Zayn al-ʿAbidin (b. 1958) was, according to anthropologist Saddeka Arebi (1994), among the most widely read female Saudi Arabian essayists of the 1980s.[22] The main themes characterising the works of Zayn al-ʿAbidin during this time were related to women and family issues as well as Islamic thought and literature, which based on the concept of *shumūliyya* was understood inclusively.

With technological advancements and the colossal institutionalisation of segregated Islamic centres, women were increasingly able to engage with men's discourses while preserving the essential condition of physical seclusion.[23] Initially, communication technology such as cassette tapes, television and radio provided *dāʿiyāt* with a medium for accessing male scholars. According to Ruqayya al-Muharib, they would listen to cassette sermons of renowned male preachers, such as al-ʿUthaymin and Bin Baz and convey them to other women.[24] With the necessary physical barriers that their institutions provided, increased cooperation with male preachers could take place in segregated rooms within these buildings. Voice and image transmissions through microphone, speakers and video projectors facilitated cross-gendered cooperation. Women would for example take part in producing television programmes behind the scenes and participate orally in radio programmes, as well as produce readable media materials, such as journals and websites.

At the turn of the twenty-first century, a number of websites began appearing, such as *ʿĀlam Ḥawāʾ* ('The world of Eve'), *Lahā Online* ('For her online'), *Wāḥat al-Marʾa* ('Women's oasis'), *Laki* ('For you') and Sīrīn, in addition to female sections in Islamic websites. As these names suggest, the websites were primarily targeting female audiences, with 'feminine' design and topics relating to women.[25] However, as the Internet provided the needed physical seclusion as well as an all-encompassing scope, it provided a powerful means to progressively engage with a range of topics online that went beyond 'feminine' and religious-specific issues. *Dāʿiyāt muthaqqafāt* increasingly spoke in the name of an Islamic epistemological 'truth', heavily furnished by the Ṣaḥwa and an understanding of social changes resulting from Westernisation that aimed to undermine Islamic culture. These women found their place and mission in the public as an oppositional force against external cultural influences, including feminism as an allegedly threatening ideology.

In recent years, the capability to reach beyond women-only spaces has been strengthened further with the advancement of social media and its provision for less gender-specific virtual platforms. As I will elucidate in the next section, the new media, as a meta-space for secluded public participation, have allowed these women to reach beyond women-only spaces and given them the opportunity to perform the roles of both religious and intellectual figures.

Secluded Public Participation

The crucial importance of new media for *dāʿiyāt* is evidenced by their numerous writings on the subject that argue for the urgent need of their presence on the World Wide Web. In this literature, we find that their online participation has been encouraged for mainly three reasons: for representing Islamist-oriented women in public; for coordination purposes; and for performing *iḥtisāb*.

The presence of conservative women

In literature by male and female figures belonging to the Ṣaḥwa, women's engagement online is advocated in terms of fulfilling a need for the presence of Islamic-oriented women in the public sphere. Contending that they represent the majority of women in Saudi Arabia, Ruqayya al-Muharib has argued for the need of *dāʿiyāt* to 'enter the daily newspapers that reach all homes and workplaces, in order to appear in the public with enlightened opinions that represent the voices of the majority of women in our conservative society' (al-Muharib 2006: 101). Citing al-Muharib some years later, Muhammad Musa al-Sharif (b. 1961), a Saudi historian and an important figure in the Ṣaḥwa, echoes her concern and urges qualified *dāʿiyāt* to participate in different media outlets, including the Internet (al-Sharif 2012). These pleas highlight how the media is seen as crucial both for representing the voice of the so-called 'conservative women' and for countering trends deemed as undermining a pious society. According to al-Sharif, Islamic-oriented women should publicise their opinions in important newspapers and participate in countering those he terms *mufsidīn* (corrupters), identifying this group as 'those who seek to corrupt the society by claiming to represent the majority but who in reality are the minority' (Ibid.: 36).

While *dāʿiyāt* early on were present in platforms online and through their own websites, they have in recent years become publicly known through their personal accounts on social media, in particular on Twitter, where they have the most followed accounts among women in Saudi Arabia.[26] In addition to their Twitter accounts, many *dāʿiyāt* are also highly active on other social media applications popular among the younger generation of Saudis, such as Instagram, YouTube and Snapchat.

Complying with physical seclusion, Twitter *dāʿiyāt* never post images of themselves. Instead, they have their own logos with their names, which they use as profile pictures. To add variation to their social media feeds, their religious invocations and religious reminders are often accompanied with illustrative images, followed by voice or text. Through these platforms, they seek to reach beyond women-only spaces and at the same time promote a self-representation that celebrates the seclusion of a woman's body and image in a stark contrast to the typical popular social media figures, such as actresses and female celebrities. Through their social media accounts, they provide an alternative representation of women, one that seeks to counter the sensationalising of a woman's body by offering an alternative secluded participation. In heterosocial physical spaces, they call for a maximalist interpretation of what constitutes a woman's hijab, which includes the covering of hands with gloves, full face veiling and wearing abaya from the top of the head to cover the shape of the body, including the shoulders.

The promotion of secluded public participation includes praising other women who have gained prominence in fields outside of religious ones but who nevertheless are perceived as conservative. Belonging to fields such as medicine and business, these women are celebrated through tweets and posting of their pictures with face covering as a show of support for the successful 'conservative woman'.

One such promotion was displayed in the nomination of the 'woman of the year' by al-Muharib's website *Laha Online*. In 2017 (1438 Hijri), winners were chosen from five different areas: the social sector (*al-ijtimāʿī*) (Nawal al-ʿId, a doctorate in sunna studies); women's issues (*qaḍāyā al-marʾa*) (Nura al-ʿUdwan, a former Shura Council member with an academic background in education); the health sector (*al-ṣiḥḥī*) (Fatin Khurshid, a professor of cell engineering known for her research on cancer); the development sector (*al-tanmawī*) (Nada al-Bawardi, a founder of a local charity, Al Bunyan); and science (*al-ʿilmī*) (Fawz al-Kurdi, a doctorate in *ʿaqīda* (theology)). The winners were publicised on Twitter with a hashtag and circulated online through re-tweets and articles by sympathising newspapers.[27] The nomination was arguably an attempt both to promote successful 'conservative women' and to demonstrate their presence in broader fields than religious sciences. The announcement of the preachers Nawal al-ʿId and Fawz al-Kurdi as winners of the social and the scientific categories respectively, illustrates how *dāʿiyāt* are consistently seeking to extend their range of activities and defy a containment of their engagement to a 'religious sphere'.

Facilitating and coordinating daʿwa

As part of a collective activist framework, the new media have provided an important venue from which women can participate in the field of *daʿwa* while safeguarding their physical seclusion. The women's *daʿwa* centre Waqf Daʿwatuha provides an important example of the institutionalisation and coordination processes accompanying virtual platforms. According to its director Mariam al-Husayn, it was established in 2006 in order to provide women engaged in *daʿwa* a common platform on the Internet, as well as with other centres and *daʿwa* institutions.[28] Since then, Waqf Daʿwatuha has expanded to become a virtual and physical meeting place for women preachers. Among other activities, they coordinate *daʿwa* gatherings with prominent *dā ʿiyāt* in their centres, publish booklets on *da ʿwa*, and provide an online venue from which different *da ʿwa* activities are announced and *da ʿwa*-related resources can be downloaded.[29]

Writing for *Laha Online*, Malik Ibrahim al-Ahmad, who has a double PhD in engineering and journalism, calls for the utilisation of social media for the purpose of spreading 'proper Islamic knowledge', for making *da ʿwa* to non-Muslims, and for its mobilising potentials (al-Ahmad 2016). Evoking the religious tradition, al-Ahmad argues that just as the Prophet Muhammad used all available means for *da ʿwa* during his time, such as reaching people in their different social spaces, so should Muslims make use of social media, which includes Facebook, YouTube and Twitter. As an example of the immense impact of Facebook, al-Ahmad mentions how this platform was ground-breaking during the 'revolution of the Arab spring', before advocating for capitalising on it in the field of *da ʿwa*. Some of the advantages he lists on the use of social media include reaching the wider masses, interactivity, global range, speed, low-cost efficiency and accessibility. Male preachers he lists as being successful in the use of Facebook are the two clerics mentioned in the introduction, Muhammad al-ʿArifi and Salman al-ʿAwda, as well as ʿAid al-Qarni (b. 1960).

Reflecting her popularity online, it is unsurprising that Nawal al-ʿId stands out in using the potential of her various social media channels to the fullest. Having the most followed Twitter account (@Nawal_al3eed_) among women in Saudi Arabia, al-ʿId's social media celebrity status in the Kingdom is unprecedented. She has an account on most social media outlets, such as Instagram (nawalal3eed), Snapchat (nawalal3eed), YouTube (أ.د.نوال العيد) and Telegram (Nawalaleid), including her own smartphone application and website.[30] Through these channels, al-ʿId invites her followers into her home and workplace, where she shares parts of her daily life and private gatherings and gives short talks on a variety of subjects. As will be shown in the next section, many of these activities are justified by the doctrine of commanding right and forbidding wrong.

Electronic iḥtisāb

While the *dā ʿiyāt*'s performance of *iḥtisāb*, commanding right and forbidding wrong, was previously performed in women-only spaces, the new media have provided them with a platform in the overall public sphere where *iḥtisāb* can reach a wider public that includes both women and men. While the commanding of good (*al-amr bi 'l-ma'rūf*) takes the form of religious invocations and enjoinders to different modes of piety, forbidding wrong (*al-nahy 'an al-munkar*) includes a range of responses to what *dā'iyāt* characterise as social awareness (*taw'iyat al-mujtama'*) endeavours.[31] The *dā'iyāt* strive to make both the public and the authorities conscious of what they regard as undermining the Islamic character of the country and overall religious piety in the society. This includes countering globalisation processes, in particular what they deem to be Westernisation, of which initiatives by the UN are especially targeted.

Condemnation of international accords, such as the UN Convention on the Elimination of All Forms of Discrimination against Women (CEDAW) and the UN Sustainable Development Agenda 2030, have been expressed in different hashtag campaigns on Twitter, such as 'Stop the transformation of our world' (#أوقفوا_تحويل_عالمنا) against the UN agenda 2030. A video, made by the *dā'iyāt*-affiliated research centre Bahethat and posted on YouTube, illustrates their negative perceptions of the UN agenda and the suitable response they perceive as necessary (Bahethat 2015). After identifying a number of issues considered dangerous and incompatible with both Islam and Saudi culture – such as sex education, the distribution of contraceptives to adolescents and complete gender equality – the video suggests a number of responses. Under the rubric of social awareness, described as 'the first step towards making the wider public aware of the dangers of these initiatives and counter their implementation', the video suggests using social media as a first means of resistance (*muqāwama*). Consequently, *dā'iyāt muthaqqafāt* engage in a power struggle in the broader public in the name of a 'truth', which is heavily predicated on protecting what they regard as the proper Islamic character of Saudi Arabia.

As examined in the discussion so far, the new media have paved the way for female intellectual preachers to engage in the Saudi public sphere more widely than before, as well as to cut across traditional gender segregation and other barriers that physical seclusion entail. However, as I will discuss in the next section, they have also led to a number of renegotiations on what constitutes seclusion and posed new challenges to gender interaction concomitant with the inherent features of these media.

Gender Interaction Dilemmas

While the new media have introduced new means of communication through image and voice, they have also presented *dāʿiyāt* with a range of gender-specific dilemmas on what kind of image and voice interaction is allowed without transgressing the seclusion that their public participation is so heavily contingent upon.[32] Much of this debate is connected with discussions related to the notions of *ʿawra* and *fitna*,[33] and what is considered appropriate interaction with men.[34]

Intimately linked with *dāʿiyāt muthaqqafāt*'s maximalist interpretation of a woman's dress code is the effort to avoid any situation that can lead to *fitna*. This is why some of the *daʿwa* literature pertaining to women's engagement in the media is also dedicated to discussing aspects related to the female body and women's interaction with men. In the work of the Saudi preacher Muhammad Musa al-Sharif, women's participation is conditioned on upholding the hijab,[35] complying with so-called 'shariʿa regulations', avoiding gender seclusion (*khalwa*), and abstaining from what he calls 'soft, or seductive speech (*khuḍūʿ bi 'l-qawl*)' (al-Sharif 2012). A term found in the Qurʾan (33:32), *khuḍūʿ bi 'l-qawl* is traditionally understood as referring to a woman's voice and is important in the discussion on women's presence in public. While some *dāʿiyāt* avoid any situation that can lead to men hearing their voices,[36] the most popular *dāʿiyāt muthaqqafāt* on social media have in common that they publish their audio lectures online, demonstrating that those who make use of the inherent features of the new media are the most successful in gaining most followers.[37]

In a 2013 radio talk on gender interaction on social media, Nawal al-ʿId emphasises the distinction between formal and seductive speech, in addition to other added precautions.[38] Exhorting women to be formal and serious (*jādda*) with men online, she also recommends that direct communication with men should be limited to writing (*al-khaṭṭ wa 'l-kitāba*), as vocal interaction (*shafāhiyya*) could lead to 'other things', without specifying. She prohibits private texting, unless there is a need (*ḥāja*), and warns against the use of informal digital images that express emotions, such as the use of kissing emojis. Ultimately, she leaves it to the individual herself to judge what is appropriate and inappropriate interaction between women and men.

According to al-ʿId, a woman who has faith and fears Allah, and whose 'heart is sound', can properly assess what is appropriate. Here we find that the cultivation of piety and raising awareness of Saudi cultural norms and social sensitivity is perceived as moral and cultural compasses that guide the individual's proper behaviour in society, including gender interactions. In practice, this leaves the boundaries flexible enough to incorporate some circumstantial interpretation of what is considered 'appropriate' interaction.

In the *dāʿiyāt*'s online participation, we find a plethora of grey areas that illustrate how the use of social media alters gender interactions and leads to instances where some degree of contextual appropriateness takes precedence over doctrinal rigidity. The most profound alteration is the publicising of what are initially women-only gatherings online. This has led to a number of renegotiations of what is considered 'permissible' for men to hear. While Nawal al-ʿId advocates formality in the interaction with men, her publicised mosque lectures feature emotional expressions and vocal tones that reflect the feelings she seeks to evoke in her female audience, such as crying and the feeling of joyfulness.[39] In her Snapchat application that allows for live video streaming, her audience is invited into her private home, where she shares her thoughts from her living room. Although without showing her image, she speaks in a gentle voice that reflects the private atmosphere. When she films her gatherings with friends and family, 'feminine' expressions become even more pronounced, with the sounds of women enjoying their time together and the showcasing of different amusements surrounding them, such as fancy holiday chalets and a range of different culinary delights.

These displays of informal speeches can arguably be understood as unintentional 'transgressions' due to the nature of social media, which make it impossible to be categorically rigid. The *dāʿiyāt* are obviously aware of this dilemma and in various degrees try to limit these transgressions. For example, in one of her weekly lectures, the female preacher Asma al-Ruwayshid asked the audience not to forward their mobile recordings to others, as her lecture was not prepared for a wider audience including men.[40] She said: 'In this setting I am speaking freely as there are only women here. As you know, there are specific rules of conduct to follow when speaking to men, such as [being careful with] the tone of one's voice' (al-Ruwayshid 2015). In such a setting, al-Ruwayshid allowed women to record the lecture and share it with other women in their private homes, provided that they did not forward it to others. Like al-ʿId, aware that she was speaking to her immediate students and followers whose shared morality could be ascertained, she was willing to show some flexibility, even when she had not prepared the lecture for male listeners as well.

The *dāʿiyāt*'s publicising of their voices illustrate some of the challenges that *dāʿiyāt* face when they engage in online forms of communication. While they call on strict gender segregation that partly includes the voice, platforms of new media necessitate some degree of adaptation in order to take advantage of the features belonging to the particular medium. Another more pertinent challenge, however, is the online engagement that they lay claim to as both public intellectuals and female preachers. As I will examine in the following section, their public interventions have resulted in an increased moral and political vulnerability as a result of being constantly under the scrutiny of both the general public and the state.

Exposure and Political Vulnerability

For female intellectual preachers, the new media have proven to be both a blessing and a curse. While increasing the *dāʿiyāt*'s access to the general public to an unprecedented level, the new media have also left them vulnerable and exposed them to both a critical audience and increased political scrutiny. Unlike the authoritative relation existing between a *dāʿiya* and her audience in women-only gatherings, the new media, characterised by reciprocal participation between users of diverging opinions, place the authority of the *dāʿiya muthaqqafa* under constant contention. This makes the *dāʿiyāt*'s authority highly contested and exposed to continuous criticism. On social media in particular, they participate in a platform that provides a range of communication opportunities that directly reach the *dāʿiyāt* through their open social media accounts. In this section, I will examine the most common criticisms of *dāʿiyāt* that I have identified, which are mainly based on intellectual, moral and political grounds.

The *dāʿiyāt muthaqqafāt*'s attempt to assume the role of intellectuals in the public sphere is challenged by those who lay claim to the same field. Most commonly, the women are accused of engaging in topics beyond their expertise, which according to their critics is limited to Islamic sciences. When several *dāʿiyāt* launched a campaign to raise awareness of the role of housewives under the hashtag 'housewife, the marginalised occupation' (#ربة_البيت_الوظيفه_المهمشه), they were met with both ridicule and criticism by opponents and critics. Alluding to what was perceived as a contradiction, most of those who belittled the campaign were quick to point out that the initiators were all employed themselves. Some users took screenshots of the *dāʿiyāt*'s self-description on Twitter as professors and experts alongside their tweets for the campaign, advising sarcastically to 'try to tell one of them to stay home and wait for the "housewife" salary'.[41] Saudi historian ʿAbd al-ʿAziz al-Khidr was more critical of the campaign's designation of housewife as an 'occupation', pointing to what he saw as a problematic understanding of family tasks in terms of economic labour.[42] Consequently, the criticism questioned the very expertise that the *dāʿiyāt* sought to represent to the public.

Perhaps the most evident opposition to the *dāʿiyāt* online is based on moral grounds. The critics spare little effort in exposing what they allege to be double standards and examples of *dāʿiyāt* not practising what they preach. Many such accusations were made under the hashtag 'Ruqayya al-Muharib, the inciter' (#المحرضه_رقيه_المحارب), created after Ruqayya al-Muharib's daughter Arwa took a picture of her diving kit while she was on vacation in the Maldives with her husband. Although it was not al-Muharib herself who was seen with a diving kit, her opponents immediately took the opportunity to expose what they perceived to be the hypocrisy of preachers who allow their children to do what they prohibit for others. One user asked whether the place was closed and for women only, while another posted the screenshot of the diving kit with one of al-Muharib's Twitter posts in which she warned against the passing of a law against sexual harassment, as it would lead to *ikhtilāṭ*, gender mixing. Clearly, it did not matter that Arwa was not under her mother's authority as a married woman and living abroad. What opponents saw was an opportunity to expose a prominent *dāʿiya* for what they considered to be double standards when it came to their own children.

Finally, with the vulnerability of public exposure comes the constant dilemma of assuming the role of an intellectual preacher in a politically authoritarian environment. In addition to what *dāʿiyāt* perceive as an obligation to perform *iḥtisāb*, their intellectual credentials are arguably substantiated by an ability to demonstrate a degree of relative independence in speaking truth to power in the broader public. This has proven to be increasingly difficult in a political context that demands the demonstration of absolute loyalty and support for political decisions. Adding to this is the frequent accusation of belonging to the Muslim Brotherhood and more recently the Ṣaḥwa movement by extension. As the Muslim Brotherhood was declared an illegal terrorist organisation by the Saudi government in 2014, any accusation of affiliation with the group can be fatal.

In the wake of the dispute with Qatar in the summer of 2017, which led to the breaking of diplomatic relations by Saudi Arabia, the United Arab Emirates, Bahrain and Egypt, many of the prominent *dāʿiyāt* remained silent. Among the officially stated reasons for the discord was Qatar's alleged support of the Muslim Brotherhood.[43] On social media, official Saudi news media outlets mobilised against Qatar, posting under a number of hashtags with fierce accusations, such as 'Qatar's treachery' (#خيانة_قطر) and 'Qatar's funding of terrorism' (#تمويل_قطر_للإرهاب). This placed an enormous pressure on the *dāʿiyāt* to support the sanctions, disassociate themselves from the accusations of belonging to the Muslim Brotherhood and consequently distance themselves from Qatar.[44] Ruqayya al-Muharib was one of the few who dared to express an opinion that could be understood as a critique of the attacks on Qatar with the following tweet, quoting the Qurʾan (17:36): '(And do not pursue that of which you have no knowledge). If everyone took heed of this principle, we would have been saved from false rumours.'[45]

Following the increasing social transformations occurring in Saudi Arabia since 2015 under the social and economic reform plan known as Saudi Vision 2030, which includes a range of entertainment projects that previously were frowned upon, such as music festivals, discos and cinemas that involve increased gender mixing, these women have arguably been put to their greatest test. For at least five days after the announcement that women would be allowed to drive in September 2017, some of the most prominent *dāʿiyāt* were silenced on social media.[46] Some days later, Ruqayya al-Muharib, the only prominent *dāʿiya* who had tweeted in disfavour of the Qatar boycott, became the first woman among the *dāʿiyāt* to be detained by the authorities, along with a number of other influential male preachers from the Ṣaḥwa movement who had been taken into custody some weeks before.[47]

Ultimately, as these women have taken upon themselves the role of intellectual preachers in the new media, they are increasingly losing the relative immunity they once enjoyed when their activities were constricted to women and more narrowly religious issues.

Conclusion

This chapter has argued that the advent of new media has revolutionised the accessibility of Saudi *dāʿiyāt*'s work and made it available to a much broader segment of the society. While women's religious gatherings were previously announced in mosques and hardly reached outside of existing religious network groups, many of their religious gatherings are now posted on social media and streamed online through audio transmission.

Importantly, the new media have also facilitated *dāʿiyāt*'s engagement in issues outside of the religious-specific ones and in the overall public sphere, reaching beyond women-only spaces and topics. Congruent with the notion of Islamic comprehensiveness (*shumūliyya*) and heavily influenced by the social activism of the Ṣaḥwa movement, *dāʿiyāt muthaqqafāt* take upon themselves the role of intellectuals as they seek to speak as experts and intervene in the name of a an Islamic 'truth' in the broader public. At the same time however, their online engagement has also led to new challenges in terms of altering modes of secluded public participation and exposing them to moral criticism and political vulnerability.

While *dāʿiyāt muthaqqafāt* call for strict gender segregation, new media platforms necessitate some degree of adaptation and what I call 'unintended transgression'. One of the most obvious transgressions is the transmission of the *dāʿiyāt*'s voice from private and women-only settings to the open channels of social media. This has led to a number of renegotiations of what is considered 'permissible' for men to hear.

A much more pertinent challenge is their claim to engage in the public discourse as both intellectuals and female preachers. While they enjoy a hierarchical authority among their adherents, *dāʿiyāt* are contested and exposed to continuous criticism on social media. Moreover, *dāʿiyāt muthaqqafāt* are constantly faced with the political vulnerability of demonstrating their independence by speaking 'truth' to power. In a political context that increasingly demands the demonstration of absolute loyalty and support of the Kingdom's political leadership, *dāʿiyāt muthaqqafāt* are faced with the dilemma of demonstrating religious and intellectual independency and consequently risk facing political repression.

Following the arrest of prominent figures belonging to the Ṣaḥwa movement, and especially the arrest of Ruqayya al-Muharib in October 2017, *dāʿiyāt muthaqqafāt* seem to be opting for a low-key presence on social media that avoids engaging in social and political issues. Continuing to cultivate piety through the publicising of religious invocations online, they keep their social media accounts active in a turbulent time while safeguarding themselves from further political crackdown. In the present and medium-term future, therefore, *dāʿiyāt muthaqqafāt* will arguably continue their online engagement, only moderated towards a less visible presence that carefully reconfigures the meaning of *iḥtisāb* in the face of political repression.

Notes

1. Available at <https://www.bbc.com/news/blogs-trending-35609249> (last accessed 15 October 2019). The male preachers are Muhammad al-ʿArifi (b. 1970), Salman al-ʿAwdah (b. 1956) and Ahmad al-Shugayr (b. 1973).
2. As of October 2019, she has 4.7 million followers on Twitter: @Nawal_Al3eed_.
3. Due to the fluid understanding of who classifies as a preacher (*dāʿiya*), it is difficult to measure the exact number of women on Twitter who identify as such. A female preacher is commonly characterised as someone intervening in the name of possessing religious credentials and being acknowledged by an audience who expects the *dāʿiya* to speak in the name of religious morals and ethics and to give religious advice (*naṣīḥa*). While some preachers exclusively use their Twitter accounts to disseminate religious invocations, others, known as intellectual female preachers (*dāʿiyāt muthaqqafāt*), intervene in wider public debates that include social and political issues. It is this latter category that this chapter is primarily concerned with.
4. In addition to the account of Nawal al-ʿId, some of the most followed Twitter accounts among female intellectual preachers include those of Ruqayya al-Muharib (@rokaya_mohareb_), Nura al-Saʿd (@Dr_NoraAlsaad), Asma al-Ruwayshid (@asyeh_books), Rim al-Bani (@reem_albani), Shaykha al-Qasim (@OmMs3ab), Amal al-Shuqayr (@AmalAlshgair) and Rim Al ʿAtif (@ReemAlatef).

5. By new media, I distinguish the media I analyse here from more conventional forms of communication, such as television, radio and newspapers. I use the definition provided by Leah A. Lievrouw (2011: 7–16) to differentiate new media from other media forms in terms of four distinct and overlapping features characterised as recombinant, networked, ubiquitous and interactive. In their design and use, new media resist stabilisation and change continuously due to being the product of people's ideas, decisions and actions (recombinant), and are continuously reorganised and dynamic as a network of networks. In terms of social and cultural consequences, new media are seen as being everywhere (ubiquitous) in societies where people use them. The fourth and essential factor of new media is their interactive feature, which supports and provides conditions for participation. The participatory potentials of the new media facilitate a more active participation of its audience than conventional media. Social media are understood here as a subset of new media and therefore appear interchangeably with new media in this chapter.
6. This chapter is developed from the work I conducted for my PhD dissertation, in which I studied the phenomenon of intellectual female preachers in Saudi Arabia (Makboul 2018). All translations from Arabic have been made by the author. Most of the material was collected between 2015 and 2018, including a year-long ethnographic fieldwork in Riyadh in 2015 and 2016, where I studied some of the most prominent preachers in the city. These women include Nawal al-ʿId, Ruqayya al-Muharib, Asma al-Ruwayshid, Rim al-Bani, Qadhla al-Qahtani and Fawz al-Kurdi. In addition to this chapter, I have published two articles related to female preachers in Saudi Arabia. The first article (Makboul 2017) studies how these women engage in issues beyond gender-specific ones, arguing that their Islamic ontology, based on a comprehensive (*shumūliyya*) view of Islam that refuses any compartmentalisation of religion to a 'private sphere', has been an important impetus for engaging in issues beyond gender and religious-specific ones. The second article (Makboul 2019) examines the intellectual female preachers' conceptualisation of politics. In line with the conception of *shumūliyya* found in the preachers' Islamic ontology, this article critiques the binary understanding of political engagement as either passivism or activism commonly found in literature dealing with political quietism in Islamic thought.
7. Added to the difficulty of providing a clear definition is also the challenge of translating *dāʿiya muthaqqafa* to 'intellectual female preacher', which also adds a semantic translation that imports a set of understandings of what it means to be a preacher and an intellectual drawn from an English terminology predisposed

to a Western context. While *da ʿwa,* from the root word *da-ʿa-wa,* has the main literal meaning of 'call' or 'invitation', *muthaqqaf* is the passive participle of the root verb *tha-qa-fa,* which literately means the 'cultured', or the 'cultivated'. Informed by Reinhart Koselleck's analytical work on concepts (1982, 2004), this chapter argues that these terms have various meanings and, as concepts, they belong to a past, present and future through constant (re)interpretations. It is from this fluid understanding of concepts as having ambiguous meanings drawn from its specific context that I situate my translation of *dāʿiya muthaqqafa* to intellectual female preachers. Although I do not claim it to be an accurate translation, it is the closest I have found to be semantically resonating.

8. Ruqayya al-Muharib is also one of the few preachers who is known as a *muftiya,* a scholar authorised by the late Grand Mufti of Saudi Arabia ʿAbd al-ʿAziz bin Baz (d. 1999) to issue fatwas.
9. Available at <https://twitter.com/rokaya_mohareb_/status/893091524031983616> (last accessed 3 August 2017).
10. Available at <https://twitter.com/rokaya_mohareb_/status/811634069113081856> (last accessed 7 November 2018).
11. Available at <https://twitter.com/rokaya_mohareb_/status/822088036062298112> (last accessed 7 November 2018).
12. In a questionnaire I prepared for my PhD thesis, I received more than seventy descriptions on the meaning of *dāʿiya muthaqqafa.*
13. In many cases, having such a religious credential would more usually also grant someone the title *ʿālima,* a female scholar.
14. This practical religious knowledge is often referred to as *fiqh al-wāqiʿ,* or the jurisprudence of reality.
15. According to Foucault, what we today in a political sense call the intellectual is someone who utilises his knowledge, his competence and his relation to truth in the field of political struggles (Foucault 1980). Truth is here understood as 'the ensemble of rules according to which the true and the false are separated and specific effects of power attached to the true'. It is also 'a system of ordered procedures for the production, regulation, distribution, circulation and operation of statements' (Ibid.: 132–3).
16. Many of the intellectual preachers I regularly followed in Riyadh had a doctorate in religious sciences and were employed at the Department of Islamic Sciences under the Faculties of Arts at the all-women Princess Noura University. Many preachers also combined an educational background within social science disciplines, education or philology with a degree in religious sciences. This illustrates

both the importance of mastering various 'secular' areas of expertise together with Islamic sciences, and the cross-pollination of disciplines.

17. According to Madawi al-Rasheed, the first generation of female Islamic activists came from known religious families such as Al al-Shaykh, al-Juraysh, al-Saʿd and al-Nasif (al-Rasheed 2013: 255).
18. Here, Salafi Muslim reformers refer to the intellectual strand of Muslim revivalists from the early twentieth century, and in particular adherents of reformist thinkers such as Rashid Rida (1865–1935). Religiously, they rejected a strict adherence to the four canonical Sunni Muslim schools of jurisprudence while following the fideist theology of Hanbalism. Socially and politically, they called for a reformist approach to Islam, influenced by the encounter with the West as both a colonial power and a pivot for scientific, technological and intellectual progress. For more on the historical concept of Salafism, see Lauzière 2016.
19. A local variation of the Egyptian version of the Muslim Brotherhood, the Ṣaḥwa movement was characterised by a hybridisation of Salafi creed and the political and social activism of the Brotherhood. The movement consisted of tendencies inspired by both Hasan al-Banna and Sayyid Qutb. Today, the movement has arguably split into three competing orientations consisting of the 'new Ṣaḥwa', which calls for moderation and is primarily occupied with social activism; the Islamo-liberals who advocate non-violent constitutional reforms; and the neo-jihadis, who support al-Qaʿida and openly criticise the Saudi government (Lacroix 2011). Arguably, the female intellectual preachers I discuss in this chapter are theologically in congruence with the Wahhabi tradition, and sociopolitically influenced by the activism of the non-violent strand of the Ṣaḥwa movement.
20. Fatwa available at <https://www.binbaz.org.sa/fatawa/74> (last accessed 20 October 2019).
21. See also my discussion on the ascendance of female intellectual preachers in Makboul 2017.
22. Today Zayn al-ʿAbidin is no longer considered to be part of the Ṣaḥwa and has departed from many of her earlier views, such as the obligation of face veiling and the prohibition of gender mixing. According to Zayn al-ʿAbidin, she previously upheld opinions of the prevailing religious discourse (*al-khiṭāb al-dīnī*), what they were taught at school and what was found in the literature available in the bookstores, which was heavily influenced by Islamists. Interview by the author, 21 September 2016.
23. According to the 2015–16 survey of the Saudi Ministry of Islamic Affairs, Dawah

and Guidance (Wizārat al-Shuʾūn al-Islāmiyya wa ʾl-Daʿwa wa ʾl-Irshād), the main governmental body overseeing *daʿwa*-related activities in the Kingdom, almost 10,000 Qurʾanic learning circles for girls exist in Riyadh, totalling more than 100,000 female students (al-Shihri and al-Najm 2016).

24. Interview by the author, 28 September 2016.
25. For more on how such websites reinforced already existing homosocial relationships, see Le Renard 2012.
26. As of July 2019, Saudi Arabia is the fourth country in the world with most user accounts on Twitter with 9.9 million active users, following the US (48.85 million), Japan (36.7 million) and the UK (14.1 million). The figures are available at: <https://www.statista.com/statistics/242606/number-of-active-twitter-users-in-selected-countries/> (last accessed 28 October 2019).
27. Available at <https://twasul.info/733787/> (last accessed 28 October 2019). The hashtag used was: (#الشخصية_النسائية_السعودية1438).
28. Interview by the author, 24 August 2016.
29. The website of Waqf Daʿwatuha can be found at www.wdawah.com, while its Twitter handle is @wdawah (last access date 14 February 2020).
30. The website address is <http://www.nawalaleid.com> (last accessed 31 January 2020).
31. For a comprehensive work on commanding right and forbidding wrong in the Islamic tradition, see Cook 2000.
32. On mediated female Muslim voices in public, see the work of Dorothea Schulz (2012).
33. *ʿAwra* is commonly translated as nakedness and generally understood as that which is forbidden for the opposite sex to see or hear. *Fitna* has several meanings depending on the context, such as sedition, tribulation and trial. In this frame of reference, it is understood as the potential seductive danger that women can pose to men.
34. For other studies related to normative discussion on women and men's interaction in the media, see Damir-Geilsdorf and Ramontini 2015.
35. Al-Sharif does not specify what 'hijab' entails here, but he encourages *dāʿiyāt* to participate in satellite channels that allow women to be present in *niqāb*, or behind the curtains.
36. The answers I received to the questionnaire I sent to *dāʿiyāt* illustrate the diverging attitudes toward a woman's voice in public. Asking whether they have any reservations against having their voice heard among men, 41 per cent answered 'no', 31 per cent replied 'yes', while 27 per cent chose 'sometimes'. During my

fieldwork, I experienced that *dāʿiyāt* who did not want their mosque lectures to be recorded would, before commencing, ask their audiences not to record their talks. Cultural as well as family-related considerations seem to play a role in whether a *dāʿiya* allows her voice to be recorded. In ultra-conservative families, husbands or other family members could disapprove of female family members speaking in public. There are also additional restrictions imposed on the modes of expression if a lecture that was initially made for a female audience is to be made public for both men and women. Finally, I also experienced that the interpretation of a woman's voice as potentially *ʿawra* was also a reason why some *dāʿiyāt* abstained from allowing their lectures to be recorded.

37. On the point of making use of the inherent features of social media, see Jon Nordenson's 2017 study of online political activism in Kuwait and Egypt.
38. Available at <https://www.youtube.com/watch?v=c9O_SrhUxYw> (last accessed 28 October 2019).
39. On the evocation of emotions through oratorical practices in Islamic homiletics, see the case of Indonesian preachers in the work of Julian Millie (2017).
40. Although I could not find her date of birth, she is most probably in her fifties as she received her BA around 1985.
41. This criticism alluded to one the claims of the campaign, which called for a compensation of women's domestic work in wages payed by the government.
42. Available at <https://twitter.com/AAlkhedr/status/837036902079430656> (last accessed 12 June 2018).
43. For a brief overview of the long-standing dispute between Saudi Arabia and Qatar, see Roberts 2017.
44. This was especially difficult due to increased cooperation between Qatari and Saudi Islamic organisations. Just months before, the Global League of Islamic Women's Organisations (GLIWO), had signed an agreement with Hadara, a Qatari-based Islamic organisation for women.
45. Available at <https://twitter.com/rokaya_mohareb_/status/871913936362360833> (last accessed 21 June 2018).
46. These include Ruqayya al-Muharib, Nawal al-ʿId, Asma al-Ruwayshid, Rim al-Bani, Nura al-ʿUmar, Malak al-Juhny, Najla al-Mubarak, Hayfa al-Rashid, Amal al-Ghunaym, Amira al-Saʿdi, Amal al-Juhaymi, Muna al-Qasim and Qamra al-Subayʿi. Considering their wide presence and engagement on social media, their silence was striking. The censorship also included women who for years had advocated for women's right to drive.

47. These include important Ṣaḥwa figures such as Salman al-ʿAwda, ʿAwad al-Qarni, ʿAli Badahdah, Muhammad Musa al-Sharif and Ahmad al-Suwayan. In August 2018, Nasir al-ʿUmar was also added to this list. Al-Muharib was released in March 2019 and has not tweeted anything since her arrest.

Bibliography

al-Ahmad, Malik I. (2016), 'Tawẓīf wasāʾil al-ijtimāʿī fī al-daʿwa [Employing social media in *daʿwa*]', *Laha Online*, 23 February, <http://www.lahaonline.com/articles/view/49770/(*)توظيف-وسائل-الإعلام-الاجتماعي-في-الدعوة.htm> (last accessed 17 October 2019).

Arebi, Saddeka (1994), *Women and Words in Saudi Arabia: The Politics of Literary Discourse*, New York: Columbia University Press.

Bahethat (2015), 'Taḥwīl ʿalaminā. Khuṭṭat al-tanmiyya al-mustadāma li-ʿām 2030 [The transformation of our world: the agenda for sustainable development of 2030]', YouTube.com, 14 November 2015, <http://www.youtube.com/watch?v=0yimXwwxZKY> (last accessed 27 October 2019).

Cook, Michael A. (2000), *Commanding Right and Forbidding Wrong in Islamic Thought*, Cambridge: Cambridge University Press.

Damir-Geilsdorf, Sabine and Leslie Ramontini (2015), 'Renegotiating Shariʿa-based Normative Guidelines in Cyberspace: The Case of Women's *ʿAwra* ', *Heidelberg Journal of Religions on the Internet* 9 <https://doi.org/10.11588/rel.2015.0.26249>.

Farquhar, Michael (2017), *Circuits of Faith: Migration, Education, and the Wahhabi Mission*, California: Stanford University Press.

Foucault, Michel (1980), *Power/Knowledge: Selected Interviews and Other Writings, 1972–1977*, New York: Pantheon.

Koselleck, Reinhart (1982), 'Begriffsgeschichte and Social History', *Economy and Society* 11 (4): 409–27.

Koselleck, Reinhart (2004), *Futures Past: On the Semantics of Historical Time*, New York: Columbia University Press.

Lacroix, Stéphane (2011), *Awakening Islam: The Politics of Religious Dissent in Contemporary Saudi Arabia*, G. Holoch (trans.), Cambridge, MA: Harvard University Press.

Lauzière, Henri (2016), *The Making of Salafism: Islamic Reform in the Twentieth Century*, New York: Columbia University Press.

Le Renard, Amélie (2012), 'From Qurʾanic Circles to the Internet: Gender Segregation and the Rise of Female Preachers in Saudi Arabia', in M. Bano and

H. Kalmbach (eds), *Women, Leadership, and Mosques: Changes in Contemporary Islamic Authority*, Leiden: Brill, pp. 105–26.

Lievrouw, Leah A. (2011), *Alternative and Activist New Media*, Cambridge: Polity Press.

Makboul, Laila (2017), 'Beyond Preaching Women: Saudi *Dāʿiyāt* and Their Engagement in the Public Sphere', *Die Welt des Islams* 57 (3–4): 303–28.

Makboul, Laila (2018), 'Pious Power: Epistemology, Discourses and Practices of Female Intellectual Preachers in Saudi Arabia', PhD thesis, University of Oslo.

Makboul, Laila (2019), 'Public Piety and the Politics of Preaching among Female Preachers', in S. al-Sarhan (ed.), *Political quietism in Islam: Sunni and Shiʿi Thought and Practice*, London: I.B. Tauris, pp. 209–24.

Millie, Julian (2017), *Hearing Allah's Call: Preaching and Performance in Indonesian Islam*, Ithaca: Cornell University Press.

al-Muharib, Ruqayya (2006), 'Ruʾya mustaqbaliyya li-l-daʿwa al-nisāʾiyya [Future vision of female *daʿwa*]', in A. al-ʿUthman (ed.), *al-Marʾa wa 'l-ʿamal al-daʿawī* [Women and *daʿwa* work], Riyadh: Dar al-Kunuz Ishibiliya li-l-nashr wa 'l-tawziʿ, pp. 96–105.

Nordenson, Jon (2017), *Online Activism in the Middle East: Political Power and Authoritarian Governments from Egypt to Kuwait*, London: I.B. Tauris.

al-Rasheed, Madawi (2013), *A Most Masculine State: Gender, Politics and Religion in Saudi Arabia*, New York: Cambridge University Press.

Roberts, D. B. (2017), 'A Dustup in the Gulf', *Foreign Affairs*, 13 June, <https://www.foreignaffairs.com/articles/middle-east/2017-06-13/dustup-gulf> (last accessed 26 January 2020).

al-Ruwayshid, Asma R. (2015), '*Kitāb al-adab fa-stamsik* [The book of ethics, so hold fast to it]', Lecture, Riyadh: Asyeh.

Schulz, Dorothea (2012), 'Dis/embodying Authority: Female Radio "Preachers" and the Ambivalences of Mass-mediated Speech in Mali', *International Journal of Middle East Studies* 44 (1): 23–43.

al-Sharif, Muhammad Musa (2012), *al-Marʾa al-Dāʿiya: Maʿālim wa ʿaqabāt wa maḥādhīr* [The female preacher: outlines, obstacles and precautions], Beirut: Dar al-Andalus al-Khadra.

al-Shihri, Hasan bin and Muhammad bin Ahmad al-Najm, (2016), *al-Kitāb al-iḥṣāʾī li-l-ʿām 1436/1437 H* [Survey book for the year 1436/1437 Hijri], Riyadh: Ministry of Islamic Affairs, Dawah and Guidance.

al-Shuqayr, Amal (2017), *Al-Nukhab al-Nisāʾiyya al-Islāmiyya fī al-Suʿūdiyya (1157–1438H/1744–2017AD)* [The female Islamist elites in Saudi Arabia

(1157–1438H/1744–2017AD)], Dubai: Al Mesbar Studies and Research Centre.

al-ʿUthaymin, Muhammad Salih (1998), *Dawr al-marʾa fi iṣlāḥ al-mujtamaʿ* [The role of women in reforming the society], Riyadh: Dar al-Qasim Press.

7

BRIEF REMINDERS: MUSLIM PREACHERS, MEDIATION AND TIME

Simon Stjernholm[1]

On 7 August 2016, the Swedish Muslim preacher Bilal Borchali (b. 1970) published the first of a series of fifteen short videos on Facebook. After initial greetings and blessings on the Prophet Muhammad in Arabic, he continued in Swedish:[2]

> Just like the logo here above me, 90 seconds, that is precisely what *insh'allah* will be here in the future, in ninety seconds we will give a message, food for thought, something that can be useful for every practising believer. Let us start with the first food for thought, my siblings [*syskon*], may Allah *subḥāna wa taʿālā* preserve you. When you buy a mobile phone, what is the first thing you buy with the phone? Exactly! Screen protection. You want to protect the screen so that in case you drop it, it won't break; you want to protect it from scratches *subḥān* Allah. When you buy a computer what do you do? You buy an antivirus software [. . .]. What about our *īmān* [faith], my siblings, how do we protect our *īmān*? How do we protect our *īmān*!? Do we really think about that which is beneficial for us, our *īmān*, that which can give us *īmān*, that which can give strength to our *īmān*, that which preserves our *īmān*, like the Prophet Muhammad *ṣallū wa sallam*, he says, *īmān* increases with good deeds and decreases with bad deeds. How *is* your *īmān*? Have you thought about, brother, have you thought about, sister, have you thought seriously about what it is that can make your *īmān*

> stronger? That is today's food for thought, so think carefully, the Prophet Muhammad *ṣallū wa sallam* said, *īmān* increases with good deeds and decreases with bad deeds, make sure to do good, make sure to take care of your *īmān* so you can be happy in this life and the coming life. See you soon again, *salām ʿalaykum wa raḥmatullāhi wa barakātuhu.* (Borchali 2016a)

The length of this video was almost two minutes, which, although longer than the promised ninety seconds, is certainly brief for being an instance of religious preaching. This type of self-imposed brevity on preachers' output in their attempts to catch the attention of an audience is this chapter's main focal point. How is preaching adapted to a short, often audio-visual, format? What can preachers' rhetorical strategies and mode of presentation in the short format tell us about their communicative aims? To elaborate on the example above: when Borchali uttered the words 'the logo here above me', an easily recognisable logo saying '90 seconds' (*90 sekunder*) appeared in the top right corner of the video, to which he pointed with his left hand. This logo was then visible all through the fifteen related videos, while two other visual characteristics changed: Borchali's dress and the background image shown behind him as he spoke. The distinct visual elements of the videos, Borchali's particular preaching style and messages, and the easy-to-consume format and distribution of these videos, should be seen as working together as a whole – using several communicative modes – aimed at influencing an audience.

The '90 seconds' series will be analysed in more detail below, together with an example of recorded oratory by another preacher, a segment of which was redacted into a short video clip. They exemplify a willingness to move beyond traditional preaching styles, and aim to engage in a direct, interactional mode of discourse with the audience, created to fit current media practices. The chapter shows how Muslim preachers in Sweden experiment with oratory genres across media as they struggle to influence young Muslims with their messages. These preachers try to exert a moral pressure on their audience to improve their behaviour in some way, consistent with preaching in general being a normative endeavour. Yet, in order to communicate effectively, they attempt to make that exertion of pressure pleasurable for their audiences (compare with Millie 2017: 135f). A key aspect in attempting to produce this pleasurable pressure in the age of social media is to keep the message short and attractive, therefore possible and apt to be consumed while scrolling through your social media flow. A preacher then aims to make a piece of religious oratory into a pleasurable pause, or diversion – while at the same time being a moment of pious or moral reflection – in people's everyday media practices. This can potentially serve to activate the viewer's pre-existing knowledge of religious norms or point them in the direction of religious messages that expand on the message.

Muslim religious oratory has been multifarious throughout its history. Its classical preaching genres, and the manuals instructing preachers in their task, show variation in terms of occasion, formality, message delivered and the speaker's intention and social role (Berkey 2001; Jones 2012). It has been – and still is – possible for a single speaker to engage in different types of public religious oratory. Yet, not all speakers can, nor may they wish to, engage in many different types of religious oratory, as various types of discourse – both in terms of content, placement, style and audience composition – are differently appraised and nested within relations of authority (Millie 2017; see also Eickelman and Piscatori 1996; Krämer and Schmidtke 2006). While historical precedence of preaching varieties must be acknowledged, it is nonetheless the case that a combination of factors – including global migration flows as well as technology and media developments – have meant that new types of and arenas for preaching have emerged. Muslim preachers have ample opportunities to experiment with different forms, employ various genres and adapt to different audiences in a more intensely diverse and globally shaped environment than their historical predecessors. A couple of examples will suffice to illustrate this point.[3] In her research on the production of Islamic television in Egypt, Yasmin Moll (2010, 2012, 2017, 2018) has shown the complex deliberations and contestations over form and content that goes into such productions, for example by ensuring that *daʿwa* programmes are as visually sophisticated as the entertainment media that the audience has become accustomed to. Through engaging with various media practices in Mali, Dorothea Schulz (2006, 2012a, 2012b) has analysed the function and meaning of particular media forms, not least radio, for how religious messages are heard and interpreted, highlighting the 'instrumental role of media technologies in facilitating particular modes of authority, assertiveness, and appeal' (Schulz 2012b: 195). These analyses suggest that the discursive possibilities, communicative choices and rhetorical strategies of preachers is a complex field of inquiry, in which both contexts (local as well as transnational) and agency are important to consider. To these and related studies, I wish to contribute a perspective that focuses on brief reminders as a form of address in contemporary media environments.

Genres, Modes and Brevity

My interest in genre lies not in categorising particular speech acts, but rather to ask what the use of different genres allow Muslim preachers to achieve in particular communicative situations. I agree with David Scott (2014: 72; see also Frow 2015), who writes that

> the interesting question to ask is not what genre a text somehow *is*, but how texts *use* the resources of genres and, in so doing, how they *activate* the knowledge and value structures and assumptions of genre in order to produce one or another sort of rhetorical work.[4]

Choosing a particular form of address, such as formulaic blessings on the Prophet Muhammad or recitation of the Qur'an in Arabic, or briefly alluding to a well-known prophetic narrative, can activate certain knowledge and value assumptions already existent in an audience. It can evoke a larger tradition that includes a set of ritual behaviours, ethical ideals, normative narratives and pious emotions, experiential knowledge of which 'constitutes a condition for its ethical reception' (Hirschkind 2006: 101).

A particular text might explicitly relate itself to an established oratory genre in Islamic tradition (for example, the Friday *khuṭba*). However, a speaker can simultaneously use resources from different other genres, for example lectures, podcasts or YouTube video clips. A type of media production that features preaching and well illustrates this fluidity of genres is what I have chosen to call the 'reminder'.[5] I use the term reminder to refer to a video clip that lasts only a few minutes which attempts to activate knowledge or values that the audience is expected to already possess, but supposedly needs to be reminded of. Focused on a particular topic and framed as urgent, it often has an emotional tone, exhorting its audience to consider a matter felt to be of pressing religious nature. Reminders are often hybrid productions that combine chosen segments of longer sermons or lectures with different media, such as still and/or moving images and music. However, reminders may also be original productions specifically created to fit the format of a particular media context, such as social media platforms. The examples studied in this chapter include both types.

A similar type of media production has been studied by Charles Hirschkind (2012: 6), who points out that a particular quality, that of being 'affecting, moving, emotional' (Ar. *muʾaththir*), is frequently used in online comments to and titles of 'short video segments of Friday sermons' that have been published on YouTube. While Hirschkind primarily studied the expressions of pious response to *muʾaththir khuṭba* segments by online audiences, my purpose is to study how some preachers strategically employ styles of communication to 'move' their potential audience as much as possible within severe time restrictions. These attempts are furthermore not limited to being segments of Friday sermons. A feature of what I call the 'reminder' that is concurrent with Hirschkind's segments, however, is that when being extracted from longer pieces of oratory, they 'tend to be those where the emotional intensity of the performance is at its most extreme' (Hirschkind 2012: 12). The second of my chosen examples, developed below, illustrates this point well.

The simultaneous use of different interacting communicative modes – including speech, gesture, still image, moving image and writing – have been labelled multimodality (see, for example, Kress 2010; Kress and van Leeuwen 2001; on Muslim discourses, see Sands 2010; El Naggar 2018). The most central communicative mode employed in the media productions studied here is speech, a salient feature of which is its reliance on the logic of time (Kress 2010: 79–83). Speech requires a certain amount of time to unfold and establishes a different relationship to its listener than does writing to its reader and image to its viewer. It is impossible for a speaker to produce all the words at once. Yet images, which can demand enormous amounts of time and work to produce, can be glanced at – and potentially dismissed – in seconds. A carefully produced piece of writing, likewise, can be skimmed through or read meticulously. A reader can begin in the middle or end of a written text, despite the intentions of its author. This is not so easily done with speech, even when recorded and thus repeatable or possible to replicate. Intonation, pitch, loudness and silences are also important aspects of speech.

The production of meaning is not only achieved through words and their referents, but also the manner in which they are uttered. Voices themselves can be ascribed different value, positive as well as negative (Sterne 2008; Schulz 2012a). Individual preachers trying to influence an audience will attempt to use the mode of speech, in combination with other modes, in the way they think most suitable to their message and aim.

The form of the reminder, including its uses of time, genre and communicative modes, is especially suitable for contemporary social media. You can (nearly) always find time for a reminder, which is not always the case with a forty-minute lecture, sermon or podcast. At the same time, being distributed through social media also means that it needs to compete for the user's attention with all sorts of messages: political propaganda, cute kittens, advertisements, film trailers, entertainment news and much more, in what can be called a 'disruptive simultaneity' (Simmel 2015: 90).[6] The setting is therefore different from that of a typical sermon in a mosque. A key challenge for preachers is thus to perform oratory in a way that responds to the particular context provided by the media habits and audience behaviours of today – including an often-short attention span.

Muslim Preachers and the Swedish Context

Similar to other European contexts, Muslim preachers have repeatedly been the topic of public attention in Sweden when criticised, arrested or otherwise related to controversy. A few examples will suffice to illustrate this tendency. In journalistic works (for example, Gadban 2015) as well as security-oriented research publications, Swedish Muslim preachers and religious activists – including the two dealt with in this chapter – have been accused of advocating radical Islamism and extremist ideas. A 2018 report from the Swedish Defence Academy has a separate section on Borchali, where the authors highlight what they see as problematic aspects of his activities (Ranstorp et al. 2018: 115–18). This includes quotes from Borchali stating that it is forbidden for Muslims to celebrate Christmas and New Year's Eve, that wives should obey their husbands, that Islam should not be adapted to become European Islam, and that a person engaging in homosexual relations cannot be considered a Muslim. Borchali's links to 'controversial foreign imams' are also mentioned (Ranstorp et al. 2018: 117). The second preacher studied here, Salih Tufekcioglu (b. 1978),[7] is mentioned in the report as a collaboration partner to Borchali. Publications like these are generally more interested in networks (who has met whom, who has invited whom to speak, and so on) rather than actual instances of preaching. When content from preaching is referred to or quoted, it consists of brief formulations, often single sentences, taken out of their context and chosen with the purpose of assessing the level of threat the preacher poses to Swedish society. My analytical interests and aims are different.

Sustained analysis regarding the messages of Muslim preachers in Sweden has been scarce. In her work on a puritan Salafi group in Sweden, Susanne Olsson (2019; see also Olsson in this volume) has partly investigated the oratory of its leaders. My own recent work has analysed messages in Muslim religious oratory on public service radio (Stjernholm 2019a, 2019b) as well as the cultural production of preachers who act independently of mosque structures and mainstream media outlets (Stjernholm 2019c). Research also exists on how Islam is taught to children in Muslim free schools (Berglund 2010). In order to gain an understanding of how locally rooted preachers try to influence young Muslims through their rhetoric, it is important to examine and contextualise their communications within a broader analytical framework than a security-oriented one.

'90 Seconds' on Facebook

Bilal Borchali has been active as a preacher and in producing online media roughly since the turn of the century. He came to Sweden when he was fifteen years old, having previously grown up as a Palestinian in Lebanon (Mogensen 2001: 66). Many are likely to be more familiar with his nickname 'SMS-Bilal', which alludes to one of his many *daʿwa* initiatives, namely a service where anyone can sign up to regularly receive a text (SMS) message containing a quote from the Qurʾan or a hadith together with a short exhortation to piety. Borchali has also co-produced ambitious websites containing information and guidance about Islam for Muslims and non-Muslims alike, as well as being central in the livestreaming service Budskapet.tv (*budskapet* translates as 'the message'), where he was one of several contributing preachers. He has for a number of years given the Friday *khuṭba* many times in various mosques in southern Sweden; quite a few of these *khuṭab* are available to download as audio or video files from his website. Moreover, Borchali has collaborated with the group United Muslims of Sweden (Sveriges Förenade Muslimer), an organisation that has been heavily criticised in recent years for the inflammatory religious messages of some of its lecturers (see, for example, Löwenmark 2017).

As mentioned in the introduction to this chapter, during the autumn of 2016 Borchali posted a series of fifteen short video messages on his public Facebook profile entitled '90 seconds'.[8] They were kept (more or less) within that length and were identified as a series by the inclusion of a logotype with the series title in each video. That the logotype was consistently used throughout the fifteen episodes shows an ambition to provide a clearly distinguishable product, immediately recognisable in form and content. Borchali also talked about the videos as episodes in a series, for example referring to 'a new episode of 90 seconds' (Borchali 2016b). With the series, he tried to offer his followers something more beneficial than the usual content of their Facebook flow. The '90 seconds' series appears to be recorded at home in front of a computer. Borchali is standing on one side of the screen and is looking straight into the camera, creating an impression of looking straight at the viewer. Often, he addresses the viewer directly: either collectively with phrases like 'my valuable siblings' (*mina dyrbara syskon*), or individually, for example by saying 'my dear brother' (*min kära bror*) or 'my dear sister' (*min kära syster*). When addressing the viewer directly, sometimes with a 'you', he often gestures or points towards the camera as if engaged in a real-life conversation.

In each episode, Borchali addresses a particular topic. Examples are: the importance of 'cleaning up' among your friends in order not to be influenced towards bad behaviour (Borchali 2016c); treating your wife nicely, for example by saying appreciative things and bringing her flowers (Borchali 2016d); teaching your children to recite al-Fatiha so that they can fulfil their daily prayer, as this will bring blessings to you even in your grave (Borchali 2016e); and the value of addressing Allah directly through *du'ā* prayers rather than asking someone else, such as a shaykh, to mediate (Borchali 2016f).

The religious messages are often introduced and underlined through metaphors taken from everyday life. In the second episode, the importance of being aware of how our actions in this life affect our fate in the hereafter, is introduced by talking about air conditioning:

> Many of us think when it is hot I need to keep the AC running, I can't travel to a country where there is no AC, I can't be in the heat, it's hard, I can't deal with it, but *subḥān* Allah we are believers, we know and we believe that [...] on Judgement Day, we will go to hell [. . .] if we don't obey Allah *subḥāna wa taʿālā*, have we thought about that heat in the hereafter with Allah ... (Borchali 2016g)

In a similar vein, one episode introduces God's promise to forgive two years' worth of sins for those who fast at Arafat Day (during hajj season) by referring to the concept of economic debt relief ('*skuldsanering*') (Borchali 2016h). By using metaphors that relate to very worldly concerns, Borchali shows a willingness to speak in ways that can resonate with everyday life. This means that his rhetoric aims to intrude into the audience's everyday life in two ways simultaneously: through the media genre itself, a short video adapted to fit into daily media habits of scrolling through social media flows, and through the actual words chosen to attract attention to the message. The relief that can be brought about by air-conditioning on a hot day, or debt relief for a person in financial debt, is said to be nothing compared to the protection from hellfire and forgiveness of sins offered by God. The message communicated can be formulated as: what I am reminding you of – pious thought and practice – is much more important than these worldly concerns of yours; so, mind your priorities.

Borchali is very often smiling in the '90 seconds' series. Even a serious phrase like 'you are responsible to Allah on Judgement Day', might be followed by the more upbeat 'I'll see you soon again' and accompanied by a friendly look and a smile. Merely reading the words that are spoken therefore does not capture the communicative potential of these videos. The smiling lips, the winking eyes looking straight at the viewer, the intonation of the voice that underlines chosen aspects, and the visual background chosen to accompany each episode, all contribute.

If we look at the visual framing of this series, it is not consistently 'Islamic' in an obvious way. These images are not commented on but are still part of the communicative process. By being more or less thematically linked to what is being said, a link that is up to the viewer/listener to establish, they play a role in how the audience will receive, interpret and reflect on the message. One example is the image of a 'straight road' that is used as background image for episode six. The photograph is taken at night, from the visual perspective of a white line on the ground in the middle of an asphalt-covered street, with streetlights on each side. In the episode, Borchali recites (in Arabic, without scriptural aid, while gesturing and looking straight into the camera at the viewer) verses 27–9 from the Qur'an's Sura 25, and afterwards comments on them:

> Allah *subḥāna wa taʿālā* says on Judgement Day one will regret not having followed the Prophet, have regrets because of one's companions [. . .] So when is the time, my siblings, for us to clean up among our bad company? [. . .] Have you thought about your life in the hereafter with Allah *subḥāna wa taʿālā*? Have you thought that you would like to make it on Judgement Day? Then it's time to start cleaning already today, my brother and my sister. (Borchali 2016c)

Borchali does not mention the image behind him – and it may well be the case that the image has been chosen after recording the message. However, by creating a particular combination of visual and auditory materials for each video, the viewer is invited to interpret this combination, to fill in the 'blanks', to use a metaphor from Wolfgang Iser (1978), so that meaning is produced through an ongoing interaction in which the reader/listener/viewer takes active part. Seen in this way, the visual background that accompanies Borchali's speech, appearance and gestures are part of shaping the viewer's experience, even though it is not explicitly addressed in words. This interpretive opening relies on a shared frame of reference (narratives, values, expressions, and so on) between preacher and viewer that is already existent before watching the video. One of the central points of the reminder video genre is to activate this shared frame through the viewer's response.

Borchali's '90 seconds' series shows an ambition to communicate in ways that both aurally, visually and temporally fit into the particular media context of the Facebook flow. He is not limited to the traditional venues, times and conventions of preaching, but experiments with different genres. This type of output must be seen as supplementary to the other regular genres of preaching in which Borchali engages; in particular Friday sermons and lectures at Islamic conferences, both of which are also often disseminated online. The

'90 seconds' series may be an attempt to reach people who do not regularly attend such events. It shows that a preacher may employ various rhetorical and communicative strategies for different settings and imagined audiences. In attempts to communicate effectively, the resources of different genres (degree of formality, type of language, physical and visual settings, and so on) are mobilised as the preacher sees fit.

Learning from the Prophet

My second example of the way a reminder communicates multimodally, is a YouTube video called 'How the Prophet Muhammad taught the Arabs that racism is wrong' (*Så lärde profeten Muhammed araberna att rasism är fel*).[9] The video, which is three minutes and fifty-four seconds long, features the voice of Salih Tufekcioglu, a Malmö-based preacher, teacher and entrepreneur. Tufekcioglu collaborated with Borchali for a number of years in editing online material and producing live-streamed Islamic lectures. More recently, however, Tufekcioglu has sought other collaboration partners and created his own channels of communication, including websites, a blog and several podcast series.[10] The video 'How the Prophet' is an illustrative example of how a conscious choice of preaching style and content can be combined with images and sound, thereby becoming something new. This hybridising mode of cultural production is reminiscent of sampling techniques in music production. By creatively using and blending different genres, such productions can potentially achieve a different kind of rhetorical work and reach a broader audience compared to the original oratory in its immediate context of delivery.

The video's speech track is an excerpt from a lecture given in Gothenburg in front of an audience consisting of Muslims with Turkish background. When I interviewed Tufekcioglu about his preaching activities, he mentioned this particular lecture as an example of having used what he called a 'preachy' style of speaking, consciously seeking to stir the audience's emotions through his oral address. He told me that his style 'used to be more, like, preachy [. . .] but I have gradually moved from arousing emotions to being more intellectually [. . .] reasoning' (interview, 10 December 2017). He furthermore described this particular occasion:

> I was talking about this thing about not marrying over national boundaries. And I had an audience of, there were only Turks, and it was, like, families, there were, like, mothers, fathers, uncles, and so on. And I was standing up there and I just – now I'm going to talk about this topic that all youths come to talk to me about, precisely about marrying over cultural boundaries – I'll just do it. (Interview, 10 December 2017)

In taking the decision to deliver a message advocating openness toward transcending national boundaries in marriage practices to a culturally homogeneous audience – consisting of people with a Turkish background – Tufekcioglu was highly aware that he was treading on sensitive ground. Yet he persisted and, importantly, he consciously chose to speak in an unusually animated manner. He decided to take the potentially negative consequences of delivering this particular speech in this particular context, because he felt a need to do so. After the lecture event, another person ('a brother') chose a segment of Tufekcioglu's speech, and together they combined it with music and moving images, producing the video in focus here. In the video, the speaker is not shown at all, only indicated by his name next to a Facebook logo (encouraging viewers to look him up). The manner of speaking here is different from most of Tufekcioglu's oratory, which is often calm and relatively casual, despite obviously being prepared in advance. In the excerpt used in the video, he speaks in short, rhythmic and exclamatory utterances with occasional rhyming. Moreover, the voice is emotionally charged, with a higher intonation than usual, at times almost shouting, then calming down, then increasing in strength again.

Tufekcioglu is talking about a scene from the *sīra* of the Prophet Muhammad. When Muhammad and his companions have – largely peacefully – re-entered Mecca after years of military conflicts, Bilal, the black former slave who is known for being the first muezzin, is instructed by Muhammad to climb on top of the Kaʿba and call to prayer, something that reportedly enraged Mecca's previous leaders (see, for example, Ibn Kathīr 2000: 411f). In Tufekcioglu's retelling, this was 'a shock' to the Arab leaders, due to their habit of ascribing status according to differences like skin colour, wealth and genealogy. In the video's conclusion, Tufekcioglu emphasises that:

> The best of you / Is the one whose fear of God is deepest / The best of you is not the one who is richest! / The best of you is not the one who is whitest! / The best of you is not the one who is male! / The best of you is the one who has *taqwā* [. . .] / Allah does not look to my skin colour / He does not look to my sex / He does not look to my wallet / He looks to my heart / And if I open my chest / If you my brother or sister open your chest / Our hearts are the same / And that is what Allah *subḥāna wa taʿālā* looks to.

There is a strong urge here to look beyond superficial differences between people – such as skin colour, wealth and gender – while instead acknowledging and acting upon the difference that God cares about. Pious fear of God (*taqwā*), how our hearts respond to the divine calling to do right – that is what should preoccupy us, according to Tufekcioglu, rather than man-made cultural and national borders. The core message that Tufekcioglu talked about in his speech – not restricting marriage to people of shared national background – is briefly made explicit in the video as well. But it is made part of a much larger morally charged urge to focus on truly important matters – piety, fear of God, the spiritual status of one's heart – instead of such petty concerns.

Simultaneous with Tufekcioglu's speech, an ensemble of fifteen different selections of moving visuals are showing. His description of the scene with Bilal on top of the Kaʿba are first accompanied by images of a windy sand desert, a man walking with camels in a sandy desert, and a man in a white robe looking at a desert sunrise (or sunset). Later the images shift into the corresponding scene from the well-known feature film *The Message* (1976), where Bilal is shown on top of the Kaʿba and people are looking up at him, listening. After retelling the narrative of Bilal, as Tufekcioglu moves into the more generalised equality-oriented rhetoric, images that are shown include a page of the Qurʾan (accompanying a recitation in Arabic followed by translation in Swedish), a child running across a green field, various nature images, and a model of the globe, rotating westwards, starting over Central Asia and moving across the Middle East and North Africa and ending the shot over the Atlantic Ocean. As Tufekcioglu says that the best person is not the one who is richest or whitest, a man in shirt and business jacket looking depressed – head in his hands – is shown. When he mentions that we need to stay away from sins, what appears to be people dancing in a nightclub are shown. As a contrast, when *taqwā* and obedience of God is mentioned, a man prostrating in prayer is in view. Accompanying the video's last words, cited above, is an image of four boys and an adult man, all dressed in white robes, standing in line, hands facing upwards, perhaps engaged in prayer. In addition to speech and images, a music track is playing on loop throughout the video. The melody might be described as solemn, in a minor key, and played on what sounds like digital strings. It adds to the seriousness and heartfelt tone of Tufekcioglu's speech.

It is left to the viewer to piece together the relationship between words and images, as well as the succession of imagery. No explanation or information of sources is provided. Parts of the visual material look like home-made videos, other parts look like material that could be used in a commercial, and parts of it is an excerpt from a feature film. Some of the visual material have a more obvious relationship to the words being uttered: the feature film scene dramatising the narrative that is recounted; the Qur'anic page accompanying a recitation and its translation; the globe when differences between cultures are referred to. Other imagery has a wider gap that needs to be filled by interpretation. Yet, it is possible to see these visual excerpts as constructing a visual narrative that supports the spoken one. When a hybrid product is successful, when its multimodality is well configured and directed, its whole can be larger – that is, be more meaningful to its audience – than the sum of its parts. This video can achieve something different than the original address in front of a physically present audience. It aims to exert moral pressure on its audience by pushing them to improve their behaviour in a particular direction: this video is not 'just entertainment'. Through its complex multimodal presentation, it aims to exert this pressure in a mediated form, a mode of circulation that is pleasurable to engage with. This shows the speaker's and video producer's awareness of the struggle to win and sustain the attention of an audience, combined with a willingness to adapt to the particular context of the potential audience.

Conclusion

In Julian Millie's work on Muslim preaching on West Java, he cites a number of cases where a preacher, sensing that the audience's attention rate is falling, uses 'refreshment strategies' like singing a song or telling a joke as a supplement to their regular spoken oratory (see, for example, Millie 2017: 27, 47, 50–66). A parallel can be drawn to how 'new preachers' in Egypt have used the entertaining affordances of television to attract broader audiences to their project of pious renewal, rather than relying on allegedly boring talking heads (Moll 2018). In both Indonesia and Egypt, consciously affect-seeking forms of mediation of preaching have sparked public critique and debate, as conservative voices have reacted against making preaching resemble entertainment. The examples of mediation of preaching that I have analysed here can be seen as analogical to the communicative strategies analysed by Millie and Moll, albeit on a much more modest and low-budget scale, and in a Muslim-minority context.

While the Indonesian and Egyptian preachers are well-known figures in society, can make a living off their preaching, and rely on multiple resources like capital, media infrastructure, and social status, the Swedish preachers I have investigated are active on the margins of society, probably with little financial remuneration, outside of established media channels, in a society where they are seen as suspect by many. Yet their efforts to engage affectively with their audience show comparable ambitions regarding how to make oneself listened to. There is an adaptiveness and creativeness in how individual preachers use different genres of oratory that engages its audience multimodally. A particular preacher is not restricted or bound to use only one genre of preaching. Although it may sometimes be in a preacher's interest to remain safely within one or two oratory genres, perhaps in order to remain being deemed 'traditional' or 'rational', it is entirely possible – and potentially rewarding in terms of audience response – to move between, or make use of, multiple genres in order to communicate messages in different ways. These messages may be very similar in terms of theological content, but a variety of oratorical media productions can broaden their appeal and potential influence. By producing reminders in the way exemplified here as a complement to other oratory output (for example, sermons and lectures), preachers may be able to capture and redirect the audience's attention to types of preaching where issues are dealt with in a more sustained and substantial manner. The examples analysed in this chapter illustrate attempts by preachers to expand the reach of Islamic religious discourses into other parts of their audience's lives than the mosque; attempts at speaking for Islam into the everyday life of their audiences, nudging them to refocus on issues of religious importance and letting attendance to these pious concerns play a larger part in their life.

More than that, this chapter has shown how preachers adapt to a certain temporal economy inherent in the media environments through which they disseminate their communications. In order to make themselves seen and heard in the 'disruptive simultaneity' (in Simmel's words) of media platforms like Facebook and YouTube – where practically everything is present and seeks attention at the same time – these preachers make brevity of address a key aspect of their productions. Through combining genre resources from more classical forms of Islamic preaching with resources from contemporary capitalist culture, preachers attempt, on the one hand, to attract and sustain an audience's attention to their own preaching video, and on the other hand to activate pious norms, emotions and values already present in the audience – but of which they need to be reminded. The effect of such reminiscence can, for example, be: to cause a brief pious reflection that ends immediately when the video ends; to affect the viewer's behaviour in a more religiously observant direction for some time following consumption of the video; or to inspire the viewer to seek out further *daʿwa* material that goes more into depth with the issues touched upon. An effective reminder video thus has the potential to achieve a different kind of rhetorical work in this particular media context than a regular lecture or sermon video, which typically lasts significantly longer and makes less use of hybrid genre resources and multimodal communicative strategies. The brief reminder category of preaching video, therefore, is an apt response by preachers to contemporary everyday media practices that supports, rather than challenges, the prevalence of more traditional forms of preaching.

Notes

1. The research on which this chapter is based was supported by Åke Wiberg's Foundation, Helge Ax:son Johnson's Foundation, and the Krapperup Foundation. I want to thank Andreas Bandak and Elisabeth Özdalga for helpful comments on a draft version of this chapter.
2. All translations from the original Swedish were made by the author.

3. In addition to the examples introduced here, see also, for example, Beekers 2015; Brinton 2016; Kalmbach 2015; Lynch 2017; Millie 2017; Sunier and Şahin 2015.
4. Italics in original.
5. The term 'reminder' is also used in emic contexts by some Muslim producers of preaching videos.
6. Georg Simmel (1858–1918) used this expression in a 1890 essay on art exhibitions, to capture the experience of being presented to a large number of artworks at the same time, leading to 'a mix of impressions endangering any deeper understanding of an individual artwork' (Simmel 2015: 90).
7. As Tufekcioglu generally refrains from using Turkish diacritical marks when writing his name, I will do the same.
8. I downloaded all episodes on 10 April 2017. At that date, the number of viewings for the individual videos ranged from around 700 to around 1,800.
9. I downloaded this video from the YouTube channel Destination Jannah Productions on 1 February 2017, at which point it had 675 views. The video had been uploaded to the channel on 31 January 2016. At the time of writing, however, the channel – and therefore the video – appears to have been removed from YouTube. The same video has been posted to other online platforms. One upload of the video to Facebook was made on 13 September 2018; when observed on 1 October 2019 it had 442 views. In addition, the original full-length lecture by Tufekcioglu has been disseminated through his own online channels.
10. For further information on Tufekcioglu along with analysis of other examples of his work, see Stjernholm 2019c.

Bibliography

Beekers, Daan (2015), 'A Moment of Persuasion: Travelling Preachers and Islamic Pedagogy in the Netherlands', *Culture and Religion* 16 (2): 193–214.

Berglund, Jenny (2010), *Teaching Islam: Islamic Religious Education in Sweden*, Münster: Waxmann.

Berkey, Jonathan P. (2001), *Popular Preaching and Religious Authority in the Medieval Islamic Near East*, Seattle: University of Washington Press.

Borchali, Bilal (2016a), 'Din Iman [Your iman]', published on Facebook.com/borchali 7 August 2016, downloaded 10 April 2017.

Borchali, Bilal (2016b), 'Gör Allah nöjd [Make Allah pleased]', published on Facebook.com/borchali 24 August 2016, downloaded 10 April 2017.

Borchali, Bilal (2016c), 'Dags att städa [Time to clean up]', published on Facebook.com/borchali 15 August 2016, downloaded 10 April 2017.

Borchali, Bilal (2016d), 'Älska din fru [Love your wife]', published on Facebook.com/borchali 17 August 2016, downloaded 10 April 2017.

Borchali, Bilal (2016e), 'al-Fatiha', published on Facebook.com/borchali 11 August 2016, downloaded 10 April 2017.

Borchali, Bilal (2016f), 'Direkt till Allah [Immediately to Allah]', published on Facebook.com/borchali 1 September 2016, downloaded 10 April 2017.

Borchali, Bilal (2016g), 'Bättre tillstånd i det nästkommande [Better condition in the hereafter]', published on Facebook.com/borchali 9 August 2016, downloaded 10 April 2017.

Borchali, Bilal (2016h), 'Två års sanering [Two years' cleansing]', published on Facebook.com/borchali 4 September 2016, downloaded 10 April 2017.

Brinton, Jacquelene G. (2016), *Preaching Islamic Renewal: Religious Authority and Media in Contemporary Egypt*, Oakland: University of California Press.

Eickelman, Dale F. and James Piscatori (1996), *Muslim Politics*, Princeton: Princeton University Press.

El Naggar, Shaimaa (2018), '"But I Did Not Do Anything!" – Analysing the YouTube Videos of the American Muslim Televangelist Baba Ali: Delineating the Complexity of a Novel Genre', *Critical Discourse Studies* 15 (3): 303–19.

Frow, John (2015), *Genre*, 2nd ed., London and New York: Routledge.

Gadban, Hanna (2015), *Min Jihad: Jakten På Liberal Islam* [My jihad: searching for liberal Islam], Stockholm: Fri tanke.

Hirschkind, Charles (2006), *The Ethical Soundscape: Cassette Sermons and Islamic Counterpublics*, New York: Columbia University Press.

Hirschkind, Charles (2012), 'Experiments in Devotion Online: The YouTube *Khuṭba*', *International Journal of Middle East Studies* 44 (1): 5–21.

Ibn Kathīr (2000), *The Life of the Prophet Muhammad*, Vol. III, T. Le Gassick (trans.), Reading: Garnet.

Iser, Wolfgang (1978), *The Act of Reading: A Theory of Aesthetic Response*, Baltimore and London: Johns Hopkins University Press.

Jones, Linda G. (2012), *The Power of Oratory in the Medieval Muslim World*, Cambridge: Cambridge University Press.

Kalmbach, Hilary (2015), 'Blurring Boundaries: Aesthetics, Performance, and the Transformation of Islamic Leadership', *Culture and Religion* 16 (2): 160–74.

Krämer, Gudrun and Sabine Schmidtke (eds) (2006), *Speaking for Islam: Religious Authorities in Muslim Societies*, Leiden and Boston: Brill.

Kress, Gunther (2010), *Multimodality: A Social Semiotic Approach to Contemporary Communication*, London and New York: Routledge.

Kress, Gunther and Theo van Leeuwen (2001), *Multimodal Discourse: The Modes and Media of Contemporary Communication*, London: Hodder Education.

Lynch, Marc (ed.) (2017), *New Islamic Media*, POMEPS Studies 23, Institute for Middle East Studies, George Washington University, <https://pomeps.org/wp-content/uploads/2017/02/POMEPS_Studies_23_Media_Web-rev.pdf> (last accessed 10 November 2019).

Löwenmark, Sofia (2017), 'SFM sprider våldsbejakande islamism för skattepengar [SFM distributes violent Islamism financed by tax money]', Smedjan/Timbro, 15 March 2017, <https://timbro.se/smedjan/reportage/sfm-sprider-valdsbejakande-islamism-skattepengar/> (last accessed 23 October 2019).

Millie, Julian (2017), *Hearing Allah's Call: Preaching and Performance in Indonesian Islam*, Ithaca, NY: Cornell University Press.

Mogensen, Lars (2001), 'Svensson, du är muslim [Swede, you are a Muslim]', *Guru*, January, pp. 66–8.

Moll, Yasmin (2010), 'Islamic Televangelism: Religion, Media and Visuality in Contemporary Egypt', *Arab Media & Society* 10: 1–27.

Moll, Yasmin (2012), 'Storytelling, Sincerity, and Islamic Televangelism in Egypt', in P. N. Thomas and P. Lee (eds), *Global and Local Televangelism*, Basingstoke: Palgrave Macmillan, pp. 21–44.

Moll, Yasmin (2017), 'Subtitling Islam: Translation, Mediation, Critique', *Public Culture* 29 (2): 333–61.

Moll, Yasmin (2018), 'Television is Not Radio: Theologies of Mediation in the Egyptian Islamic Revival', *Cultural Anthropology* 33 (2): 233–65.

Olsson, Susanne (2019), *Contemporary Puritan Salafism: A Swedish Case Study*, Bristol: Equinox.

Ranstorp, Magnus, Filip Ahlin, Peder Hyllengren and Magnus Normark (2018), *Mellan salafism och salafistisk jihadism* [Between Salafism and Salafi jihadism], Stockholm: Försvarshögskolan.

Sands, Kristin Zahra (2010), 'Muslims, Identity and Multimodal Communication on the Internet', *Contemporary Islam* 4 (1): 139–55.

Schulz, Dorothea E. (2006), 'Promises of (Im)Mediate Salvation: Islam, Broadcast Media, and the Remaking of Religious Experience in Mali', *American Ethnologist* 33 (2): 210–29.

Schulz, Dorothea (2012a), 'Dis/Embodying Authority: Female Radio "Preachers" and the Ambivalences of Mass-Mediated Speech in Mali', *International Journal of Middle East Studies* 44 (1): 23–43.

Schulz, Dorothea Elisabeth (2012b), *Muslims and New Media in West Africa: Pathways to God*, Bloomington, IN: Indiana University Press.

Schulz, Dorothea E. (2015), 'Mediating Authority: Media Technologies and the Generation of Charismatic Appeal in Southern Mali', *Culture and Religion* 16 (2): 125–45.

Scott, David (2014), *Omens of Adversity: Tragedy, Time, Memory, Justice*, Durham, NC and London: Duke University Press.

Simmel, Georg (2015), 'On Art Exhibitions', *Theory, Culture & Society* 32 (1): 87–92.

Sterne, Jonathan (2008), 'Enemy Voice', *Social Text* 26 (3 (96)): 79–100.

Stjernholm, Simon (2019a), 'Muslim Religious Oratory on Swedish Public Service Radio', *Journal of Contemporary Religion* 34 (1): 57–73.

Stjernholm, Simon (2019b), 'Sounding Sufi: Sufi-Oriented Messages on Swedish Public Service Radio', in F. Piraino and M. Sedgwick (eds), *Global Sufism: Boundaries, Structures, and Politics*, London: Hurst & Co, pp. 193–208.

Stjernholm, Simon (2019c), 'DIY Preaching and Muslim Religious Authority', *Journal of Muslims in Europe* 8 (2): 197–215.

Sunier, Thijl and Mehmet Şahin (2015), 'The Weeping Sermon: Persuasion, Binding and Authority within the Gülen-Movement', *Culture and Religion* 16 (2): 228–41.

'Så lärde profeten Muhammed araberna att rasism är fel [How the Prophet Muhammad taught the Arabs that racism is wrong]', uploaded to YouTube.com 31 January 2016, downloaded 1 February 2017.

PART IV

IDENTITIES

8

ADVISING AND WARNING THE PEOPLE: SWEDISH SALAFIS ON VIOLENCE, RENUNCIATION AND LIFE IN THE SUBURBS

Susanne Olsson

The speaker, Moosa Assal, is dressed in a long white robe, sitting in front of shelves of Arabic books, looking relaxed, with long hair and beard. He is about to speak about the 'chaos' in Swedish suburbs, for example riots where young people have thrown stones at police and firemen as well as set cars on fire. Initially, he speaks Arabic and welcomes the viewers. He then speaks Swedish in a distinct suburban Stockholm dialect, likely shared by many of the expected viewers.[1]

> This is sincere advice, advice from me to those who listen. As a person in this society. As a person who is born, and has grown up, in the suburbs. In Husby, Rinkeby and Tensta.[2] So I speak from my heart to peoples' hearts tonight. [. . .] I do not make any money from this. There is nobody who told me 'you have to speak about this'. This is something that I really want to talk about. I want to give advice. Specifically, to my brothers out there in the suburbs. To the Muslims. Because I can talk from our own religion.[3]

Assal then turns specifically to those of his Muslim 'brothers' whom he knows to be criminals, and advises them to fear God:

> Fear Allah! Be afraid of Allah! Know that one day you will stand in front of your Lord. You will be responsible for your actions. Don't think that you

> can do whatever you want in this world and then in the next life you are not responsible! No! You are responsible for your actions!
> We have a Lord who sees us and hears us, whom we will meet one day. When our deeds will be brought up, and Allah will judge us based on what we have done and what we have said. So, I ask you, my brother who commits such evil acts: do you yourself think this is something good? Do you feel good from this? Impossible!

Instead of getting involved in evil acts, Assal stresses that 'brothers' should be a source of positive energy in society, which would be in accordance with Islam.

Assal's speech also contains explanations of the present situation in the suburbs, where he refers to theological themes, the Qur'an and the Prophet, and stresses the responsibility of each individual:

> The first reason for all of this is, of course, Satan. It is the Devil who whispers and fools people into doing these crimes and these evil acts. But this does not mean that you can sit at home or do this and say, 'It is Satan who is saying this to me!' No! We have been ordered in the Qur'an to meet Satan as an enemy! [. . .] You can end up in Hell due to your deeds. You know and I know that our deeds will be weighed. In which of the scales will drugs be put? Good deed or bad deed? Burglary, and riots, and similar stuff, when you throw stones at people. The Prophet forbade hitting someone in the face. Hitting! What should we then say about throwing stones at a person's face?!

As a contrast, Assal advises the viewers to use their energy to become good role models and leave criminal life behind. The solution is to return to God in fear and repentance:

> The solution to this is to fear your Lord. To return in repentance. To reflect on your life. [. . .] That you people, you Muslims, return to religion, and are afraid of Allah and fear Allah, and know that these acts bring you to the fire of Hell, and know that the fire of Hell is real, and that you will burn in it.

The above-mentioned video and its messages are examples of the *da'wa* of a Swedish Salafi group that runs a website (islam.nu) and a YouTube channel.[4]

In a shorter video, Assal is standing on a snowy street in a thick winter jacket, speaking about violence. He refers to cases where young men have been killed in Stockholm suburbs. He speaks directly to young men, who may be involved in suburban gang criminality:

> I believe that those of you who commit crimes like this have many feelings inside and I think that you can instead use these feelings in a good direction and do positive things. Because nobody in the suburbs likes these acts, and nobody wants it like this! We want to have safety! We want love! We want harmony! We want to feel good! This is my advice to people, to try to think in different ways, and try to solve it through peaceful means, and not in this way. And I don't think that people always have these motives to want to kill someone, but because they have weapons and maybe they use drugs and other stuff; it makes them commit these evil acts, unfortunately, and they do not think seriously about the consequences of it. [. . .] To kill someone is not a small thing. God says in the Qur'an that 'whoever kills a person, except (in retaliation) for another, or (for) fomenting corruption on the earth, (it is) as if he had killed all the people. And whoever gives (a person) life, (it is) as if he had given all the people life'. [Q. 5:32][5] So my last piece of advice to you is, put down your weapon! Thank you very much.[6]

It is obvious from these examples that the Salafi group focused on in this chapter is concerned about the concrete social ills they are facing in the local community. The group calls itself the Ibn Abbas Centre. It insists that it is apolitical and against violence, instead carrying out missionary activities focused on piety, correct practice and behaviour. In the 'About' section of its website, the Ibn Abbas Centre states that it strives to spread 'correct, authentic information about Islam in Swedish':

> We spread knowledge about Islam based on the Qur'an, the Prophet's sunna *ṣallā allāhu ʿalayhi wa sallam*, as well as the understanding of the companions and the imams of the first three generations, and those who follow them in [doing] good. This is based on the Prophet's saying (*ṣallā allāhu ʿalayhi wa sallam*): 'Hold on to my sunna and the rightly guided caliphs' sunna.' The Ibn Abbas Centre is run by educated students with recommendations from the scholars as well as having a degree [in a theological

> discipline] from the Islamic University of Medina. The same applies to all of our lecturers. All our activities are voluntary.[7]

In line with the aims, its Medina-educated leaders give lectures on various topics, which are published on the website and YouTube channel. This chapter analyses lecture videos from the YouTube channel that claim to present 'true Islam', as well as shorter videos with brief advice and warnings. The videos can be seen as part of the Islamic *waʿẓ* tradition in which preachers throughout the centuries have presented pious advice and warnings, as well as religious knowledge more broadly, to their audiences.

Salafism functions as an umbrella term framing fragmented and contradictory attitudes. Salafis can be characterised as fundamentalist, due to, for example, the mimetic relationship to an idealised past, a highly scripture-oriented approach, an emphasis on pious practices as a purifying shield from polluting surroundings and viewing oneself as 'chosen' (for a useful conceptualisation of fundamentalism, see Stadler 2009). Muslims using Salafi as a self-designation claim authenticity based on a return to authoritative sources, that is, the Qurʾan and the sunna. As an ideal, Salafis promote imitation of pious behaviour as recorded in these sources, without interpretation. The term Salafi further relates to *al-salaf al-ṣāliḥ*, referring to the first generations of Muslims, the 'pious predecessors'. To emulate (*ittibāʿ*) their examples is stressed among Salafis and thus constitutes a third source for their vision of Islam.

Salafi preaching and teaching in this manner seem to be growing in many parts of Europe.[8] Salafism is not only a movement of the last couple of decades. In late nineteenth- and early twentieth-century Egypt, a movement developed that is often designated as Salafi (or Salafiyya). It was led by Muhammad Abduh (1849–1905) and Jamal al-Din al-Afghani (1839–97), who responded positively to the West and welcomed modernist interpretation, while at the same time arguing for a return to Islamic sources (Meijer 2009: 7). Rashid Rida (1865–1935), who is often portrayed as part of this movement, turned to a more scriptural and literal view of the sources later in his life, sharing more traits with contemporary Salafism. Since contemporary Salafism is radically different from modernists like Abduh, Henri Lauzière (2010) has suggested 'Sunni anti-rationalist Purism' as an alternative term. However, the term Salafism will be used here. Saudi Wahhabism has influenced contemporary Salafism to a great extent, even though Salafis generally reject the imitation (*taqlīd*) of any particular Islamic school of law. Thus, Salafis do not have much in common with the modernist reformers of nineteenth- and twentieth-century Egypt. The idea of returning to the sources may look similar at first sight, but at closer scrutiny it is not.

Salafism is divided into three categories by Roel Meijer (2009: 17): (1) quietist and discrete, (2) quietist but still acting politically and (3) openly activist. The third type comes closer to Islamism, as in the Saudi Ṣaḥwa movement (see also Haykel 2009: 48). The Ibn Abbas Centre fits in the first type, that is, quietist and discrete. Openly activist Salafi groups are, for example, al-Qaʿida and Islamic State, who stress the literalist mimetic stance towards the sources, while Islamist groups are more positively inclined to interpretation of the sources, rather than promoting detailed emulation of them. This stance does not necessarily lead to a modernist or liberal reading of the sources, but the interpretative stance is clearly different from the Salafi stance.

Advice and Warning

The concept of *waʿẓ* differs from *naṣīḥa*, which in its basic forms means simply (friendly) advice or admonishing.[9] As we will see below, however, *naṣīḥa* has become a term also used by the Ibn Abbas Centre, even when directed at larger anonymous audiences. Today, various forms of media create a landscape of multiple Islamic voices. This also makes categorisations of various forms of Islamic speeches more difficult. For example, whether the speech of a preacher is a sermon or not depends on the setting and the social context, the style and content of the speech, and whether it is delivered through new media or in traditional settings, such as a mosque. A speech may be a lecture (*muḥāḍara*), a lesson (*dars*), or a traditional Friday sermon (*khuṭba*), even though it may be difficult to establish clear boundaries between various speech acts (Radtke and Jansen 2012). A *wāʿiẓ* can warn and admonish people through different kinds of speech acts. The videos studied here can be seen as a kind of *waʿẓ* directed at an audience not physically present; in fact, the intended audience may not know about or choose not to watch the video, for example youngsters living in suburbs or locked up in prison.

Not all people who preach or teach Islam today are Islamic scholars. Yet in the Ibn Abbas Centre, lecturers or 'missionaries' (*duʿāt*, sing. *dāʿī*), have their education from the Islamic University of Medina (IUM, on which see Farquhar 2016). In general terms, a *dāʿī* is someone who calls people to Islam and is expected to live up to high moral standards. Today, many different people act as missionaries. *Daʿwa* 'has increasingly become a space for the articulation of a contestatory Islamic discourse on state and society' (Hirschkind 2005: 32). It is often an individual practice aimed at improving the morality of the wider community. Moral reform, in the framework of *daʿwa*, is connected to various forms of public or social activism, for example social and educational services (Hirschkind 2005: 32). The Salafi group studied here is a part of this broader transnational missionary tendency, and individuals are encouraged to participate in and perform *daʿwa* activities. The Ibn Abbas Centre has a focus on moral reform in general. They strongly condemn violence, including suburban riots and acts of terrorism. This social commitment to a peaceful society may contribute to strengthening their social capital in the community, for example in contacts with local authorities.

The *Duʿāt*

Salafis in Sweden constitute a minority among the Muslim minority. In my recent book, *Contemporary Puritan Salafism: A Swedish Case Study* (2019), a more thorough contextualisation of the Swedish setting and the Salafi environment is given. The Ibn Abbas Centre presents itself as taking 'the middle path' and stresses typically Salafi sources of authority. In the following, the research material will be presented in more detail, introducing first the selection of the three main *duʿāt* appearing in the chosen videos. All of them have studied or are studying at the IUM. Only videos posted on the YouTube channel islam.nu are included. The empirical material does not allow me to offer any generalising conclusions about Salafism in Sweden or elsewhere, nor of all aspects of this particular group.

The videos feature local lecturers talking in Swedish. Two of them are Swedish converts, who use the names Abu Dawud Abdullah as-Sueidi and Abdul Wadud. The third is Moosa Assal. Assal, who is from the suburb Husby, participated in a televised series about Muslims in Sweden aired on Swedish public service television (SVT) in spring 2017, called *Jag är muslim* ('I am Muslim'). In the series, he was portrayed as a very popular Swedish

Salafi imam, working hard against violent radicalisation. He has received positive media coverage (for example, Tenstabons videoursäkt 2016).

Abdul Wadud has a leadership position. In contrast to Assal, he has received negative treatment in the Swedish media, showing that the relationship to journalists is problematic. One video published on islam.nu is specifically concerned with the alleged 'media frenzy' against Islam.[10] One critical article concerning how Swedish Shiʿites are threatened by, among others, Salafis, referred to a lecture by Abdul Wadud (Orrenius 2017a). The video was called *Sanningen om Shia* ('The truth about Shiʿa'), and it was removed after the publication of the article.[11] In another article where Abdul Wadud and Assal are mentioned, the government agency Swedish Board of Student Finance's (CSN) financing of Swedish students at the IUM was criticised (Orrenius 2017b). In the mentioned video on media frenzy, an image of the world appears where certain countries and ideologies are shown as being threats to Islam and Muslims. The speakers argue that a certain group of people are responsible for the hostile media environment; they are said to belong to liberal think tanks connected to the US or Israel. Abu Dawud urges the viewers to acknowledge this and to engage in defending their religion. He states that there are people with an immigrant or Muslim name who are given media space to criticise the situation in the suburbs, such as the existence of Muslim moral policing there. It is true that several articles have been published in the Swedish media that warn against increased 'moral policing', especially in the suburbs and mainly targeting women (see Pekgul 2017).[12]

The Videos

The YouTube channel was created on 27 August 2015, but the first video referred to here was published on 23 October of the same year and the last video referred to was published on 7 June 2017.[13] Some videos are between thirty and sixty minutes long and consist of reflections on prayer, the Qurʾan, the pious predecessors and *ʿaqīda* (creed). Some are also related to more mundane topics, such as advice on using Snapchat. The speaker usually sits in recognisably Salafi clothing with a long beard at a desk and in front of bookshelves carrying books in Arabic, thus embodying an image of a proper Salafi scholar. However, we can also note that Assal often dresses and speaks in a more youthful or suburban manner, which may be a conscious outreach strategy. Other clips are merely a few minutes long and address questions related to something that has recently happened in Sweden, such as cases of suburban gang criminality. In these shorter clips, it is usually Assal who is speaking outside, standing on a street, as in one of the videos mentioned initially, or sitting in the metro speaking directly into the camera.

My selection of videos is based on the titles of videos that indicate a focus on violence and renunciation. All topics explicitly deal with topics young people meet or hear about in the media. The videos reject violence and violently inclined groups. Most videos refer to the authority of the Qurʾan and sunna as well as the importance of emulating pious authorities through presenting prophetic narratives (hadith) and parables. Islamic scholars are also often referred to as authorities. Yet there are exceptions, which lack any explicit authoritative references, for example a short video in which Assal stands outside the upper secondary school in the suburb Tensta, dressed in a winter jacket, and speaks about the need to stop bullying in schools, without mentioning Islam.[14]

The following presentation of the research material is divided into three main themes: (1) renunciation, (2) terrorism and (3) suburban violence. The themes may appear in one and the same video, but in this study the chosen material is structured according to these themes for sake of clarity.

1. Reaching Paradise through renunciation

The theme of renunciation (*zuhd*) is a central topic; it requires a certain lifestyle and functions as a motivation to join the Ibn Abbas Centre. It is explicitly addressed in a video with Abdul Wadud entitled *Avhållsamhet – Zuhud* ('Renunciation – *zuhud*'), which is introduced here in order to outline and frame common ideas and strategies.[15] Abdul Wadud wears a grey robe and a Saudi-style red and white chequered shawl over his head. He sits next to a minbar with his notes on a small table. After reciting from the Qurʾan, he states that they will hear a hadith about *dunyā* (this world) and *zuhd*. He admonishes the audience, saying that this world will come to an end and that we only have a short time to live here. He explains that renunciation means not to be obsessed with *dunyā*. When someone neglects prayer in order to get a job, or postpones prayer until the time of the prayer has passed, or when a woman removes her head-covering in order to be accepted in school, be liked or get a job, he or she has placed *dunyā* above *ākhira* (the hereafter). Such a person belongs among the losers. People should be pleased with what they have been given from God.

Abdul Wadud states that each prayer should be performed like a farewell prayer, where one would make *tawba* (repent) to God and focus on God, not on *dunyā*. Related to this, he refers to a hadith frequently used by Salafis, showing how they are a part of the chosen group:

> You must have and fulfil certain criteria in order to enter Paradise. Why do you think that from humanity, when divided on Judgement day, only one out of a thousand will enter Paradise. One from each thousand. And 999 will be thrown into Hell. This means that Paradise is not for free. It is not something easy but demands sacrifices. It demands *ṣabr* [patience]. It demands obedience to Allah *subḥāna wa ta'ālā*: that you meet Allah with good deeds, with a clean heart. [. . .] In these times of *fitna* [disturbances, rebellion], you shall reflect upon Paradise, because it is like a carrot that drives people forward.

The common theme of *zuhd* is expressed in a requirement not to be obsessed by the this-worldly, but rather to focus on and continuously strive for Paradise, knowing that death can come at any time. Imitating the Prophet would lead you to practise *zuhd*. This message runs through most videos and is a basic attitude found in all of the material on the website. Being renunciant is a part of being a good role model. In the following, we shall consider videos that deal more explicitly with contemporary problems, concerning violence and criminality of various kinds.

2. Establishing a non-violent strategy

A main focus for the Ibn Abbas Centre is to publicly present itself as representing a non-violent interpretation of Islam, where it dissociates itself from all groups and individuals who promote or commit violent acts. Such videos are often, but not always, responses to a recent terrorist attack. They address their understanding of the reasons why people are attracted to such ideas and groups, and present a solution to the problem, which is to return to the allegedly true understanding and practice of Islam, and to follow selected learned Islamic scholars.

One short video features Assal commenting on the fact that young people in Sweden have joined Islamic State and other groups who promote violence. Assal asks those joining such groups if they have considered the consequences of what they do, and stresses that their actions negatively affect Muslims around the world. As a result, he claims, Muslims are harassed, and governments establish new rules making life harder for all Muslims. He says: 'People have become afraid of Islam and the Qur'an! Is this what you want? You will be responsible! If you don't repent, this will lay on your neck on Judgement day.'[16]

Another recurrent idea is that violence, according to the Ibn Abbas Centre, has no support in authentic Islamic sources. This is problematic, since scriptural 'proof' is needed in order to deem something legitimately Islamic. Assal states, in the same video:

> Return to the Qur'an and sunna and return to listening to the scholars. This is my short piece of advice to the young people who have joined these groups. And I hope that you regret this and return for real, and I mean it!

In a video entitled *Islam är fri från terrorism* ('Islam is free from terrorism'), Abdul Wadud also stresses that terrorism is not Islamic. He sits at a desk, dressed in a black robe and wearing a white scarf on his head, and he speaks about how Islam becomes connected to terrorism in the media. The video illustrates the centrality ascribed to the need to establish scriptural proof in Islamic sources:

> Of course, the sources must be the Qur'an and sunna. They are the sources of proof in Islam. That which is not in the Qur'an or sunna does not have anything to do with Islam. So, if you really want to know what Islam says about these questions you must return to the Qur'an, the sunna and to the understanding of *ṣaḥāba* [companions of the Prophet] of this, in order to *insh'allah* get the correct picture of this question.[17]

Another video is presented as advice (*naṣīḥa*) directed to those who are a part of or sympathise with groups like Islamic State. Assal says in this video that many young people do not speak Arabic and they do not have much knowledge, and then it is easy to go astray. He warns them of taking knowledge from certain websites and individuals, such as the American jihadi preacher

Anwar al-Awlaqi (d. 2011).[18] He mentions meeting a young man who sympathised with such dangerous websites: this young man did not even know how to perform *wuḍū* (ablutions before prayer), but spoke about topics such as who is and is not a Muslim. Assal also said that listening to jihadist songs (*anāshīd*) and watching war videos in which Muslims are hurt and killed, can lead you to form a black and white image of the world.[19] Abdul Wadud likewise emphasises, in the above-mentioned video 'Islam is free from terrorism', that the terrorists lack knowledge: 'They have no *ʿālim* on their side and are young and stupid.' He points out that the audience must avoid 'popcorn-ʿulamaʾ', those who just 'pop up' from anywhere.

One particular sin brought up by Abdul Wadud in the video 'Islam is free from terrorism', is disobedience to parents, relating to jihadi foreign fighters. He says that most parents would not allow their children to travel to join Islamic State and that those who travelled without their parents' permission are sinners. He also states that even if parents would allow their child to join Islamic State, it is not allowed according to Islam. Here, we also get a glimpse of the conservative views on women:

> And it is even worse when it is a woman who runs away from home to join [Islamic State]. Even worse! Women are not allowed to travel without a *maḥram*. Right? Women are not allowed to travel without a *maḥram*. Women should not even make jihad. [. . .] The jihad of women is to make hajj and *umra*. This is the jihad of women. Not to stand with weapons and make war. This is mentioned in the books of *fiqh* by the ʿulamaʾ. One of the conditions of a *mujāhid* is that it is a man. The physique of women is not adapted to take part in these fights.

Women who run away from home to join Islamic State thus disobey their parents. Moreover, they travel without a *maḥram* (unmarriageable man), and get married without a *wālī* (legal guardian). Abdul Wadud refers to the Prophet, who said that someone getting married without a *wālī* does not have a legal marriage, which makes the woman a *zāniya* (fornicator). Those familiar with these terms would immediately understand that these major sins would bring one closer to the fires of Hell.

3. Social development: suburban strategies

Many Swedish Muslims live in suburbs with socio-economic distress, lower education levels and unemployment, and high rates of criminality and violence.[20] The videos mentioned in the introduction touched upon this situation explicitly. One issue that the *duʿāt* often deal with is to define what they claim to be underlying causes of a problematic situation and speak about how it can be prevented. As their activities are mainly located in the suburbs, the situation there is a recurring topic. Moreover, should they succeed in contributing to reduced criminality in the suburbs, they would most likely gain in popularity in the local population, among other Muslims and perhaps in the media. In the video *Råd kring livet i förorterna* ('Advice on life in the suburbs'), Assal recommends renunciation: being too focused on *dunyā* and material things, one risks beginning a life of criminality, or taking loans with interest, in order to finance a certain lifestyle. We are tempted, he argues, via music, films and social media to lead a materialistic life.[21]

In another video, Abu Dawud gives advice to Muslims on how to behave following the terror attack in Stockholm on 7 April 2017.[22] The video is recorded the day after the attack when not all the information about the suspect was known. The video repeats several themes that have previously been mentioned. But Abu Dawud also gives practical advice to Swedish Muslims, such as not to spread rumours, to think positive, stay calm, behave well and be a good role model, which he stresses is everyone's responsibility.[23] The Ibn Abbas Centre believes that as a consequence of people joining it and becoming truly practising Muslims, terrorism and other violence will decrease. Assal says that he has participated in social projects in the suburbs for over twenty years, for example arranging concerts in the suburbs. Yet he does not see that such events help:

> These are not solutions. And I say that openly. And people can say what they want. 'But what should we say then: "Islam, Islam"?' Yes, Islam! Let people hear about Islam! Islam leads people to truthfulness, to honesty! Not to hurt people. Not to lie. Not to steal. [. . .] Treat people as you yourself want to be treated. This is what Islam teaches humanity. [. . .] Islam is what made our youngsters stop smoking, give up chewing tobacco [*snus*], give

> up drugs, give up all of this. And everybody knows this really. People know this. And I know 100 per cent that the police know this. [. . .] That when a person becomes religious, we don't have to worry anymore about these crimes.[24]

This quote shows an aim to spread knowledge about Islam, the ethical aspects that they promote and the practical effects this allegedly has of people giving up criminality and drugs. A central argument is that everybody already knows that becoming religious will solve all such problems.

Concluding Comments

The authority of a preacher or teacher depends on how the audience perceives him. In this respect, a validation of his knowledge is an important criterion for authority (Radtke and Jansen 2012). The *duʿāt* have studied at the Islamic University of Medina, which can be used in claims of authority. They repeat and rely on what is written in the authoritative traditional sources. The stress on having scriptural proof (*dalīl*) for what is said is constantly emphasised. The local *duʿāt* hold high positions of authority and play important roles as religious specialists as well as social role models.

Identification with the in-group and brotherhood (and sisterhood) is stressed, meaning that 'cooperation is not only motivated by rational interests but also by a sense of fellowship or "brotherhood" which makes it easier to gain trust and acquire social capital' (Pall and de Koning 2017; see also Sik 2012). By taking part of and showing themselves concerned with life in the socially troubled Stockholm suburbs, these Salafi preachers and teachers can acquire a position that goes beyond their purely religious qualifications, potentially making their *daʿwa* relevant to a larger group of people. The Salafi group wishes to spread an image of themselves that publicly stresses non-violence, and a vision of Islam as contributing to reduce all forms of violence. This is a response to the current situation in Sweden, where hundreds of people have travelled to join Islamic State, where Stockholm recently suffered a terrorist attack with five casualties, and where suburbs experience gang criminality.

The Salafi missionaries present their activities as part of Islamic tradition, an authentic Islamic method, where admonishing people and giving advice is an established form of teaching and preaching. They strive to reach out to young people in the suburbs in a language and style that they will recognise and through media that are likely to attract them. In the view of the *du ʿāt*, true Islam will help clean up the suburbs, contribute to the development of well-behaved people, as well as create nice and safe suburban areas. Through *da ʿwa* activities directed at youths who might otherwise be attracted to criminality and radicalism, they work to achieve their goal. They aim to develop good role models who renounce the this-worldly in favour of striving to reach Paradise. They even claim that 'everybody knows' – even the police – that Islam will make people quit drugs and criminal activities. With such a message, it is not surprising if young people in segregated suburbs listen to them. Rather than abstract and removed from daily concerns, the message is straightforward and self-assured as it attempts to disrupt the positive images some young people may have of violent lifestyles and create new role models to emulate. They are thereby striving to present a positive message: if people join their project of moral reform and renunciation, they might contribute to strengthening the suburbs and creating a peaceful environment. At the same time, in-group identity construction is strong and exclusionist. The Salafi preachers present themselves as belonging to the selected group with good chances of reaching Paradise. The rest, they claim, will go to Hell.

Notes

1. All quotes from the original Swedish were translated by the author. 'Suburbs' here refers to socially and economically weak areas on the outskirts of Swedish cities, whose population is often disproportionally made up of people with immigrant background.
2. Suburbs located in the western parts of Stockholm.
3. The video *Lägg ned gängkrigen. Påminnelse med Moosa Assal* ('Stop gang wars. Reminder with Moosa Assal'] was uploaded to YouTube.com on 11 March 2017 and is available at <https://www.youtube.com/watch?v=FokD_S3KID8> (last accessed 18 May 2017).
4. Islam.nu has previously been described as working against terrorism, suicide, Usama bin Laden and related ideas (see Stjernholm 2013: 180, n. 181).
5. Here, Droge's translation of the Qur'an is used to render the quote's Swedish translation into English.

6. The video *Stoppa våldet i förorterna!* ('Stop suburban violence!'] was uploaded to YouTube.com on 16 January 2016 and is available at <https://www.youtube.com/watch?v=OfCkb2OBi10> (last accessed 21 April 2017).
7. Available at <https://islam.nu/om-oss> (last accessed 17 May 2017).
8. It is not possible to ascertain statistically whether or not the number of Salafi adherents is increasing. There are also indications that Salafism functions as a kind of framework that influences Muslims at large and their perceptions of what Islam is, or should be. In many cases, it seems that non-Salafis are influenced by Salafis in, for example, dress codes. This may give the false impression that there are more devout Salafis than there actually are (Olsson 2019: 10). Moreover, the increase of Salafi propaganda in social media is not in itself proof for a growing Salafi presence.
9. *Naṣīḥa* can also be translated as 'advice for rulers' (*Fürstenspiegel*), which historically is a genre consisting of advice on politics, statecraft, comportment towards God and his subjects (Bosworth 2012).
10. The video *Mediadrevet mot Islam. Fajr Påminnelse med Abu Dawud & Imran Sheikh* ('Media frenzy. Fajr reminder with Abu Dawud and Imran Sheikh') was uploaded to YouTube.com on 17 June 2017 and is available at <https://www.youtube.com/watch?v=0njcAig7EuA> (last accessed 25 August 2017).
11. For an overview of Salafi rhetoric against the Shiʿites and Shiʿa Islam, see Olsson 2017.
12. The view on media may be affected by negative press that was mentioned above. Furthermore, Abdul Wadud also appeared in an episode of *Uppdrag granskning* ('Mandate review'), aired on 16 May 2012, entitled *Imamernas råd* ('The advice of the imams'), by the Swedish National Television (SVT). In the documentary, two women with hidden cameras and dressed in *niqāb* went to several Muslim congregations to ask for help, arguing that the husband of one of the women beat her and she wondered whether she should report him to the police; Abdul Wadud was one of those advising against it.
13. Even though the number of views or visitors does not say anything about the popularity or impact of the site, it may be interesting to note that the number has increased. The total number of views were as follows: 7 June 2017 – 96,600; 25 August 2017 – 119,559; 21 February 2018 – 178,698; 27 March 2018 – 194,418.
14. The video *Stoppa mobbningen i skolorna* ('Stop bullying in schools') was uploaded to YouTube.com on 25 February 2016 and is available at <https://www.youtube.com/watch?v=hKxkFSgy2Zo> (last accessed 21 April 2017).

15. The video *Avhållsamhet – Zuhud* ('Renunciation – *zuhud*') was uploaded to YouTube.com on 23 October 2015 and is available at <https://www.youtube.com/watch?v=jBRO683SBNM> (last accessed 21 April 2017).
16. The video *Viktigt råd till dig som stödjer Isis!* ('Important advice to you who support Islamic State!') was uploaded to YouTube.com on 11 January 2016 and is available at <https://www.youtube.com/watch?v=8tmzvu0ofq4> (last accessed 21 April 2017).
17. The video *Islam är fri från Terrorism* ('Islam is free from terrorism') was uploaded to YouTube.com on 7 November 2015 and is available at <https://www.youtube.com/watch?v=rSj21URcvIk> (last accessed 19 May 2017).
18. Anwar al-Awlaqi, often spelled al-Awlaki, was a Yemeni American (1971–2011), who was killed in Yemen by an American drone. He had been recruiting to al-Qa'ida and published treatises to motivate people to join in violent jihad (see Olsson 2016: 170–89). The Salafi website kalamullah.com was also mentioned.
19. The video *Varför vi inte stödjer ISIS, al Qaida och liknande…* ('Why we do not support Islamic State, al-Qa'ida and the like…') was uploaded to YouTube.com on 10 August 2016 and is available at <https://www.youtube.com/watch?v=MwtqUDyO3qU> (last accessed 7 June 2017).
20. The website <http://statistik.stockholm.se/> presents statistics over various areas in Stockholm that can be used to compare (last accessed 7 June 2017). <http://statistik.bra.se/solwebb/action/start> has statistics on criminality (last accessed 7 June 2017).
21. The video *Råd kring livet i förorten. Fajr Påminnelse med Heykel & Moosa* ('Advice on life in the suburbs. *Fajr* reminder with Heykel and Moosa') was uploaded to YouTube.com on 3 June 2017 and is available at <https://www.youtube.com/watch?v=Cv4KtFDOzFQ> (last accessed 7 June 2017).
22. Five people were killed in a truck attack in central Stockholm, for which Rakhmat Akilov was convicted to life in prison. A collection of articles about the attack and its aftermath (in Swedish) can be found at <dn.se/om/attentatet-pa-drottninggatan/> (last accessed 21 October 2019).
23. The video *Ett råd till muslimer efter dådet i Stockholm* ('Advice to Muslims after the deed in Stockholm') was uploaded to YouTube.com on 9 April 2017 and is available at <https://www.youtube.com/watch?v=W26KumRGP_E> (last accessed 18 April 2017).
24. The video *Vågorna: En föreläsning om lösningar på Gatuvåldet* ('The waves: a lecture about solutions to street crime') was uploaded to YouTube.com on 10 August

2016 and is available at <https://www.youtube.com/watch?v=wjpXZMqSERk> (last accessed 28 April 2017).

Bibliography

Bosworth, Clifford Edmund (2012), 'Naṣīḥat al-Mulūk', in *Encyclopaedia of Islam*, 2nd ed., consulted online 28 April 2017 at <http://dx.doi.org/10.1163/1573-3912_islam_COM_0850>.

Droge, Arthur J. (2013), *The Qur'ān: A New Annotated Translation*, Sheffield: Equinox.

Farquhar, Michael (2016), *Circuits of Faith: Migration, Education, and the Wahhabi Mission*, Stanford: Stanford University Press.

Gobillot, Geneviève (2012), 'Zuhd', in *Encyclopaedia of Islam*, 2nd ed., consulted online on 14 December 2016 at <http://dx.doi.org/10.1163/1573-3912_islam_SIM_8201>.

Haykel, Bernard (2009), 'On the Nature of Salafi Thought and Action', in R. Meijer (ed.), *Global Salafism: Islam's New Religious Movement*, London: Hurst, pp. 33–57.

Hirschkind, Charles (2005), 'Cassette Ethics: Public Piety and Popular Media in Egypt', in B. Meyer and A. Moors (eds), *Religion, Media, and the Public Sphere*, Bloomington, IN: Indiana University Press, pp. 29–51.

Lauzière, Henri (2010), 'The Construction of Salafiyya: Reconsidering Salafism from the Perspective of Conceptual History', *International Journal of Middle East Studies* 42 (3): 369–89.

Meijer, Roel (2009), 'Introduction', in R. Meijer (ed.), *Global Salafism: Islam's New Religious Movement*, London: Hurst, pp. 1–32.

Olsson, Susanne (2016), *Minority Jurisprudence in Islam: Muslim Communities in the West*, London: I.B. Tauris.

Olsson, Susanne (2017), 'Shiah as Internal Others: A Salafi Rejection of the "Rejecters"', *Islam and Christian Muslim Relations* 28 (4): 409–30.

Olsson, Susanne (2019), *Contemporary Puritan Salafism: A Swedish Case Study*, London: Equinox.

Orrenius, Niklas (2017a), 'Svenska shiamuslimer hotas från två håll [Swedish Shiʿa Muslims are threatened from two angles]', *Dagens Nyheter*, 26 May, <https://www.dn.se/nyheter/sverige/niklas-orrenius-svenska-shiamuslimer-hotas-fran-tva-hall/> (last accessed 10 November 2019).

Orrenius, Niklas (2017b), 'Studiemedel går till saudisk mission i Sverige [Student funding is used for Saudi mission in Sweden]', *Dagens Nyheter*, 2 June, <https://

www.dn.se/arkiv/nyheter/studiemedel-gar-till-saudisk-mission-i-sverige/> (last accessed 10 November 2019).

Pall, Zoltan and Martijn de Koning (2017), 'Being and Belonging in Transnational Salafism: Informality, Social Capital and Authority in European and Middle Eastern Salafi Networks', *Journal of Muslims in Europe* 6 (1): 76–103.

Pekgul, Nalin (2017), 'Vi måste ta ställning mot fundamentalisterna [We must take a stand against the fundamentalists]', *Expressen*, 24 June, <http://www.expressen.se/kultur/ide/vi-maste-ta-stallning-mot-fundamentalisterna/> (last accessed 25 August 2017).

Radtke, Bernd and Johannes J. G. Jansen (2012), 'Wāʿiẓ', in *Encyclopaedia of Islam*, 2nd ed., consulted online on 18 April 2017 at <http://dx.doi.org/10.1163/1573-3912_islam_COM_1332>.

Sik, Endre (2012), 'Trust, Network Capital, and Informality: Cross-Border Entrepreneurship in the First Two Decades of Post-Communism', *Review of Sociology* 4: 53–72.

Stadler, Nurit (2009), *Yeshiva Fundamentalism: Piety, Gender, and Resistance in the Ultra-Orthodox World*, New York: NYU Press.

Stjernholm, Simon (2013), 'Våldsbejakande och antidemokratiska islamistiska budskap på internet [Violent and anti-democratic Islamist messages on the Internet]', in Statens medieråd, *Våldsbejakande och antidemokratiska budskap på internet*, <http://www.regeringen.se/49bb8d/contentassets/c6460146d8de486eabf7f209b3a9093a/valdsbejakande-och-antidemokratiska-budskap-pa-internet> (last accessed 18 May 2017).

Tenstabons videoursäkt (2016), 'Tenstabons videoursäkt efter stenkastningen: "Så här kan man inte bete sig" [The excuse of the Tensta-inhabitant: 'You cannot behave like this']', *Metro*, 8 February, <https://www.metro.se/artikel/tenstabons-videours%C3%A4kt-efter-stenkastningen-s%C3%A5-h%C3%A4r-kan-man-inte-bete-sig-xr> (last accessed 28 March 2018).

'Zuhd' (2003), in J. L. Esposito (ed.), *The Oxford Dictionary of Islam*, Oxford University Press.

9

DISCOURSES ON MARRIAGE, RELIGIOUS IDENTITY AND GENDER IN MEDIEVAL AND CONTEMPORARY ISLAMIC PREACHING: CONTINUITIES AND ADAPTATIONS

Linda G. Jones[1]

Islamic homiletics on marriage and spousal relations provide insights into the construction of religious and gender identities, the human–divine relationship and gender roles within a given society. Typically, Muslim canonical nuptial orations (*khuṭab al-nikāḥ* or *khuṭab al-zawāj*) cite Qur'anic verses and the Prophet Muhammad's hadiths expressing a clear preference for marriage as the ideal relationship between men and women (al-Bukhārī: Book 67; Muslim: Book 16; Ibn Mājah: Book 9), and emphasise the spiritual, emotional and social benefits it holds for the individual and society (Q. 30:21 and Q. 4:1, 4:21). Preachers may also discuss these topics in the Friday *khuṭba* and in the non-canonical hortatory sermon (*wa'ẓ/maw'iẓa*). Because homiletics has been associated with marriage since the origins of Islam, analysing sermons on marriage from different historical periods allows us to identify continuities within the homiletic tradition and detect developments reflecting the preacher's adaptation of his message to suit the needs, expectations and values of his audience. Contemporary Muslim preachers face the added challenges of needing to negotiate the globalising moral contexts of contemporary Muslim communities.

Since I have discussed specimens of Islamic nuptial orations elsewhere (Jones 2012: 123–30; Jones 2013), this chapter analyses Islamic homiletic discourses about marriage and marital relations in a pre-modern *maw'iẓa* and a contemporary Friday *khuṭba*. This cross-cultural diachronic analysis of two distinct homiletic sub-genres has two broad goals. First, it seeks to explore how each preacher interprets the meaning of marriage, represents spousal relations and defines gender identities and roles for his audience. In terms of methodology, I examine the homiletic and rhetorical strategies employed in each text with the following questions in mind: how does each preacher conceptualise marriage and spousal relations? How does he envisage marriage in light of the *'ibādāt* (religious obligations)? How does marriage shape Muslim gendered identities? What rhetorical devices does the preacher employ to convey his vision of marriage, spousal relations and the roles of wives and husbands? The responses to these questions will engage with academic discussions about gender and spousal relations in Islam, the relationality of gender identities, and gender justice and equality (Ali 2010; Baranzagi 2013).

The second goal entails a comparative meta-level of analysis in which the two case studies of Islamic preaching on marital relations allow for an exploration of the broader question of the continuities and adaptability of a religious tradition in light of changing social, cultural, political or other circumstances. Despite the historical and geographic divide between the two sermons under study, the continuities between them invite the question of how to account for the adaptability or flexibility of Islam as a religious tradition. In other words, what elements, instruments, or practices within Islam and the Islamic homiletic traditions contribute to religious continuities and adaptability? To answer these questions, I draw inspiration from Andrea Nicklisch's observations (2018) regarding the dual ability of cultures 'to adapt to new conditions, to borrow, modify or discard features of other cultures, and to undergo changes within themselves'. At the same time, cultures are able 'to preserve elements of themselves over long periods of time in spite of adverse circumstance'. Another source of theoretical insight comes from Vered Noam (2009: 41–3) who has criticised the post-Enlightenment thesis that identifies the 'perspective of continuity' with pre-modern religious tradition and ascribes to the modern period acknowledgements of the need for religious change. Noam shows that the impulses for continuity and change coexist in pre-modern and contemporary religious traditions. Significantly, she highlights the role of the Jewish homiletic interpreter who, though obligated to show that his interpretations of Halakha are grounded in the Bible, nevertheless enjoys 'a tremendously broad exegetical space' for interpreting his sources. I hope to show that a similar situation obtains in the case of Muslim preachers' interpretations of the Qur'an and hadith sources on marriage.

Islamic Orations on Marriage: A Brief Introduction

Homiletics has been associated with marriage since the origins of Islam. In fact, Muhammad followed the pre-Islamic Arabian custom whereby the marriage oration (*khuṭbat nikāḥ* or *khuṭbat zawāj*) fulfilled a specific socio-legal function as the verbal articulation of the marriage contract, and it continues to do so today (Pasha 2005; Qutbuddin 2008: 196–7, 2019: 378–82; Tarmanini 1989; Nasir 2009: 20–34; Ali 2010; Saleh 2010). If we compare the extant text of the *khuṭba* that the Prophet's uncle Abū Ṭālib reportedly delivered for Muhammad's marriage to Khadīja with subsequent *khuṭab* that the Prophet and other Muslim orators pronounced, the continuity of certain core elements becomes clear. In the pre-Islamic period and under Islam such *khuṭab* necessarily contained initial praises to the deity, identified the bride and groom, affirmed the volition of both parties to wed and specified the details of the dower (Qutbuddin 2008: 226). Yet Muhammad is credited with introducing other elements, notably, the profession of faith in the oneness of God and the prophethood and messengership of Muhammad, specific doxological formulas, prayers and the recitation of certain Qur'anic verses. Since these elements became part of the Prophet's sunna, they are commonly found in marriage *khuṭab* throughout the ages all over the Muslim world (compare with Ibn al-Murābiṭ 1992–3: Vol. 2, 650–6; Pasha 2005).

Yet as noted in the introduction to this chapter, the *khuṭbat nikāḥ* is not the only homiletic genre in which Muslim preachers discuss marriage and gendered spousal roles. These topics also appear in Friday *khuṭab* and in non-canonical hortatory preaching (*wa'ẓ/maw'iẓa*). As is well known, the Friday *khuṭba* is one of the prescriptive orations (*khuṭab shar'iyya*) that, like other Islamic rituals, must be delivered at specific times, for specific occasions and performed in a specific way (Wensinck 1999; Qutbuddin 2008; Jones 2012: 48–67). Orators usually discuss *taqwā* (piety, fear or consciousness of God), one of the prescriptive exhortations, in the main body of the sermon and address other relevant religious, social or political topics of their own choosing or at the behest of the congregation (Jones 2012: 52–8; Qutbuddin 2008: 198–210). Thus, the Friday preacher (*khaṭīb*) could address the topic of marriage within the framework of preaching on social issues affecting the community. In this respect, in both pre-modern and contemporary times the best Friday *khuṭba* is a dialogical, rather than strictly a top-down experience because a good preacher is aware of the social composition of his audience, attendant to their spiritual and practical needs and concerns, and adjusts his advice, instructions, rhetoric, exemplary stories and exhortations accordingly.

As for the homiletic exhortation (*waʿẓ*) or hortatory sermon (*mawʿiẓa*), this genre of non-canonical preaching was practised in a variety of contexts. Eyewitness accounts from pre-modern Muslim jurists, biographers, travellers and other preachers attest that these preachers, known in Arabic as *wuʿʿāẓ* (sing. *wāʿiẓ*), delivered their sermons in preaching assemblies called *majālis al-waʿẓ*. These assemblies could take place in any space deemed appropriate for the religious instruction and edification of the general populace – a congregational or private mosque, a designated public square, the courtyard of the ruler's palace or an individual's home. Topics varied widely, but typically included Muslim eschatology, ethics and morality (Berkey 2001; Jones 2012: 158–92). Some ʿulamaʾ criticised these so-called 'popular preachers' for their insufficient religious knowledge or performative histrionics (Berkey 2001; Swartz 1986). Yet many *wuʿʿāẓ* were scholarly elites who were trained in Islamic jurisprudence, Qurʾanic exegesis, hadith transmission or Sufism. Some even preached both extra-canonical hortatory and liturgical sermons (Jones 2012: 218–25). Not surprisingly, social concerns regarding the legitimacy of hortatory preaching reverberated in divergent customs and juridical opinions concerning the propriety of women's attendance of these sermons. Significantly for the present chapter, evidence from late medieval Egyptian sources indicates that women indeed attended these sessions (Ibn al-Ḥājj 1981: Vol. 2, 13–16). Moreover, there are medieval Arabic biographical notices of female hortatory preachers (*wāʿiẓāt*) operating in al-Andalus, the Maghrib, Egypt, Iraq and Mecca, among other places, where they usually – but not always – preached before all-female audiences (Ibn al-Ḥājj 1981: Vol. 2, 13–16; Jones 2012: 226–30).

While there is some continuity in the homiletic themes, recurring

Qurʾanic verses, hadith narratives and rhetorical strategies concerning marriage across the sub-genres, these are by no means homogenous or static. In his study of thirteenth-century marriage sermons from Latin Christendom, medievalist David d'Avray discovered that marriage symbolism reflects the varied and changing historical circumstances, values and attitudes of a given society. He found that the composition of the target audience also determined the reception and function of a given theme. Accordingly, sermons on a particular theme took on different meanings in distinct audiences (Cistercian monks versus the laity) (d'Avray 2001).

We can expect to encounter variations and transformations in Islamic homiletic discourses about marriage as well. Islamic societies and cultures are no less diverse than their Christian counterparts. For one thing, there were multiple types of marital arrangements in Sunni and Shiʿi Islam (Nasir 2009: 20–8; Sindawi 2013), which would account for variations in the legal aspects of the marriage *khuṭba*. Moreover, Islamic preaching on marriage and spousal relations does not exist in a vacuum. It is not immune from historical and cultural phenomena, such as misogyny, Islamophobia, the rise of Islamic feminism or the emergence of self-styled progressive Islamic communities. The tasks of reinterpreting and contextualising the Qurʾan and the hadith in the pursuit of gender justice began with scholar activists such as Fatima Mernissi (1987) and continues with Kecia Ali (2010), Nimat Barazangi (2013), Nighat Saleem (2014) and Carmen del Río Pereda (2016), among many others. Much of their attention has focused on exposing and challenging the interpretations of scripture, hadiths and reports about the pious ancestors (*salaf*) that traditionally have been deployed to denigrate women. Many of these disputed verses and reports appear in Islamic sermons on marriage and marital relations, giving rise to diverse homiletic discourses that range from fetishising a hierarchical dominant husband–subservient wife relationship to idealising marital relations based on equality, reciprocity and love. As we shall see in this chapter, both discourses exist in the Islamic homiletic tradition. Hence, we must acknowledge the existence of discursive and thematic diversity in Muslim homiletics focused on marriage and spousal relations and attempt to explain the prevalence of certain themes, symbols or discourses over others according to the relevant factors – historical, social and religious contexts, homiletic genre, target audience, and so forth.

As a contribution to this endeavour, this chapter analyses two case studies of Islamic homiletic discourses about marriage and marital relations in a pre-modern *maw ʿiẓa* and a contemporary Friday *khuṭba*. The pre-modern source is an anonymous sixteenth-century *maw ʿiẓa* on 'the inalienable rights of the two spouses (*ḥuqūq al-zawjayn*)' (BnP, Ms. Arabe 1248, fols 300v–306v). This sermon belongs to an unedited manuscript of hortatory sermons (Ms. Arabe 1248 of the Bibliothèque nationale de Paris) titled, *Ḥuqūq ikhwat al-Islām* ('The reciprocal inalienable rights of brothers and sisters of Islam') (BnP, Ms. Arabe 1248, fols 286v–329v). The contemporary source is a Friday *khuṭba* posted online on the website of an American Muslim organisation, the Islamic Center of Southern California. I will discuss the *khuṭba* titled, 'The Path to a Healthy Marriage', which Imam Hassan Zeenni preached on 1 April 2016 (icsconline 2012).

Case Study 1: The Manly Reputation (*Muruwwa*), Hyper-masculinity and Fragile Masculinity

This anonymous hortatory sermon is preserved in an unedited manuscript of Arabic homilies from Cairo and is dated 922/1516, a year before the Ottoman conquest of Egypt from the Mamluks (Hess 1973: 55–76). The original cataloguer of the manuscript attributed the sermonary to the Egyptian Shafiʿi scholar, jurist and Sufi ʿAbd al-Wahhāb al-Shaʿrānī (d. 973/1565) (Winter 1982, 1996; Geoffroy 1995). Yet the text's early date (1516) makes it improbable that al-Shaʿrānī could have composed it at such a young age (Vajda and Sauvan 1985: 122–3). Still, the anonymous preacher of these hortatory sermons must have a cultural profile (Sufi, Sunni scholar and jurist) and literary style sufficiently similar for the mistaken identity to have occurred in the first place. Hence, I shall refer to the author interchangeably as Pseudo-al-Shaʿrānī or 'the anonymous preacher' and assume that he composed (and delivered) his homilies in a milieu similar to that in which the real al-Shaʿrānī operated. The milieu in question is late Mamluk Egypt within the context of what scholars have called the 'popularisation' of Islamic piety (Hofer 2015; Shoshan 1993, 2006; Berkey 2000, 2001). Many popular religious movements coincided with the emergence of Sufi orders such as the Shādhiliyya and the Shaʿrāwiyya (named after its founder al-Shaʿrānī). Charismatic preachers from these shariʿa-minded confraternities spread their teachings and ethical values to all strata of society (Mojaddedi 2003). They often invited the public to attend their lessons (sing. *dars*), sessions of hadith narration, ritual ceremonies invoking God (*dhikr* and *samāʿ*), as well as their liturgical and hortatory sermons (Berkey 2001; Shoshan 2006; Jones 2012).

Pseudo-al-Shaʿrānī's homilies on the 'inalienable rights' governing relations between Muslims fit the paradigm of the preacher-scholar and/or jurist engaged in ethico-religious preaching aimed at a general mixed audience. The preacher employed simple vocabulary, eschewed rhymed prose or other sophisticated rhetorical embellishments, and relied extensively upon hadiths – with minimal source attribution – and copious use of narratives to convey his message. Many of these reports feature or were transmitted by women, which strongly suggests a mixed-gender audience. The prologue of the sermon reveals that Pseudo-al-Shaʿrānī envisaged two categories of social relationships. The first category exemplifies relations between social equals or in which power relations are balanced: 'the friend with the friend (*al-ṣadīq maʿā al-ṣadīq*), the loved one with the loved one (*al-ḥabīb maʿā al-ḥabīb*), the boon companion with the boon companion (*al-khalīl maʿā al-khalīl*)', among others. The second class consisted of hierarchical relations: the master with the disciple, the ruler (amir) and the subject, the rich man and the poor man, one of the spouses over the other (*wāḥid al-zawjayn maʿā al-ākhar*), the master with the slave (*al-sayyid maʿā al-mamlūk*), and so forth (BnP Ms. Arabe 1248, fol. 300v).

In each of these hierarchical relationships, Pseudo-al-Shaʿrānī privileged the more powerful partner by naming them first. He employed the gender-neutral term *zawj* (spouse/mate) yet asserted the husband's uncontested authority over the wife. Although he purported to discuss the rights, obligations and claims that each spouse may make upon the other, he focused almost exclusively on the duties and responsibilities that the wife owes the husband. He set the tone by opening with a bold authoritative declaration:

> Marriage is a form of enslavement (*al-nikāḥ nawʿatu raqqin*). And the wife who is his possession owes her husband absolute exclusive obedience (*wa-man raqīqati-hi fa-ʿalay-hā ṭāʿatu l-zawj muṭlaqan*) in everything that he asks of her, as long as it does not contradict God's will. (BnP Ms. Arabe 1248, fol. 300v)

There was nothing controversial about this conception of marriage. Early Hanafi, Maliki and Shafiʿi jurists habitually drew analogies between marriage and the ownership of slaves or property to conceptualise marriage in terms of the husband's dominion and the wife's servitude (Ali 2010). Al-Ghazzālī stated this in introducing his 'examination of the husband's rights' in his chapter on marriage in *The Revival of the Religious Sciences* (al-Ghazzālī 1984: 120). Pseudo-al-Shaʿrānī quoted al-Ghazzālī extensively although he did not cite him by name.

The preacher/al-Ghazzālī announced that: 'There are many reports (*akhbār kathīra*) that magnify the rights of the husband.' He narrated some of them in the same order as they appear in *The Revival* (BnP Ms. Arabe 1248, fol. 300v; al-Ghazzālī 1984: 1).[2] The reports feature the Prophet and other exemplary figures from the *salaf* who corroborate this conception of marriage and marital relations. I have identified three salient themes. First, the preacher sanctified the dominant husband–submissive wife dynamic and idealised the figure of the obedient wife. According to Pseudo-al-Shaʿrānī, '[Muhammad] said: "If I were to have commanded anyone to prostrate themselves to anyone else I would have commanded the wife to prostrate before her husband" due to the magnitude of his rights over her' (BnP Ms. Arabe 1248, fol. 300v; al-Ghazzālī 1984: 121). The preacher provided no further commentary on this hadith even though certain versions are considered weak (*ḍaʿīf*) and others sound (*ḥasan*) (Ibn Mājah: Vol. 3, Book 9, nos 1852 and 1853, respectively). He went on to cite a succession of hadiths in the same order as they appear in *The Revival*, consecrating the dominant husband–submissive wife relationship and conjoining wifely obedience to women's other obligatory acts of worship: 'If a woman dies while her husband is satisfied with her, she will enter Paradise.'

> The Prophet said, 'If the wife performs her five ritual prayers, fasts the month of Ramadan, and guards her private parts she will enter the paradise of her Lord.' And [Muhammad] added the obedience of the husband to the exigencies of submission to God and the foundations upon which Islam was built (*mabānī l-Islām*). (BnP Ms. Arabe 1248, fol. 300v; al-Ghazzālī 1984: 120)

Another hadith warned that the wife who performs acts of devotion, such as voluntary fasting, without her husband's permission would not receive a heavenly reward (BnP Ms. Arabe 1248, fol. 300v). Such reports elevate the wife's submission to her husband from the mundane legal plane to the realm of eschatology. The wife's salvation literally depends upon her obedience to and satisfaction of her husband's will. The preacher (and al-Ghazzālī) repeatedly invoked prophetic rather than Qur'anic authority to subordinate the wife's other acts of worship and deeds to her obedience to her husband.

The second set of narratives exhorts the wife to 'place the rights of [her husband] over her own rights and those of the rest of her relatives' (BnP Ms. Arabe 1248, fol. 301v). Here Pseudo-al-Shaʿrānī narrated a story featuring Muhammad and an anonymous woman whose husband had to travel abroad. The husband made the wife promise that she would not descend from the top floor of the house to the bottom while he was away. One day the woman's father came to the house, so the woman sent a message to the Prophet asking permission to go downstairs. The Prophet responded, 'Obey your husband.' Subsequently the woman's father died, and she asked permission from the Prophet to come downstairs to attend the funeral, but he responded the same. After the father's burial, Muhammad sent a message to the woman informing her that God had forgiven all the sins of her father 'due to the obedience of his daughter' (BnP Ms. Arabe 1248, fol. 300v; al-Ghazzālī 1984: 121). The wife's recompense for not fulfilling her duties as a daughter by visiting her sick father was to become an instrument of his posthumous eschatological salvation.

Kecia Ali has demonstrated that husbands often attempted to ensure an exclusive claim over the sexuality of their wives by controlling their mobility (Ali 2010: 71–3). Pseudo-al-Shaʿrānī exhibited similar concerns judging from the numerous hadiths and anecdotes he narrated warning that a wife must never leave the house without her husband's permission, as well as his directives restricting the movement of the wife who has been granted permission by her husband to leave the home. Among other things, she must cover her face and body so that no man could recognise her by her shape or the sound of her voice. She should avoid walking in the streets or the markets 'where the Devil roams'. Moreover, she should only go out for a specific essential purpose, not simply to look around or for any frivolous matter 'because this violates the manly reputation (*muruwwa*) [of her husband]' (BnP Ms. Arabe 1248, fol. 303v; al-Ghazzālī 1984: 101). Al-Ghazzālī's version does not include the comment about the husband's *muruwwa*, which suggests that the fragility of the husband's manly reputation particularly worried Pseudo-al-Shaʿrānī. The anonymous preacher's attitude in this regard could also reflect urban Egyptian social norms that recognised the need of working women to go out in public for work-related purposes but restricted this permission to unmarried women who did not have marital support (Rapoport 2007: 24). The third narrative strategy Pseudo-al-Shaʿrānī applied consisted of deploying female voices and invoking female authority to reinforce the dominant husband–submissive wife dynamic. Towards this end, he quoted several hadiths transmitted on the authority of ʿAʾisha bt. Abī Bakr; as she was Muhammad's favourite wife, she spent more time with him and transmitted more hadiths than any of the other wives. Of particular relevance is a hadith the preacher narrated to validate the aforementioned exigency that a wife must not leave the home without the husband's permission. ʿAʾisha declared, 'If the Prophet knew what innovations the women have introduced (in their way of life) he would definitely have prevented them from going out at all' (BnP Ms. Arabe 1248, fol. 303r; al-Ghazzālī 1984:). The preacher has altered this saying to make it more restrictive. In the established Sunni versions of this hadith, ʿAʾisha indicated that the Prophet would have prevented women from going to the mosque as the Israelites had prohibited women from entering the temple, had he been aware of their misconduct there (Malik: Book 14.6, nos 12–15; Abū Dawūd: Book 2, 569; Muslim: 445a [= Book 4, no. 895]; al-Bukhārī: 869 [= vol. 1, Book 12, no. 828], et alia). In its original context, the saying is conditional and relates this hypothetical restriction placed on women's movement to the specific circumstances of their misconduct in the mosque. Yet Pseudo-al-Shaʿrānī, following al-Ghazzālī, presented it as a global prohibition on women going out in public. More to the point, the preacher eluded any mention of the numerous sound hadiths to the contrary, transmitted by ʿAʾisha and others, which affirm that the Prophet explicitly instructed men not to prevent women from going out to the mosque (for example, Muslim, 4: 442a; al-Bukhārī, 67: 5238; Muslim, 4: 442 a and c; and Bukhārī, 11: 899; Saleem 2014:160). Moreover, other hadiths depict women attending the congregational mosque for canonical and supererogatory prayers and show Muhammad conversing with women inside the mosque, not only his wives but also non-*maḥram* women (Saleem 2014: 127–70).

ʿAʾisha was not the only famous woman whom the preacher cited as an authority in reaffirming the husband's dominion over the wife. He reproduced a speech attributed to Asmāʾ bt. Khārijah, one of the first generation of Muslim women, which reports the advice she gave to her daughter when she got married. She advised her on how to create a relationship of mutual respect and support: 'Be an earth for him and he will be your sky. Be a resting place for him and he will be your pillar. Be his bondmaid and he will be your slave.' The relationship of reciprocity described here tempers previous images of the all-powerful husband. Yet her subsequent counsel evinces the fundamental imbalance of power in favour of the husband:

> Do not make excessive demands, for he will then desert you. Do not become too distant from him for he will then forget you. Should he draw near, then draw close to him; should he become distant, stay away from him. Shield his nose, ears, and eyes so he will smell nothing from you but that which is sweet, hear nothing but that which is good, and look at nothing but that which is beautiful. (BnP Ms. Arabe 1248, fol. 303v; al-Ghazzālī 1984: 123)

Asmāʾ's maternal advice for remaining in the good graces of the husband highlights her daughter's vulnerability and weaker position vis-à-vis her spouse.

Pseudo-al-Shaʿrānī's anecdotes generally follow al-Ghazzālī's discussion of the husband's rights. Yet he largely ignored the lengthy section al-Ghazzālī devoted to explaining the husband's obligations vis-à-vis his wives (al-Ghazzālī 1984: 93–9). He also minimised Qurʾanic references to women's rights. For instance, he mentioned that God spoke of 'the magnitude of the right of wives when He said, "and they (f.) have taken from you (m. pl.) a firm and strong covenant (*wa-akhadhna min-kum mīthāqan ghalīẓan*)"' (Q. 4:21);[3] however, he did not elaborate on the significance of the verse. (This attitude contrasts with that of the preacher in the second case study who, as we shall see, singled out this verse as a proof text for taking marriage seriously and working to build a relationship that is mutually satisfying for both spouses.) A number of Qurʾanic commentators agree that Q. 4:21 admonishes husbands contemplating divorce or marrying another wife against repossessing the current wife's dowry if they have consummated the marriage. In so doing, they would abrogate the 'firm', 'solemn', 'inviolable' pledge they gave to treat their wives with goodness, honour and respect (Ibn al-ʿAbbās/al-Firūzabādī 2007: 86; al-Qushayrī 2017: 389; al-Maḥallī and al-Suyūṭī 2007: 88).

To be fair, al-Ghazzālī also cited this verse without further comment; however, he placed it within an extended discussion on 'the obligations incumbent upon the husband', which is in line with the interpretations of the aforementioned Qurʾanic commentators. Among other things, al-Ghazzālī urged husbands to 'tolerate the bad manners' of their wives, 'to consort with them in kindness' (Q. 4:19) and to emulate the Prophet's 'forbearance and kindness' in the face of his wives' anger (al-Ghazzālī 1984: 94). By contrast, Pseudo-al-Shaʿrānī simply went on to recite Q. 4:34, which allows men to admonish, sexually abandon or strike women who commit *nushūz* (misconduct) against their husbands, and then he cited several reports validating the use of physical violence against wives.

Elsewhere Pseudo-al-Shaʿrānī returned once more to al-Ghazzālī's comments on the husband's obligations toward the wife – again without acknowledging him explicitly – when he spoke of reciprocity in spousal relations and encouraged mercy and patience towards wives. For instance, he quoted the prophetic hadith:

> Whatever man shows patience towards the misconduct (*sūʾ khalq*) of his wife, God will grant him a recompense like that he granted to Job for his tribulations. And whatever wife shows patience toward the misconduct of her husband, God will grant her a reward like that he gave to Āsiya the wife of Pharaoh. (BnP Ms. Arabe 1248, fol. 302r; al-Ghazzālī 1984: 94)

He quoted another hadith extolling the Prophet as the perfect man because he was

> the most compassionate of men towards his wives and womenfolk. No one surpassed him in his penchant for joking, teasing and playing with his wives, for this is what delights the hearts of women. The Prophet joked with his wives and came down to their level of their intellect.

He also cited Muhammad's saying, 'The best of you are the men who treat their wives the best. And I am the best of you in the treatment of my wives' (BnP Ms. Arabe 1248, fol. 302r–302v). Yet rather than elaborate on these themes, he reprised the motif of the husband's rights over his wife, declaring,

'It is a man's right to be followed, not to be a follower (*ḥaqq al-rajul an yakūna matbūʿan lā tābiʿan*)' (BnP Ms. Arabe 1248, fol. 302v; al-Ghazzālī 1984: 97). The remainder of the homily refocused attention on the husband's rights, control and prerogatives over his wife.

To sum up so far, Pseudo-al-Shaʿrānī delivered a hortatory sermon that drew primarily from hadith sources, mostly cited in al-Ghazzālī's *The Revival of the Religious Sciences*, and to a lesser extent from the Qurʾan. Although he purported to speak about the mutual rights of each spouse, in fact he focused his sermon on presenting a traditional paradigm of marriage that places the husband in a position of domination and ownership over his wife, who owes him 'absolute obedience'. He skilfully exploited the 'broad exegetical space' and rhetorical liberties, characteristic of the hortatory preaching assembly (*majlis al-waʿẓ*), which allowed him to reinterpret and make selective use of his sources to achieve his homiletic goals. This is apparent in the way he glossed over certain Qurʾanic verses (Q. 4:21), reinterpreted certain hadiths (for example, ʿAʾisha's saying about prohibiting women's access to the mosques) and suppressed or restructured al-Ghazzālī's anecdotes, all of which acknowledged the rights of the wife. Pseudo-al-Shaʿrānī's homiletic message, selected use of sources and rhetorical techniques are consistent with the descriptions of hortatory assemblies delivered before popular mixed audiences (*al-ʿāmma*). It is reasonable to suppose that the principal target audience of mostly male and female urban poor, and 'working class' artisans, shopkeepers and labourers would not have received the kind of higher education in the Islamic sciences that would have equipped them to challenge Pseudo-al-Shaʿrānī's interpretation of the Qurʾanic verses, hadith narratives and anecdotes he presented.

Pseudo-al-Shaʿrānī's general vision of the husband's hegemony over the wife was normative for his time. Yet the comparison with al-Ghazzālī's text shows that the anonymous preacher preferred the most expansive interpretation of the husband's domination. For this reason, Pseudo-al-Shaʿrānī's sermon exemplifies the kind of source manipulation that modern feminists such as Fatima Mernissi, Kecia Ali and so many others have criticised the ʿulamaʾ of committing in order to perpetuate and justify patriarchal attitudes and practices that, they would argue, are not as present in the Qurʾan. The second case study of a contemporary liturgical sermon invites intriguing comparisons precisely because the preacher and his audience espouse a worldview shaped by feminist sensibilities. Although their visions of marriage and the ideal spousal relationship are extremely disparate, the two sermons exhibit parallels in the preachers' selection of Qur'anic verses and hadith narratives, the processes of interpreting their sources and the deployment of carefully selected anecdotes and reports to achieve their homiletic goals.

Case Study 2: A Contemporary Friday *Khuṭba* on 'The Path to a Healthy Marriage'

The second text to be analysed is a Friday liturgical sermon on the subject of 'the path to a healthy marriage', which Hassan Zeenni, the imam of Islamic Center of Southern California (ICSC), delivered on 1 April 2016.[4] Located in Los Angeles, the ICSC is one of thousands of Islamic centres catering to the needs of the Muslim communities across the US. According to Abdelhamid Lotfi's typology of Muslim spaces in the US, the ICSC fits the paradigm of the 'Islamic centre', so-called because of its 'programmatic use of space involving a number of activities, both sacred and mundane, such as an Islamic school on Sundays, conferences, bookshops and kitchens'. While a few of these structures are purpose-built mosques, most are of the 'storefront mosque' variety. This means that they are 'owned by associations or individuals' who typically lease space in a pre-existing structure (an abandoned church, movie theatre, commercial building, and so on) and adapt it for Muslim liturgical and cultural uses by introducing elements such as a mihrab, a minbar or a modest minaret (Lotfi 2001: 240). The ICSC's website includes a history of the Center, which states that it originated in the mid-1960's as the initiative of 'a group of guys who wanted to get together to pray'. By the end of the decade, the ICSC was able to purchase a building 'from members of the Jewish community, which also used the building for their congregation meetings'. In 1976, the ICSC sold that building and purchased its present location, a building that had housed an insurance company.

The founding and evolution of the ICSC coincided with a period of intense growth of Muslim communities in the US and the concomitant emergence of prominent Muslim leaders eager to 'construct a modern universal Islamic culture that is not only relevant, but also appealing in the American environment' (Yazbeck Haddad 2004: 37). American Muslim spokespersons such as Ismail Raji al-Faruqi, Fathi Osman and Maher Hathout (the latter of whom was president of the ICSC until 2018) inspired Muslims to adopt positive American practices and participate in American society. Likewise, they urged Muslims to avoid defensive attitudes of 'retrenchment' and victimisation and make more of an effort to reach out and engage in inter-religious dialogue. Gender considerations also played a role in fashioning modern socially engaged American Muslims. For instance, al-Faruqi advocated adopting the African American tradition of 'mak[ing] the mosque a family-centered place, where women attended and participated in mosque services' (Yazbeck Haddad 2004: 37–8).

The ICSC website projects an image of openness, tolerance, diversity, modernity and gender equality. It achieves this by posting dynamic images of Muslim men and women of all ages interacting, recordings of Friday sermons in English and its policy statements on the Center's mission and approach to Islam. The mission statement emphasises its aim to create an 'American Muslim identity' that transcends the particularisms of cultural, ethnic and geographic origins. The ICSC encourages its members to self-identify as 'American Muslims', rather than as members of 'a particular ethnic group, color, or tribe', and it expressly forbids 'exclusionary activities' in the Center.[5] Of particular relevance are points six and seven of the ICSC's 'approach to Islam', which address the subject of gender:

> Men and women are equally encouraged to participate in the activities of the Center and equally responsible for their efforts. The Center does not believe in segregation of the sexes to attain righteousness. Rather, righteousness is attained through modesty, decency, purity of heart, clarity of conscience, and the observance of the dictates of God and His apostle.

This dialogical spirit and responsiveness to the needs, mission, zeitgeist and gender values of the Islamic Center of Southern California inform the Friday *khuṭab* posted on the Center's website.[6] Several of these *khuṭab* indicate that the topics of women and gender have served as a means of reflecting upon societal, political or ethical issues. Some sermons connect the mission of promoting gender equality to the need to refute negative images of Islam stemming from the misogynist terror tactics of Islamic State and Boko Haram, which have been used to inflame hostile images of Islam and Muslims.[7]

Most of Hassan Zeenni's sermons posted on the ICSC website address gender-neutral topics on spirituality, scriptural exegesis, ethics or sociopolitical problems affecting the entire community. However, he delivered a Friday *khuṭba* on 28 March 2014 titled 'Are Men and Women Equal in Islam?', and on 25 September 2015, he preached on 'Making Progress towards Equality'. These precedents help us contextualise and interpret his *khuṭba* on 'The Path to a Healthy Marriage'. In this sermon, he used three rhetorical devices to apply the ICSC's principles of gender equality to this Friday sermon. First, he immediately established complicity between himself and the audience. Second, he recited and commented upon Qur'anic chapters that portray marriage in a positive light. Third, he embellished the Qur'anic concepts with narratives about the exemplary marriages and spousal relations featuring the Prophet and prominent heroes of the *salaf*.

Zeenni began by announcing that someone from the congregation had requested him to deliver a sermon on this topic and he acknowledged that 'in the last few years this institution has been within our community under tremendous pressure'. By framing the *khuṭba* in this way, Zeenni demonstrated responsiveness to the community's concerns and awareness of the challenges implicit in sustaining marriage as an institution in modern societies. Such preliminary remarks serve as rhetorical devices to establish a positive rapport with the audience by showing that he understands the difficulties of making a marriage work.

He then recited from verse twenty-one of Sūrat al-Nisā' to impress upon his audience the weightiness of marriage as an institution: 'while you have gone into one another and they (f.) have taken from you (m. pl.) a firm and strong covenant (*wa-qad afḍā ba'ḍu-kum ilā ba'ḍin wa-akhadhna min-kum mīthāqan ghalīẓan*)'. It bears recalling from the analysis of the first sermon case study that Pseudo-al-Sha'rānī also cited this very same verse; however, he refrained from further commentary in order to avoid addressing the gender implications of acknowledging the rights and honour husbands owe their wives. Zeenni adopted the opposite approach of making this verse the proof text of his central message about the gravity of marriage as an institution. Where Pseudo-al-Sha'rānī employed understatement by glossing over the significance of this verse, Zeenni deployed hyperbole by claiming that 'the only time in the Qur'an, in the entire Qur'an that Allah *subḥāna* speaks to us the believers' is to speak about the 'strong and firm commitment (*mīthāqan ghalīẓan*)' of marriage. It suffices to read Sūrat al-Nisāʾ in its entirety to realise that Zeenni's claim is contradicted by the numerous verses in the Qurʾan in which God addresses the believers and uses the second person plural forms of speech. Here hyperbole serves Zeenni as an instrument of rhetorical effect, which he strengthened with the insertion of a subsequent accurate statement concerning the rare occurrence of the phrase '*mīthāqan ghalīẓan*' in the Qurʾan. For Zeenni, this concept is crucial because God uses the same expression only two other times in the Qurʾan (4:154 and 33:7, respectively) to enjoin Moses and then to enjoin Muhammad, Noah, Moses and Jesus, the son of Mary, to fulfil their prophetic missions with a 'strong firm pledge'. Employing analogical reasoning, Zeenni inferred 'that we equally should use and invest the same effort and the hard work' to make marriage work, thereby establishing a parallel between 'the hard work' of marriage and the 'weightiness' of the prophetic mission.

Thereupon he recited verse twenty-one of Sūrat al-Rūm (Q. 30:21):

> And among His signs is that He created for you from yourselves mates that you may find tranquillity in them; and He has instilled, engendered between you affection and mercy. Indeed, in that are signs for a people who give thought.

Zeenni first reiterated the emotional benefits of marriage as a source of tranquillity, mercy and loving affection between the couple, before connecting these positive aspects to the aforementioned idea of the weightiness and divine design of marriage as an institution. Since God portrays spousal relations as one of his 'signs and wonders', 'the institution of marriage is a gift; it has a purpose and is not to be taken lightly'. It is 'a wonder to be marvelled at, it is a gift, and should be taken seriously'. Here Zeenni used repetition, parallel structures and semantic parallels to emphasise his message.

Having established the underlying divine inspiration and solemnity of the marriage covenant and its affective benefits for the couple, Zeenni expounded his path to a happy marriage. For Zeenni, Q. 30:21 contains three conceptual pillars upon which a healthy marriage should be based: maintaining tranquillity (*sakīna*), nurturing the loving affection (*mawadda*) that God has instilled in the couple, and cultivating mercy (*raḥma*), 'the glue that keeps the marriage together'. Zeenni reiterated that marriage is an equal partnership in which both spouses have to work hard to maintain marital tranquillity, sustain loving affection, and show mercy and forgiveness towards each other, and that both spouses have the right to be happy and fulfilled in the marriage. To illustrate this, he narrated various anecdotes about the married life of the Prophet and the *salaf.* His first exemplum related how the venerable judge of Kufa al-Qāḍī Shurayḥ (d. 87/706) built and maintained tranquillity in his marriage. A friend had asked al-Qāḍī Shurayḥ what the secret of the success of his marriage was, and he replied that he had looked for a woman with similar interests to his and they got married. Then right after the wedding she stood up and said, '*bismillāh, ammā ba'd*'[8] (in the name of God, what comes after) and he said, 'Oh no, I've married a woman who likes to give speeches.' She continued,

> Look, I am a stranger to you and you are a stranger to me. I could have married somebody else and you could have married somebody else, but God Almighty chose for us to come together for this institution. So, you tell me what you like and don't like and I tell you what I like and don't like from the beginning.

Although Imam Zeenni did not mention al-Qāḍī Shurayḥ's wife by name, he presented her as a model for both spouses: 'We have to let each other know what is bothering us, what is on our mind, what we dislike', and he stressed 'the importance of communication to maintain tranquillity at home'. Framing the wife's speech as a *khuṭba*, by noting that she 'stood up and said, "*bismillāh, ammā ba'd*"', signals that she was not addressing her husband from a position of subservience or self-abnegation. Rather, she spoke from a position of equality by asserting her right to have her dislikes acknowledged and respected as well as those of her husband.

Another story illustrated that the Prophet maintained the *sakīna* in his marriage with 'A'isha by 'never bringing his external problems home'. Despite Muhammad's numerous responsibilities as a leader, prophet and judge, one day when he returned home, 'A'isha received him and immediately sought his attention by telling him a long story about which she wanted his opinion. Zeenni noted that in al-Bukhārī's version 'A'isha's story took up five pages and yet the Prophet patiently responded showing that he had listened attentively. The preacher interjected a personal anecdote for rhetorical effect, confessing that when he gets home and his wife and 'kids' want to talk to him, 'the only thing' he wants to do 'is to be left alone' and most of the time when they talk to him he 'tunes out' and is not listening. 'But not the Prophet. He listened … he did not bring the external negative load to the relation.'

Zeenni also narrated an anecdote about the famed jurist Ibn Ḥanbal (d. 241/855) and his wife of twenty years who had just died. First, Zeenni defended Ibn Ḥanbal's tears of grief as manly and appropriate given the circumstances, thus criticising the 'male chauvinistic society' of the time. He then quoted what Ibn Ḥanbal said about his wife, first in Arabic for veracity and dramatic emphasis, then in English:

> I lived with her for twenty years and she never disturbed the peace … because *idhā ghaḍibat ghaḍaytu-hā wa-idhā ghaḍibtu ghaḍat-ī*, when she gets angry I go and do whatever I can to make her happy and whenever I got angry, she did everything to make me happy.

For Zeenni this was an exemplary marriage because they dealt with their problems 'by being there for each other'. The lesson he emphasised was that 'whatever disturbs the peace, deal with it immediately'. The anecdote demonstrates the right of both spouses to get angry and the duty of both spouses to strive to make the other happy.

After instructing the congregation that the path to a healthy marriage must begin by 'preparing' and 'fertilising the soil' by establishing 'peace at home', the next step consisted of 'planting the seeds of love'. Couples should express love verbally, but 'because words can be cheap, actions are louder'. Once again, he drew from the hadiths about Muhammad and ʿAʾisha's marriage to demonstrate both kinds of love: ʿAʾisha once asked the Prophet, 'Do you love me?' He said, 'Yes, I do, and I love you like the knot in a rope.' Imam Zeenni used the image of how hard it is to untie a knot to warn that for love to become this 'tight' it has to be nurtured by actions. To demonstrate this, he mentioned the familiar anecdotes of how the Prophet 'dedicated a third of his time to serving his wives and the people he loved' and how 'he literally did housework to help and be there for his spouses'.

Imam Zeenni briefly addressed the third pillar of a healthy marriage, 'mercy, *raḥma*, the glue that cements the relationship on two fronts'. Here he resorted to direct inclusive speech, first warning that: 'We will not remain the same whether in health or financial conditions and this is where mercy comes.' A successful marriage requires 'our hearts to be filled with mercy' so that spouses can keep on embracing each other as they inevitably change with the passage of time. Second, he explained that *raḥma* is 'the door to forgiving one another' because 'no one can avoid making mistakes'. Zeenni concluded the *khuṭba* by quoting the same hadith that Pseudo-al-Shaʿrānī cited in his homily: 'The best of you are the men who treat their wives the best. And I am the best of you in the treatment of my wives.' In keeping with the general theme of this sermon's onus on gender equality, Zeenni reinterpreted this saying as a model for both spouses and, indeed, for all Muslims, while recalling his original theme of the weightiness of marriage. He told them just as you would 'bring your best' to playing a game, closing a business deal or any other important matter, so too must you imitate the Prophet and 'bring your best' when dealing with your marriage, spouse and family.

In order to appreciate the significance of Zeenni's comments on this hadith, it is necessary to consider briefly how previous ʿulamaʾ have interpreted it. Both the Sufi Abū Ṭālib al-Makkī (d. 386/996) and al-Ghazzālī, whom al-Makkī influenced, quoted and commented upon this saying within the context of discussing the proper etiquette of marital relations and specifically the best practices for husbands to follow in fulfilling the duty of providing financial support (*nafaqa*) for their wives (Immenkamp 1994: 104). Although Pseudo-al-Shaʿrānī probably cited this saying from al-Ghazzālī's *The Revival* rather than directly from the hadith collections (compare with Ibn Mājah: Vol. 3 Book 9, nos 1977 and 1978), he provided no further commentary. As noted, he quoted the saying within a chain of other hadiths relating how the Prophet enjoyed 'dallying with his own wives' and how Muhammad praised the heavenly rewards for exercising patience and restraint with one's wives. In other words, Pseudo-al-Shaʿrānī placed the onus on the affective, as opposed to the financial dimension of the best treatment of one's wife. It is also important to note that structurally, Pseudo-al-Shaʿrānī 'sandwiched' these sayings within two more extensively commented series of anecdotes that emphasised the husband's right to dominate his wife. Many of these reports featured warnings that the husband who 'becomes the slave of his wife' by failing to command her obedience, control her movement or simply by being too indulgent in fulfilling her wishes, would lose his manly reputation (*muruwwa*). Pseudo-al-Shaʿrānī's rhetorical treatment allows him to acknowledge these popular sayings about the Prophet's marriages while maintaining the audience's attention fixed on the paradigm of the domineering husband. By contrast, Zeenni made the message gender inclusive by reinterpreting the original message, 'the best of you are the men (*al-rijāl*) who treat their wives the best' as a general advice to both spouses to 'bring your best' to every aspect of their married life. Moreover, he magnified the importance of this message by placing it at the climactic end of the sermon, thereby according it a privileged place in his recipes for 'a healthy marriage'.

Conclusions: Continuities and Adaptations in Islamic Sermons on Marriage

The striking differences between Pseudo-al-Shaʿrānī's conception of marriage 'as a form of enslavement' in which the wife owes the husband unconditional obedience and Imam Zeenni's recipe for a healthy marriage as an equal partnership built upon mutual peace-making, affectionate love and mercy merely reflect their very different historical contexts, cultural zeitgeists and gender perspectives. Yet we must not allow these differences to obscure important similarities in their homiletic and rhetorical strategies or lose sight of the larger continuities within the Islamic homiletic tradition. The analysis of samples of Muslim homiletics from contexts that are worlds apart – early modern Cairo and twenty-first century California – illuminates the extent to which both preachers made conscious ideological choices about which visions to promote regarding marriage, spousal relations and gender identities. Both preachers had access to the same canonical sources and quoted some of the same Qurʾanic verses (4:21) and hadiths, yet they used these sources in different ways and for different ends. Pseudo-al-Shaʿrānī based his sermon on the 'mutual rights of spouses' on al-Ghazzālī's notion of 'marriage as a form of enslavement' and relied overwhelmingly on hadiths and reports about the companions and the *salaf* – including many women – to promote an androcentric patriarchal view of spousal relations. This anonymous preacher consciously chose to ignore or gloss over Qurʾanic verses, hadiths and reports that portray greater reciprocity between spouses, that give due weight to the wife's rights or that recognise women's autonomy in their religious obligations. These choices align with his classification of the married couple among the hierarchical relationships, analogous to the master and slave or the ruler and subject, wherein one person dominates the other by divine design. Pseudo-al-Shaʿrānī's sermons echo the social and gender conventions of a highly stratified society. Slaves obviously occupied the lowest rungs of society, followed by semi-professional beggars, the working poor and 'those engaged in the lowly trades (*ahl al-hiraf al-safila*)', merchants and artisans, the mercantile bourgeoisie, prominent shaykhs, members of the ʿulamaʾ and Sufis, and the military and political ruling class (Winter 1992; rpt. 2005: 238–41). Independent of their social class, married women were subjected by law to obey the authority of their husbands; however, an against-the-grain reading of Pseudo-al-Shaʿrānī's obsession with the dangers of disobedient wives hints at the fragility of the image of absolute husbandly hegemony.[9] In this sense, the anonymous preacher's thematic and rhetorical choices served the homiletic project of attempting to rectify and restore the proper social and gender orders.

Imam Zeenni also made strategic ideological and rhetorical choices to promote his vision of marriage based on gender equality, reciprocal rights to happiness, serenity and mutual love and mercy. The foremost of these choices was to base his Friday *khuṭba* on two Qurʾanic verses (4:21 and 30:21) that depict marriage as a 'strong firm covenant' that must be taken seriously and emphasise the spiritual and emotional benefits for the couple, and to complement the verses with edifying anecdotes about Muhammad, the pious forefathers and their wives. As noted, Pseudo-al-Shaʿrānī mentioned in passing Q. 4:21 but Zeenni made it the centrepiece of his *khuṭba*. While Qurʾanic recitation is one of the prescriptive liturgical conditions of the Friday *khuṭba*, the privileging of the Qurʾan serves other purposes. For Zeenni, it provides definitive scriptural proof that progressive values of gender equality and marital couplehood founded on reciprocal love and mercy, rather than solely on legalistic rights and obligations, are intrinsic to Islam. Privileging Qurʾanic authority in sermons addressed to general audiences appeases certain progressives and feminists who attribute Islamic misogynist or patriarchal attitudes to an overreliance upon hadiths and other fallible human sources. Perhaps for this reason, Zeenni strategically selected reports about the Prophet and about Ibn Ḥanbal and al-Qāḍī Shurayḥ, two pious *salaf* particularly revered by conservatives, which challenged the images of the hegemonic domineering husband. Muhammad is 'the best of men' because he treated his wives the best: he listened attentively to them, helped them with the chores and satisfied them sexually. Ibn Ḥanbal, al-Qāḍī Shurayḥ and their respective wives emerge as exemplars of marriages built upon mutual love, trust and open communication. But in constructing these idyllic images of marriage for his American Muslim audience, Zeenni had to suppress other inconvenient narratives about polygamy or domestic violence – according to one report, al-Qāḍī Shurayḥ beat his wife, although he later repented (Ibn Khallikān 1842: Vol. 1, 621).

Finally, Pseudo-al-Shaʿrānī and Imam Zeenni demonstrate the power of homiletic narratives in modelling gender scripts (Gagnon and Simon 1973). As we have seen, Pseudo-al-Shaʿrānī deployed the sayings of Muhammad, his wives and the male and female *salaf* to perpetuate the scripts of hegemonic masculinity and female subjugation. Challenges to the divinely defined hierarchical order of spousal relations had clear gender implications. The husband who cannot control his wife's sexuality and mobility and who fails to impose his 'right to be followed, not to be a follower' loses his *muruwwa*. He is socially emasculated, which exposes the fundamental fragility of hypermasculinity. For his part, Zeenni narrated reports about masculine heroes (Muhammad, Ibn Ḥanbal and al-Qāḍī Shurayḥ) in dialogue with their wives in order to challenge male chauvinism and subvert the traditional gender script that defines masculinity as domination over women. Instead, he fostered gender equality and promoted a gender script that portrays the wife as an empowered agent co-responsible with her husband for making marriage work. In both cases, and despite their enormous differences, Islamic preaching plays a fundamental role in articulating, perpetuating and transforming societal ideals about marriage, spousal relations and gender relations more generally. Indeed, we could say that Muslim preachers were in a privileged position to fulfil this mission because of the prestige of the *khuṭba* and, to a lesser extent, the hortatory preaching assembly, as institutions that reproduce and routinise the charismatic authority of the Prophet. Moreover, preachers speaking before the mass public typically possessed greater knowledge of the Qurʾan, the hadith and reports about the pious ancestors than most members of their audience did. This scholarly advantage, combined with a charismatic preacher's rhetorical skills, enabled both preachers to present and interpret traditional Qur᾽anic, hadith and other sources in the manner most suitable to their vision of marriage and gender relations, whether to justify patriarchy or to foster greater gender and spousal equality. In sum, Islamic preaching as a practice represents and derives its authority from continuity with tradition. Yet it is this very 'perspective of continuity' that endows the preacher with the legitimacy to reinterpret his sources and adapt his message to the novel conditions, exigencies and challenges affecting his congregation.

Notes

1. Research for the original conference paper and this revised chapter was undertaken within the framework of the Spanish government-funded research projects, nos FFI2015-63659-C2-2-P, MINECO/FEDER, UE (2016–19) and PGC2018-093472-B-C32, MICINN/FEDER, UE (2019–22). The author wishes to thank Dr Elisabeth Özdalga and Dr Simon Stjernholm for their invitation to contribute to this volume and for their comments on an earlier draft of this chapter.
2. Where Pseudo-al-Shaʿrānī appears to have quoted al-Ghazzālī's text verbatim I utilise Madelain Farah's English translation.
3. The term, *mīthāq*, is usually translated as covenant, pledge or commitment. I use these translations interchangeably in the text to avoid redundancy.
4. Available at <http://www.icsconline.org/media/khutbas/ThePathToAHealthyMarriage.mp3> (last accessed 22 October 2019).
5. 'Who we are', available at <http://www.islamiccenter.com/about/who-we-are/> (last accessed 22 October 2019).
6. 'Friday Khutbas', available at <http://www.icsconline.org/2012-08-18-20-36-22/fridaykhutbas> (last accessed 22 October 2019).
7. In addition to the sermon studied here, an illustrative example is Tarek Shawky's sermon 'Women as the Cornerstone of Islam', delivered on 2 October 2015 and available at <http://www.icsconline.org/media/khutbas/WomenAsTheCornerstoneofIslam.mp3> (last accessed 22 October 2019).
8. The expression *ammā baʿd* was reportedly used by the Prophet Muhammad as a transition to starting a *khuṭba*, and has been incorporated in later Muslim ritual tradition as well.
9. This is borne out in the late Mamluk biographical and juridical sources, which record incidents of female adultery, greater female autonomy in choosing their

spouses, in curtailing the husband's right to take another wife and in initiating divorce. The sources also evince the husband's accumulation of the debts owed to the wife as part of the marital support in accordance with her social position (Rapoport 2007: 26–37).

Bibliography

Abū Dawūd ibn Sulaymān al-Ash'ath, *Sunan Abī Dawūd*, <https://sunnah.com/abudawud> (last accessed 5 February 2020).

Ali, Kecia (2010), *Marriage and Slavery in Islam*, Cambridge, MA: Harvard University Press.

'Ḥuqūq ikhwat al-Islām', Bibliothèque nationale de Paris, Ms. Arabe 1248, fols 286v–329v.

d'Avray, David (2001), *Medieval Marriage Sermons: Mass Communication in a Culture without Print*, Oxford: Oxford University Press.

Barazangi, Nimat H. (2013), 'Why Muslim Women are Reinterpreting the Qur'an and Hadith: A Transformative Scholarship Activism', in M. A. Failinger, E. R. Schiltz and S. J. Stabile (eds), *Feminism, Law, and Religion*, London: Ashgate, pp. 257–80.

Berkey, Jonathan P. (2000), 'Storytelling, Preaching, and Power in Mamluk Cairo', *Mamluk Studies Review* 4: 53–73.

Berkey, Jonathan P. (2001), *Popular Preaching and Religious Authority in the Medieval Islamic Near East*, Seattle: University of Washington Press.

Brinton, Jacquelene G. (2016), *Preaching Islamic Renewal: Religious Authority and Media in Contemporary Egypt*, Berkeley: University of California Press.

al-Bukhārī, Muhammad, *Ṣaḥīḥ al-Bukhārī*, Book 67, no. 2, <https://sunnah.com/bukhari/67> (last accessed 5 February 2020).

Gagnon, John H. and William Simon (1973), *Sexual Conduct: The Social Sources of Human Sexuality*, Chicago: Aldine.

Geoffroy, M. Éric (1995), *Le Soufisme en Égypte et en Syrie sous les derniers Mamelouks et les premiers Ottomans: Orientations spirituelles et enjeux culturels*, Damascus: Presses de L'Ipfo.

al-Ghazzālī, Abū Ḥāmid (1984), *Marriage and Sexuality in Islam: A Translation of al-Ghazzālī's Book on the Etiquette on Marriage, Book XII of Iḥyā' 'ulūm al-dīn*, M. Farah (trans.), Salt Lake City: University of Utah Press.

Hess, Andrew C. (1973), 'The Ottoman Conquest of Egypt (1517) and the Beginning of the Sixteenth-century World War', *International Journal of Middle East Studies* 4 (1): 55–76.

Hofer, Nathan (2015), *The Popularisation of Sufism in Ayyubid and Mamluk Egypt, 1173–1325*, Edinburgh: Edinburgh University Press.

Ibn al-ʿAbbās, ʿAbdullah/al-Firūzabādī, M. (2007), *Tanwīr al-miqbās min tafsīr Ibn ʿAbbās*, M. Guezzou (trans.), Yousef Meri (ed. and Intro.), Amman: Royal Aal Bayt Institute for Islamic Thought.

Ibn al-Ḥājj (1981 [1960]), *Madkhal al-sharʿ al-sharīf*, ed. (s. i.), 4 vols, Cairo: Maṭbaʿat Muṣṭafā al-Bābī, rpt. Dar al-fikr.

Ibn Mājah, *Sunna*, Vol. 3, Book 9, hadith no. 1852. Cited in online version: <https://sunnah.com/ibnmajah/9> (last accessed 10 November 2019).

Ibn al-Khallikān (1842), *Ibn Khallikan's Biographical Dictionary*, B. Mac Guckin de Slane (trans.), Vol. 1, Paris: Oriental Translation Fund for Great Britain and Ireland.

Ibn al-Murābiṭ, M. (1992–3), *Zawāhir al-fikar wa-jawāhir al-faqar li-Ibn al-Murābiṭ*, Aḥmad al-Miṣbaḥī (ed.), 3 vols, Rabat: Jāmiʿat Muḥammad al-Khāmis (University of Muhammad V).

Immenkamp, Beatrix (1994), 'Marriage and Celibacy in Medieval Islam: A Study of Ghazālī's *Kitāb Ādāb al-Nikāḥ*', PhD thesis, University of Cambridge.

Jones, Linda G. (2006), 'Ibn ʿAbbād of Ronda's Sermon on the Prophet's Birthday Celebration: Preaching the Sufi and Sunni Paths of Islam', *Medieval Sermon Studies* 50 (1): 31–49.

Jones, Linda G. (2012), *The Power of Oratory in the Medieval Islamic World*, New York: Cambridge University Press.

Jones, Linda G. (2013), 'A Nuptial Sermon by Ibn al-Jannān: A Surprising Source on Commercial Relations between Murcia and Genova (1245)', in J. Mutgè i Vives, R. Salicrú i Lluch and C. Vela (eds), *La Corona catalanoaragonesa, l'Islam i el món mediterrani. Estudis d'història medieval en homenatge a la doctora Maria Teresa Ferrer i Mallol*, Barcelona: CSIC, pp. 405–11.

Lotfi, Abdelhamid (2001), 'Creating Muslim Space in the USA: Masājid and Islamic Centers', *Islam and Christian–Muslim Relations* 12 (2): 235–54.

al-Maḥallī, J. D. and J. D. al-Suyūtī (2007), *Tafsīr al-Jalālayn*, Feras Hamza (trans.), G. b. M. bin Talal (ed.), Amman: Royal Aal Bayt Institute for Islamic Thought.

Mālik ibn Anas, *Al-Muwatta*, Aisha Bewley (trans.), <https://bewley.virtualave.net/muwcont.html> (last acessed 5 February 2020).

Mernissi, Fatima (1987), *Beyond the Veil: Male–Female Dynamics in Modern Muslim Society*, revised edition, Bloomington and Indianapolis: Indiana University Press.

Mojaddedi, Jawid A. (2003), 'Getting Drunk with Abū Yazīd or Staying Sober with

Junayd: The Creation of a Popular Typology of Sufism', *Bulletin of the School of Oriental and African Studies* (*BSOAS*) 66 (1): 1–13.

Muslim ibn al-Ḥajjāj, *Ṣaḥīḥ Muslim*, Book 16, no. 1, <https://sunnah.com/muslim/16> (last accessed 5 February 2020).

Nasir, Jamal J. (2009), *The Status of Women Under Islamic Law and Modern Islamic Legislation*, Leiden: Brill.

Nicklisch, Andrea (2018), 'Continuity and Discontinuity in 17th- and 18th-century Ecclesiastical Silverworks from the Southern Andes', *Religions* 9 (9), <https://www.mdpi.com/2077-1444/9/9/262/htm> (last accessed 10 November 2019).

Noam, Vered (2009 [2007]), 'Tradition: Continuity or Change – Two Religious Options', in M. Halbertal and D. Hartman (eds), *Judaism and the Challenges of Modern Life*, New York: Continuum, pp. 31–47.

al-Qushayrī, Abū l-Qāsim 'Abd al-Karīm (2017), *Laṭā'if al-Ishārāt, Subtle Allusions: Great Commentaries on the Holy Qur'ān, Sūras 1–4*, Kristin Zahra Sands (trans.), Louisville, KY: Fons Vitae/Royal Aal al-Bayt Institute for Islamic Thought.

Qutbuddin, Tahera (2008), '*Khuṭba*: The Evolution of Early Arabic Oration', in B. Greundler and M. Cooperson (eds), *Classical Arabic Humanities in Their Own Terms: Festschrift for Wolfhart Heinrichs on His 65th Birthday*, Leiden: Brill, pp. 176–273.

Qutbuddin, Tahera (2019), *Arabic Oration: Art and Function*, Leiden: Brill.

Pasha, Kareen Saeed (2005), *Khutba in-Nikkah, Marriage Sermon Delivered by Dr Abdul Kareen Saeed Pasha*, <http://aaiil.org/text/books/others/abdulkarimsaeed/khutbanikahmarriagesermon/khutbanikkahmarriagesermon.pdf> (last accessed 10 November 2019).

Rapoport, Youssef (2007), 'Women and Gender in Mamluk Society: An Overview', *Mamluk Studies Review* 11 (2): 1–47.

del Río Pereda, Carmen (2016), *La soberanía de la mujer en el Corán*, Madrid: Editorial Almuzara.

Saleem, Nighat P. (2014), 'Muslim Women & Public Space: The Debate between Conservative and Feminist Thinkers', PhD thesis, University of Birmingham.

Saleh, Waleed (2010), *Amor, sexualidad y matrimonio en el islam*, Seville: Guadarrama, Madrid: Fundación Tres Culturas del Mediterráneo.

Shoshan, Boaz (1993), *Popular Culture in Medieval Cairo*, Cambridge: Cambridge University Press.

Shoshan, Boaz (2006), 'Popular Sufi Sermons in Late Mamluk Egypt', in A. Ayalon and D. J. Wasserstein (eds), *Mamluks and Ottomans: Studies in Honor of Michael Winter*, New York: Routledge, pp. 106–13.

Sindawi, Khalid (2013), *Temporary Marriage in Sunni and Shiʿite Islam: A Comparative Study*, Wiesbaden: Harrassowitch Verlag.

Swartz, Merlin L. (1986), *Ibn al-Jawzī's 'Kitāb al-Quṣṣāṣ wa 'l-mudkhakkirīn'*, Beirut: Dār al-Machreq.

Tarmanini, ʿA. S. (1989), *Al-Zawāj ʿindā l-ʿarab fī l-jāhiliyya wa 'l-Islām: dirāsa muqārana fī majāl al-taʾrīkh wa 'l-adab wa 'l-sharīʿa*, Ḥalab, Syria: Dār al-Qalam al-ʿArabī.

Vajda, Georges and Yvette Sauvan (1985), *Catalogue des manuscrits arabes. Deuxième partie: Manuscrits musulmanes*, T. III, nos 1121–464, Paris: Bibliothèque nationale de Paris.

Wensinck, Arent J. (1999), 'Khuṭba', *Encyclopaedia of Islam*, 2nd ed., Vol. 5, Leiden: Brill, pp. 74–5.

Winter, Michael (1982), *Society and Religion in Early Ottoman Egypt: Studies in the Writings of ʿAbd al-Wahhāb al-Sharānī*, New Brunswick and London: Transaction Publishers.

Winter, Michael (1996), 'al-Shaʿrānī, ʿAbd al-Wahhāb b. Aḥmad', *Encyclopaedia of Islam*, 2nd ed., Vol. 9, Leiden: Brill, p. 316.

Winter, Michael (2005 [1992]), *Egyptian Society under Ottoman Rule, 1517–1798*, London and New York: Routledge/Taylor & Francis.

Yasbeck Haddad, Yvonne (2004), *Not Quite American? The Shaping of Arab and Muslim Identity in the United States*, Waco, TX: Baylor University Press.

Zomeño, Amalia (2000), *Dote y matrimonio en al-Andalus y el Norte de África: estudios sobre la jurisprudencia islámica medieval*, Madrid: CSIC.

EPILOGUE

Simon Stjernholm and Elisabeth Özdalga

The fact that a Muslim Friday noon service, including its sermon, the *khuṭba*, does not look or sound very different today compared to what it did a hundred or several hundred years ago, should not deceive us into thinking that the wider dynamics into which it is embedded have been left untouched. The deep transformations of modernisation have struck religious institutions and communities as much as it has hit economic, social and political structures and relationships. Considering Muslim homiletics, the wider sphere of preaching of which the *khuṭba* is but one genre, there are perhaps two forces of change that have been especially significant: the emergence of the nation-state and the development of modern mass media. Without denying the impact of other forces, this epilogue will briefly discuss the significance of changes within these two fields, as well as point to series of questions they give rise to.

With respect to the Middle East, the development of the modern nation-state is closely connected to colonialism and the outcomes of the two world wars. Access to and use of modern mass media among broad population groups, including television, cassettes and the Internet, is of more recent date. Yet, however strong the power of transformation, the forces of tradition do not yield so easily. Concerning Muslim homiletics, much of its liturgies, discourses of authority, and willingness (or need) to invoke the same authoritative sources are preserved, while the uses to which they are put, and negotiations of their potential meanings, are subject to change.

The Emergence of the Nation-state

The modern nation-state is a centralised and complex organisation of more or less formal institutions. The effects of its growth on religious life have varied both between and within different cultural contexts. Modern Turkey offers a striking example of how the state, in its capacity as a newly born nation-state, took control over religion and, in a few years' time, gave it a new organisational structure. During this process, a large number of previously vital religious institutions and practices were put under direct state control. For instance, all judicial functions were taken over by the secular state; education of religious personnel was transferred to the Ministry of Education; Sufi brotherhoods of all kinds were banned. 'Religion' thus got a new, circumscribed definition, more or less limited to worship, prayers and oratory in the mosques. What was left of religious life was henceforth organised under the Directorate of Religious Affairs, Diyanet, which meant that Islam gradually was rendered a centralised organisation within the borders of the Turkish nation. This also brought a standardisation of religious practices, meaning that local variations in how people were addressed by preachers gradually diminished.

Key words in this process are state control, centralisation, standardisation and an emphasis on national culture. The development in Turkey sketched here is by no means unique, except for the fact that in this heir to the imperial Ottoman state it was carried through by a revolutionary-minded, impatient and authoritarian leadership. Similar processes have been taking place in many other Muslim countries, but in every country along its own trajectory. In Egypt, for example, authorities have intensified control over religious affairs by means of incorporating private mosques into the governmental system. When this was not entirely successful, focus changed to the preachers and the quality of their training. As these initiatives also proved insufficient, the government accepted local volunteers, but then in combination with increased governmental supervision (Gaffney 1994: 265–6). In Jordan too, religious activities were gradually drawn under governmental control. At the end of the 1940s a village imam would still be appointed and paid by the villagers themselves. Later on, however, religious personnel became more and more incorporated into the governmental bureaucracy through formal certificates of learning and official appointments (*khaṭīb*, marriage official and pilgrim's guide or *murshid*). The government would also intervene into the preaching act itself, but not all imams or preachers would be happy to deliver so-called 'canned' sermons (Antoun 1989: 85, 136). To sum up, attempts at top-down streamlining and standardisation of preaching and other religious activities has been a general trend in Middle Eastern countries.

The impact of the state on Muslim preaching occurs in especially four areas: organisation of mosques and mosque administrations; education of imams and preachers; regulations concerning the qualifications required to hold a *khuṭba* or a *wa'ẓ*; and efforts to directly influence the contents of preaching, for example through authorised collections of sermons, state-sponsored periodical publications, and/or directly delivered texts, which preachers are obliged to read. As a consequence, official preaching discourses risk being deemed predictable, standardised and unsatisfactory – by preachers as well as the audience. The sketched developments in several Muslim-majority states therefore points to a series of questions: what happens to Muslim religious oratory under these conditions? More specifically, how does the fact that Muslim preaching is incorporated into the auspices of a centralised and tightly ramified official organisation affect preaching practices and their significance? What kinds of resistance, adaptation and innovation to these changes can be seen in relation to preaching? How do global and local actors, discourses and practices interact? One possibility is that when official discourses and practices fail to satisfy, alternative modes and paths of expression are sought. This means that another key development is the development and use of various new media, as they open up spaces for a plurality of voices, expressions and audiences.

Media Developments

The development of various technologically advanced media has allowed increased possibilities to disseminate messages to larger, and new, audiences. With important media formats like audio cassettes, television and the Internet – with its various platforms and social media – many preachers have been able to reach audiences beyond their local, national or regional horizon. Moreover, these media have made possible experimentation with different types of products, aiming at different audiences; both traditional and highly unconventional forms of preaching have proliferated. Furthermore, these modes of circulation offer possibilities of archiving, reusing, mixing together and repeating recorded instances of preaching, all of which facilitate changing modes of audience engagement with and redistribution of preachers' orations.

In recent years, the interactive and privacy-transgressing dimensions of digital media, together with the abundance of possibilities for practically anyone to distribute homemade audio and video productions, have had an almost universal impact. This has had implications also for Muslim preachers and forms of preaching. Partly, it has opened up opportunities for challenging state or market control over broadcast media and public places, in Muslim majority as well as minority contexts. At the same time, new and unconventional communication channels are not necessarily used for politically radical purposes; the messages that are distributed can often be socially conservative and anti-liberal. What is generally true, however, is that specific media formats, due to their different affordances, require and encourage particular types of communication skills and strategies, while downplaying or discouraging others. While not mutually exclusive in this regard, audio cassettes, television and online social media all in their own way affect the form that preaching takes within its particular communicative framework.

When thinking about the significance of contemporary digital media, one should not only focus on the possibilities they provide, but also be aware of the dangers accompanying them. These include, for example, increased opportunities for surveillance of large amounts of data, individual vulnerability to state repression, and global possibilities for networking and circulation of propaganda by militant groups. Preachers, their messages and sympathisers are affected by these and similar processes as well.

All of this leads us to pose another series of questions: how do preachers adapt to the specific media formats available to them, and what effects does this have on their output and audiences? And conversely, what uses do states and other official actors make of the new media available to them, perhaps in order to control or counter independent preaching discourses? What roles do more or less self-appointed preachers play – in local contexts where Muslims are both in majority and in minority – in comparison to preachers who are officially appointed or traditionally schooled religious scholars? What new forms and genres of preaching are developed as an effect of new media, and how are traditional oratorical practices incorporated and adapted? How do various audiences consume and interact with preaching and preachers through new media? Several chapters in this volume touch upon aspects of these questions, but they would be relevant to pursue in a number of different contexts and periods, as well as through multiple modes of analysis.

The diversity of cases included in this book points to many possible research strategies and relevant materials, focusing on different time periods as well as geographical, cultural, political and media contexts. In continued work along the lines indicated through the questions posed in this epilogue, we believe it would be useful to consider the multifariousness of Muslim preaching in order to see, for example, how the old is present in the new, how dissimilar contexts can exhibit both differences and similarities, and how religious practices reflect and relate to broader tendencies in culture and society. The exploratory approach of this volume, as well as the specific perspectives and data of its individual case studies, can hopefully provide a stimulating point of reference in further studies on the rich world of Muslim preaching, regardless of where, when, or how that preaching is carried out.

Bibliography

Antoun, Richard T. (1989), *Muslim Preacher in the Modern World: A Jordanian Case Study in Comparative Perspective*, Princeton: Princeton University Press.

Gaffney, Patrick D. (1994) *The Prophet's Pulpit: Islamic Preaching in Contemporary Egypt*, Berkeley: University of California Press.

INDEX

Abbasid revolution, 26
Abduh, Muhammad, 158
al-ʿAbidin, Suhayla Zayn, 111, 126n
Abū Bakr, 25
Abu Dawud, Abdullah as-Sueidi, 160–1, 166
Abu-Lughod, Lila, 38
al-ʿAdawiyya, Rabiʿa, 33
adhān (call to prayer), 4, 19–20, 30–1
al-Afghani, Jamal al-Din, 39, 158
ahlak (ethical rules), 86
al-Ahmad, Malik Ibrahim, 115
ʿAʾisha bt. Abī Bakr, 182, 185, 190–1
AKP (Justice and Development Party), 98
Akseki, Ahmed Hamdi, 95
Aksum, Ethiopia, 25
ʿĀlam Ḥawā ('The world of Eve'), 112
Algeria, 37
Ali, Kecia, 181, 185
ʿAlī Wafā, 71, 79–80
ʿālim (religious scholar), 30, 32–6, 39, 80, 165; *see also* ʿulamaʾ
ʿālimāt (female religious scholars), 110, 125
Altıkulaç, Tayyar, 87–94, 100–1n, 100n, 101n
al-Aʿmash, 74–5
Ankara, Turkey, 93
'the anonymous preacher', 178–86, 188–9, 192–5
al-ʿAqqad, Mustafa, 33, 35
Arab Spring, 115
Arabia, 21, 24, 26
pre-Islamic, 24
Arabiyya language, 21, 27–8n
al-ʿArd ('The land'), 34
Arebi, Saddeka, 111
al-ʿArifi, Muhammad, 115
Armstrong, Lyall, 72
Asmāʾ bt. Khārijah, 183
Assal, Moosa, 155–7, 160–2, 164–7
audience response, 5, 76, 132–47
al-ʿAwda, Salman, 115
al-Awlaqi, Anwar, 165, 170n
ʿawra, 117, 127n, 128n
al-Azhar, Shaykh, 39

Bab al-Ouad City, 37
al-Badawi, Ahmad, 33
Baghdad, 76
al-Baghdadi, Abu Bakr, 1
Bahethat research centre, 116
Bahrain, 121
al-Banna, Hasan, 126n
Banū Isrāʾīl, destruction of the nation of, 77
al-Barudi, Shams, 39
Basra, 75

Bayna 'l-qaṣrayn ('Palace walk'), 36, 42
BBC, 107
Becker, Carl, 23
bidaʿ (innovations), sing. *bidʿa*, 72, 77
Bilal (Muhammad's companion), 143–4
  Bilal, muʾadhdhan al-rasul ('Bilal, the Prophet's muezzin'), 34–5, 45n
Bin Baz, ʿAbd al-ʿAziz (Grand Mufti), 110–11
biographical dictionaries, 71
Bitlis, Turkey, 100n
Boko Haram, 187
Borchali, Bilal, 132–3, 137–42
Bosnia, 58–61, 62–3n
  guidance and governance, 61–2
  women, 48–65
  Yugoslav period, 53
Bosnian Muslim Women's Rituals: Bulas Singing, Reciting and Teaching in Sarajevo (film), 62n
Bowen, John, 48–9
Brinton, Jacquelene G., 41
broadcast media, 204
van Bruinessen, Martin, 48–9
Budskapet.tv, 138
al-Bukhārī, 75, 190
Bulliet, Richard, 76
Bulqīnī family, 71

Cairo, 38–9, 71, 72, 78, 178, 193
California, 193
'canned' sermons, 203
cassettes, 3, 37, 111, 201, 203–4
censorship, 128n
Chahine, Youssef, 34
Christianity
  Eucharist, 23
  and khuṭba, 23–5
  liturgy, 23
  and Muslim sermons, 36
Christina, Queen of Sweden, 26
civil Islam, 83
'clean cinema' (*sīnimā naẓīfa*), 33
communication technology, 111–12, 204
Convention on the Elimination of All Forms of Discrimination against Women (CEDAW), 116
Copts, 42

daʿī (missionary preacher), plural *duʿāt*, 7, 45, 160–1, 166–8
dāʿiyāt, 108–23, 123n, 127–8n
dāʿiyāt muthaqqafāt, 107–23, 124–5n
Damascus, 25
Darius the Great, 25
dars (religious lesson), 2, 39, 44, 159, 179
d'Avray, David, 177
daʿwa
  Borchali, Bilal, 138
  facilitating and coordinating, 114–15
  female education, 127n
  female preachers, 117, 125n
  islam.nu, 156–7
  preaching videos, 147
  state and society, 160
  Sweden, 167–8
  TV programmes, 134
  women, 110–11
Demirel, Süleyman, 91, 101n
ders (lessons), 53, 55, 58, 62; *see also dars*
dhikr, 20, 21, 179; *see also zikr*
DISK, 84–7
'disruptive simultaneity', 137, 148, 148n
Diyanet, 87–98, 99n, 100–1n, 100n, 101n, 202
  Law 633, 92
Diyanet Aylık Dergi, 95
Diyanet Gazetesi, 84–6, 93–7
Doğan, Dr Lütfü, 88
Doğan, Lütfü, 88, 90, 101n
duʿāt (missionary preachers), sing. *daʿī*, 7, 45, 160–1, 166–8
dunyā (this world), 162–3, 166

Ebussuud, Mehmed Efendi, 99n
Ecevit, Bülent, 91
education, 109–10
Egypt
  compared to Turkey, 83, 97
  film, 30–4
  Islamic television, 134
  Mamluk, 178
  Mubarak era, 42
  nation-state, 202
  'new preachers', 146
  and Qatar, 121
  Ṣaḥwa movement, 126n

Egypt (*cont.*)
Salafism, 158–9
TV serials, 37–41
'Uncle al-Sha'rawi', 41–3
women, 176
Erbakan, Necmettin, 101n
Ethiopia, 25
Ethiosemitic language, 24–5

Facebook, 115, 132–3, 138–42, 143, 148
false traditions of preaching, 74–6, 79
al-Faruqi, Ismail Raji, 187
Faysal, King, 33
female preachers
exposure and political vulnerability, 119–22
gender interaction dilemma, 117–19
new media, 107–31
Saudi, 107–31
speaking to the sisters, 54–8
see also women
film
Egyptian, 30–4
French-produced, 32
historical epic films, 34–5
role of 'ulama' in, 32–4
fitna, 117, 127n
Foucault, Michel, 109, 125n
France, Anatole, *Taïs*, 34
Friday sermon (*khuṭbat al-jum'a*), 1, 6, 7, 9

Gaffney, Patrick, *The Prophet's Pulpit*, 43
al-Ghazali/al-Ghazzālī, 99n, 192, 193
The Revival of the Religious Sciences, 180–5, 192
Geez, 24–5
Germany, 92, 98
Ghaddafi, Muammar, 33
Goitein, Shlomo D., 23–4
Gonzalez-Quijano, Yves, 41
Gözaydın, Iştar, 101n
Great Mosque of Qayrawān, Tunisia, 26
Gülen movement, 100n

al-Ḥadaq yafham ('The clever guy will understand'), 36–7, 44
hadiths
al-Suyūṭī, 99n
authority, 9
Diyanet, 95
false traditions of preaching, 79
female preachers, 8, 52, 55–8, 61
marriage, 173, 177, 179–82, 185, 191–4
Medieval preachers, 68–9, 72–6
TV serials, 40–1
Wadud, Abdul, 162–3
Hadžijska Mosque, 62n
hafiz, 49, 99–100n
hafiza, 50, 52
ḥalqa (study group), 2, 42, 44–5
Hanafi School, 99n
Hanbalism, 126n
Ḥassan wa Murquṣ ('Hassan and Morqos'), 36, 42
hatib/hatip (preacher), 53, 63n, 86, 93–6, 100n; *see also khaṭīb*
High Committee for Religious Affairs (Din Işleri Yüksek Kurulu, DIYK), 93, 96, 99–100n
hijab, 110–11, 113, 117, 127n
ḥimā, 21
Hirschkind, Charles, 136
hortatory discourse, 4–6
hortatory speeches, 22
'How the Prophet Muhammad taught the Arabs that racism is wrong', 142–3, 148n
al-Husayn, Mariam, 114
Hussein, Taha, 32–3
hutbe, 53, 56, 62, 84–6, 92–8, 99–100n; *see also khuṭba*

'ibādāt/ibadet (worship, religious obligations), 55, 57, 174
Ibn Abbas Centre, 157–71
Ibn al-Jawzī, 71, 73–7, 80
Kitāb al-quṣṣāṣ wa 'l-mudhakkirīn, 71
Ibn Ḥanbal, Aḥmad, 75, 191, 195
Ibn Jubayr, 76
Ibn Taymiyya, 71, 73, 75
İbn-i Melek, 99n
Iceland, 22
al-'Id, Nawal, 107, 108, 114, 115, 117–18
'īd al-aḍḥā, 2
'īd al-fiṭr, 2
'iffa (modesty), 110–11

iḥtisāb (commanding right and forbidding wrong), 108, 110–11, 115–16, 120–1, 123
electronic, 115–16
ijāza (licenses), 69
ikhtilāṭ (gender mixing), 111, 120
ikhtiṭāṭ, 21
ʿilm (knowledge), 68, 77
ʿilm al-ijtimāʿ (social knowledge), 109
Imām al-duʿā ('The first among preachers'), 41–3
Imamernas råd ('The advice of the imams'), 169n
ʿImārat Yaʿqūbiān ('The Yacoubian building'), 35–6
Indonesia, 83, 146
Instagram, 113, 115
internet, 98, 113, 114–15
Iran, TV serials, 38
Iraq, 27
Iser, Wolfgang, 141
Islam är fri från terrorism ('Islam is free from terrorism'), 164–5
Islamic awakening, 33
Islamic Center of Southern California (ICSC), 186–93
Islamic Community, 59, 60–1
Islamic Faculty, 59
Islamic Middle Period, 69, 70, 72, 73
Islamic State, 1, 159, 164–5, 167, 187
Islamic University of Medina (IUM), 160, 167
islam.nu, 160–7
Isparta, Turkey, 91
Israelites, 182
israīʾliyyāt, 73, 74
Istanbul, 90
istikamet (straight path), 55, 57
itikat (set of beliefs), 86
ittibāʿ, 158
ʿIzz al-Din, Ibrahim, 32–3

jādda (formal and serious), 117
Jag är muslim ('I am Muslim') TV series, 160–1
Jones, Linda Gale, 80n
Jordan, 83, 97, 202–3
journals, 111
Judaeo-Christianity, 24
Judaism
homiletic interpreter, 174–5
ICSC, 186
Sabbath, 23, 26
services, 23–4
tradition, 25, 26
Justice and Development Party (Adalet ve Kalkınma Partisi, AKP), 83, 101n

Kahraman, 34
khalwa (seclusion), 111, 117
Khariji movement, 77
khaṭīb (preacher), 6–8, 19–20, 25, 37, 45, 69–70, 176, 203; *see also hatib/hatip*
al-Khidr, ʿAbd al-ʿAziz, 120
khuḍūʿ bi ʾl-qawl (soft, or seductive speech), 117
khuṭab, sing. *khuṭba*, 6–9, 12, 135, 136, 138, 159, 201, 203
in the age of the prophet, 20–2
ammā baʿd, 196n
in films and TV dramas, 30–47
framework of Islamic rhetoric, 19–29
khuṭbat al-jumʿa (Friday sermon), 1, 6, 7, 9
khuṭbat nikāḥ (marriage oration), 175
and marriage, 173–8, 194–5
Medieval preachers, 69–70
minbar, 24–27
origins of the ceremony, 23–4
'The Path to a Healthy Marriage', 186–93
ritual, 1–2, 19–29
videos, 138–9
Korazin synagogue, Galilee, 25
Koselleck, Reinhart, 125n
Kufa, 74–5
al-Kurdi, Fawz, 114
Kurds, 100n

Lahā Online ('For her online'), 112, 114, 115
Laki ('For you'), 112
Lambek, Michael, 48–9
Latin Christendom, 177
Lauzière, Henri, 158
lecture recordings, 118–19, 155–71
lectures, live-streamed, 142

Libya, 33
Lieuvrouw, Leah A., 124n
Lord, Ceren, 100n
Lotfi, Abdelhamid, 186

McGregor, Richard, 71
Mahmud, ʿAbd al-Halim 39–40
majālis al-waʿẓ, 176
majlis, 21–2
al-Makkī, Abū Ṭālib, 192
Malaysia, 83
Mali, 134
Mamluk Egypt, 70, 178–86, 196–7n
al-Maraghi, Mustafa, 40–1
marriage, 173–200
  hierarchical relationships, 179–81
  husband's obligations, 183–4
  orations on, 175–8
  Islamic sermons on, 133–4, 193–6
  wife's mobility, 181–2
  see also women
Maryām al-Muqaddasa ('The Holy Mary'), 38
masculinity, 178–86, 195
masjid, 21–2, 25
mawadda (nurturing and loving affection), 189–90
mawʿiẓa, 174, 178; *see also waʿẓ*
Mecca, 33
media, 5, 159, 168,
  developments, 134–5, 201, 203–5
  Diyanet, 87, 94, 98
  films and TV dramas, 30–45
  negative treatment, 161, 169n
  newspapers, 84
  practices, 11, 133–4, 147
  Saudi female preachers in new media, 107–31
  Swedish online preachers, 132–51
  videos, 162, 164
  see also mediation; new media; 'reminder'; social media
mediation, 2, 3, 5, 10–11
  Swedish online preachers, 132–51
Medieval preachers, 4, 67–82, 173–200
  authority, 80–1n
Medina, 22, 23–4, 26
Medina Constitution, 24
Medina document, 22
medresa, 53, 59
Meijer, Roel, 159
Mernissi, Fatima, 185
Mesopotamia, 27
The Message, 144
mevlud, 57, 62n
militant Islamism, 33
Millie, Julian, 102n, 128n, 145–6
minbar, 2, 6, 19–20, 24–7, 186
  in film, 36
  misuses of, 93
  in TV dramas, 38, 40, 42–4
  used in titles, 31
  in videos, 162
Ministry of Education, Turkey, 90
Ministry of Justice, Turkey, 90
mīthāqan ghalīẓan (strong and firm commitment), 183, 188, 189
Mittwoch, Eugen, 23
MNP (National Order Party), 88
modernity, 43, 62n, 187
Moll, Yasmin, 134, 146
Moses, 25
Mosul, 1
MSP (National Salvation Party), 92, 101n
muʾaththir, 136
Muʿāwiya, 25
mufsidīn (corrupters), 113
muḥāḍara (lecture), 159
Muhammad, Prophet
  against racism, 142–5
  ammā baʿd, 196n
  Asrı Saadet, 99n
  daʿwa, 115
  Facebook videos, 132–3, 135, 141
  false traditions of preaching, 75
  'Farewell Sermon', 35, 67
  film, 32–5
  'heirs of', 68
  hutbe, 53–4, 85
  khuṭab, 1–2, 6–7, 20
  marriage, 173, 175, 180–2, 184, 188–95
  masjid, 21–2
  minbar, 24–6
  'popular preachers', 73, 77
  public speech in the age of, 20–2
  'sound dream', 79–80

TV dramas, 38–9, 44
vaiza, 56–7
videos, 156, 164–5
zuhd, 163
al-Muharib, Ruqayya, 108, 110, 111–14, 120–3, 124n, 125n, 128n, 129n
mukabela, 49–55, 57–8, 60–1
multimodality, 136, 145
muruwwa, 178, 181–2, 193, 195
mûsaf-prayer, 23
musalsalāt (Arab TV serials), 37–41, 43–4
Muslim Brotherhood, 38, 100n, 110, 121, 126n

namaz (ritual prayer), 56
narratives, 4–5
Borchali, Bilal, 141
film, 30–2, 35
genre, 135
marriage, 177, 181–2, 185–6
Medieval preachers, 73
Tufekcioglu, Salih, 144–5
vaiza, 55–8
videos, 162
women, 179
Zeenni, Hassan, 188, 195
naṣīḥa, 159, 164–5, 169n
Nasser era, 33
National Order Party (Milli Nizam Partisi, MNP), 88
National Salvation Party (Milli Selamet Partisi, MSP), 92, 101n
nation-state, emergence of the, 202–3
Nedvi, Süleyman, *Asrı Saadet*, 99n
neo-jihadis, 126n
Nesil Dergisi, 100–1n
new media
definition, 124n
Saudi female intellectual preachers, 107–31
'new preachers', 146
newspapers, 84, 112–14, 124n
Nicklisch, Andrea, 174
van Nieuwkerk, Karin
'90 Seconds' series, 138–42
niqāb, 127n, 169n
Noam, Vered, 174–5
Norwegian Parliament, 26
Nurcu movement, 100n
al-Nuri mosque, 1
Nursi, Bediüzzaman Said, 100n

Okutan, Ahmet, 88
Olsson, Susanne, 138
Contemporary Puritan Salafism: A Swedish Case Study, 160
online preaching, 107–31
oratorical tradition, 1, 3
Ottomans, 54, 69, 76, 99n, 178, 202
Özgüneş, Mehmet, 88

'The Path to a Healthy Marriage', *khuṭba*, 186–93
'popcorn-ʿulamaʾ', 165
Pope, 26
'popular preachers', 70–6, 78–80, 176
Princess Noura University, Department of Islamic Science, 125–6n
Prophet Muhammad *see* Muhammad, Prophet
proskynesis, 21–2
Pseudo-al-Shaʿrānī, 178–86, 188–9, 192–5

al-Qāḍī Shurayḥ, Kufa, 190, 195
al-Qaʿida, 126n, 159, 170n
al-Qalqashandī, 69
qāriʾ al-kursī (one who reads while sitting down), 70
al-Qarni, ʿAid, 115
qāṣṣ (storyteller), plural *quṣṣāṣ*, 8, 70–8, 81n
Qatar, 31, 121, 128n
qiṣaṣ al-anbiyā, 73
Qurʾan, 14n, 28n, 43, 100n
4:19, 184
4:21, 183, 185, 193, 194
4:34, 184
4:154, 189
5:32, 157
25:27–9, 141
30:21, 189, 194
33:7, 189
33:32, 117
49:10, 85
62:29, 20
ʿAbd al-Halim Mahmud, 39–40
Altıkulaç, Tayyar, 88

Qurʾan (*cont.*)
Assal, Moosa, 156, 164
authority, 9, 12
female preachers, 8
gender justice, 177
Judaeo-Christianity, 24
khuṭba, 20–1, 23
marriage, 173, 175, 183–5, 188–9, 193–6
Medieval preachers, 68, 72–3
Ramadan, 49–51
recitation, 4, 20, 23, 49–50, 52, 54, 88, 100, 135, 144–5, 194
Ṣaḥwa, 110
Salafism, 158
Süleymancı community (*cemaat*), 100n
tefsir, 95, 99n
text messages, 138
TV dramas, 39
Tufekcioglu, Salih, 144–5
vaiza, 55, 58
videos, 157, 161–2
women, 61, 110, 127n
quṣṣāṣ, see *qāṣṣ*
Qutb, Sayyid, 126n
Qutbuddin, Tahera, 14n
Arabic Oration: Art and Function, 80n

Rabıta (Saudi Arabia), 100n
Råd kring livet i förorterna ('Advice on life in the suburbs'), 166
radio programmes, 88, 111, 117–18, 134
Rağıb-ı-Isfehânî, 99n
raḥma (mercy), 189–90, 192
Ramadan, 31, 37, 54, 58
al-Rasheed, Madawi, 126n
Raudvere, Catharina, 62n
'The Many Roads in Modernity: The Transformation of South-East Europe 1870 to the 21st Century', 62n
religious identity, 173–200
'reminder', 135–7
renunciation, 162–3, 166
Sweden, 155–72
see also zuhd
Rida, Rashid, 126n, 158
al-Risala ('The message'), 33, 35
ritual, 1–9, 19–28, 43, 48–62, 135, 175–6, 179–80
Riyadh, 124n, 125–6n, 127n
Roman Empire, 27
al-Ruwayshid, Asma, 118–19

al-Sadat, Anwar, 41
Ṣaḥīḥ al-Bukhārī, 75
Şahin, Kamil, 99–100n
Ṣaḥwa, 110–13, 121, 123, 126n, 159
'new Ṣaḥwa', 126n
sakīna (tranquility), 189–91
salaf, 177, 180, 188, 190, 193, 195
al-salaf al-ṣāliḥ, 158
Salafism, 110, 126n, 138, 169n
Salah al-Din, Muhammad, Bey, 32–3
al-Salam, Shadi Abd, 36
ṣalāt, 7, 20, 23
Samarra, Iraq, 26
Sanningen om Shia ('The truth about Shiʿa'), 161
Saqf al-ʿAlam ('Roof of the world'), 39
Sarajevo, Bosnia, 49–51
Saudi Ministry of Islamic Affairs, Dawah and Guidance, 126–7n
Saudi Vision 2030, 121
Saudi Arabia, 33
female preachers and new media, 107–31
Scandinavia, 22
Schulz, Dorothea, 134
Scott, David, 135
al-Shaʿrānī, ʿAbd al-Wahhāb, 178
al-Shaʿrawi, Shaykh, 41–5
Shafiq, Viola, 33
sharʿi movement, 26
shariʿa, 67, 76–7, 86, 117, 178–9
al-Sharif, Muhammad Musa, 113, 117, 127n
Shaykh Hassan, 34
Shiʿi Islam, 177
shumūliyya, 110, 111, 122, 124n
Şibli, Mevlana, *Asrı Saadet*, 99n
Sidqi, Ismail, 34
Simmel, Georg, 147, 148n
Sippar, 27
sīra, 22, 143
Sīrīn, 112
'SMS-Bilal' *see* Borchali, Bilal
Snapchat, 113, 115, 118, 161

social media, 10–11, 98, 132–4, 136–7, 140, 166, 169n, 203–4
Bosnia, 51, 53
Saudi Arabia, 107–31
see also media; new media
'sound dream', 79–80
South Arabia, pre-Islamic, 21–2
South East Asia, 83
Soviet Union collapse, 95
Spahić-Šiljak, Zilka, 62n
speech
genres, modes and brevity, 135–7
importance of the human voice, 4–5
voices, 136–7
YouTube, 142–5
see also khuṭba; voice
Stockholm terror attack 2017, 166, 167, 170n
'Stop the transformation of our world', 116
al-Subkī, 70
Sudanese Islam, 40, 44
Sufi/Sufism, 33, 40–1, 51, 176, 192, 194, 202
brotherhoods/orders, 100n, 178
defense of popular preachers, 71, 79, 81n
lodges, 2, 53
Süleyman the Magnificent, 99n
Süleymancı community (*cemaat*), 100n
Süleymancılar, 101n
sunna, 75, 77, 114, 157–8, 162, 164, 175
Sunni Muslims, 77, 126n, 177, 182
Sūrat al-Nisā, 188–9
Sūrat al-Rūm, 189
al-Suyūṭī, 76
Câmi'uṣ-Ṣağîr, 99n
SVT, 160–1, 169n
Sweden, 26, 132–3, 147, 155–72
Muslim preachers, 137–8
suburban strategies, 166–7
Swedish Board of Student Finance (CSN), 161
Swedish Defence Academy, 137
Syria, 31, 74
TV serials, 37, 38–9

tafsīr, 73, 99n
Taksim Square, Istanbul, 84–7
taqwā (piety, fear or consciousness of God), 144–5, 175–6
tefsir, 73, 95, 99n
Telegram, 115
television, 111, 134, 146
channel, 98
historical dramas, 38–9
'religious serials', 38–9
religious TV dramas, 37–41
terrorism, 164–5
text (SMS) messages, 138
time, 132–53
Torah, 23
Trabzon, 99–100n
TRT Diyanet, 98
Tufekcioglu, Salih, 138, 142–5
al-Tukhi, Ahmad, 34–5
Tunagür, Yaşar, 87–8, 100n
Tunahan, Süleyman Hilmi, 100n
Turkey, 202
administrative reforms, 89–92
Friday sermons in a secular state, 83–105
General Staff (High Military Command), 90
'hidden unemployment', 89–90
hutbe regulations, 92–4
May Day 1977, 84–7
religious institution-building in modern, 83–105
Republican People's Party (Cumhuriyet Halk Partisi, CHP), 91
Turkish background, 142–3
Turkish constitution (Article 2), 83, 98–9n
Turkish Hearth (Türk Ocağı), 100n
TV serials, 'social serials,' 38
Twitter, 107, 108, 113–16, 120, 123n, 127n
'housewife, the marginalised occupation', 120

ʿulamaʾ, 5, 165, 176, 185, 192, 194
depiction of in film and TV, 30–47
marriage, 192, 194
Medieval preachers, 68–73, 76–9, 80–1n
see also ʿālim
Umayyads, 25, 26
UN Sustainable Development Agenda 2030, 116
United Arab Emirates, 31, 121

United Kingdom, State Opening of Parliament, 26
United Muslims of Sweden, 139
United Nations (UN), 116
Uppdrag granskning ('Mandate review'), 169n
al-ʿUthaymin, Muhammad Salih, 111
ʿUthmān ibn ʿAffān, 25

vaiza, 53, 54–8, 60, 62
vaz (homilies), 53, 55; *see also wa ʿẓ*
videos, 161–7
  images, 139–45
violence, Sweden, 155–72
voice, 52, 137
  agents', 51, 80, 159, 203
  narrative, 32, 35
  of the nation/official, 42, 95
  preachers', 4–5, 10–11, 43, 55, 86, 140, 142–3
  women's, 108, 111, 113, 117–19, 122n, 128n, 181–2

Wadud, Abdul, 160–4, 169n
Wāḥat al-Marʾa ('Women's oasis'), 112
Wahb b. Munabbih, 27–8n
Wahby, Yusuf, 32
Wahhabi theology, 110–11, 126n, 159
wā ʿiẓ (admonisher), plural *wu ʿʿāẓ*, 70, 72, 159, 176
wā ʿiẓāt (female hortatory preachers), 176
Waqf Daʿwatuha centre, 114–15
wa ʿẓ (freer form of preaching), 2, 12, 158, 159, 203
wa ʿẓ/maw ʿiẓa, 173, 175–6
websites, 112, 113, 157–8
West Java, 145–6
Widengren, Geo, 26–7
women
  Bosnian preachers, 48–65
  conservative women, 112–14
  false traditions of preaching, 75
  genres, spaces and speakers, 58–61
  guidance and governance, 61–2
  'popular preachers', 78
  in public, 74, 110–11, 176
  secluded public participation, 112–16
  Wadud, Abdul, 165, 169n
  'woman of the year', 114
  see also female preachers; marriage
wu ʿʿāẓ (admonishers), sing. *wā ʿiẓ*, 70, 72, 159, 176

The Yacoubian Building, 37–8
Yathrib, 21–2, 25
Yemen, 170n
YouTube
  al-ʿId, Nawal, 115
  Bahethat research centre, 116
  dā ʿiyāt, 113
  female preachers, 107
  Hirschkind, Charles, 136
  'How the Prophet Muhammad taught the Arabs that racism is wrong', 142–3, 148n
  learning from the prophet, 142–5
  Sweden, 155–71
Yusuf, Hassan, 39
Yūsuf al-Ṣaddīq ('The righteous Joseph'), 38

Zaghlul, Saad, 35–6
al-Zahir Baybars, 38–9
zawj (spouse/mate), 179–80
al-Zawja al-thāniyya ('The second wife'), 34
Zeenni, Hassan, 186–95
  'Are Men and Women Equal in Islam?', 188
  'Making Progress Towards Equality', 188
zikr, 57; *see also dhikr*
Zuhar al-islam ('The appearance of Islam'), 32–3
zuhd (renunciation), 162–3, 166
  Sweden, 155–72

EU representative:
Easy Access System Europe
Mustamäe tee 50, 10621 Tallinn, Estonia
Gpsr.requests@easproject.com

www.ingramcontent.com/pod-product-compliance
Lightning Source LLC
Chambersburg PA
CBHW070353240426
43671CB00013BA/2483
9781474467483